Museum of the Southwest

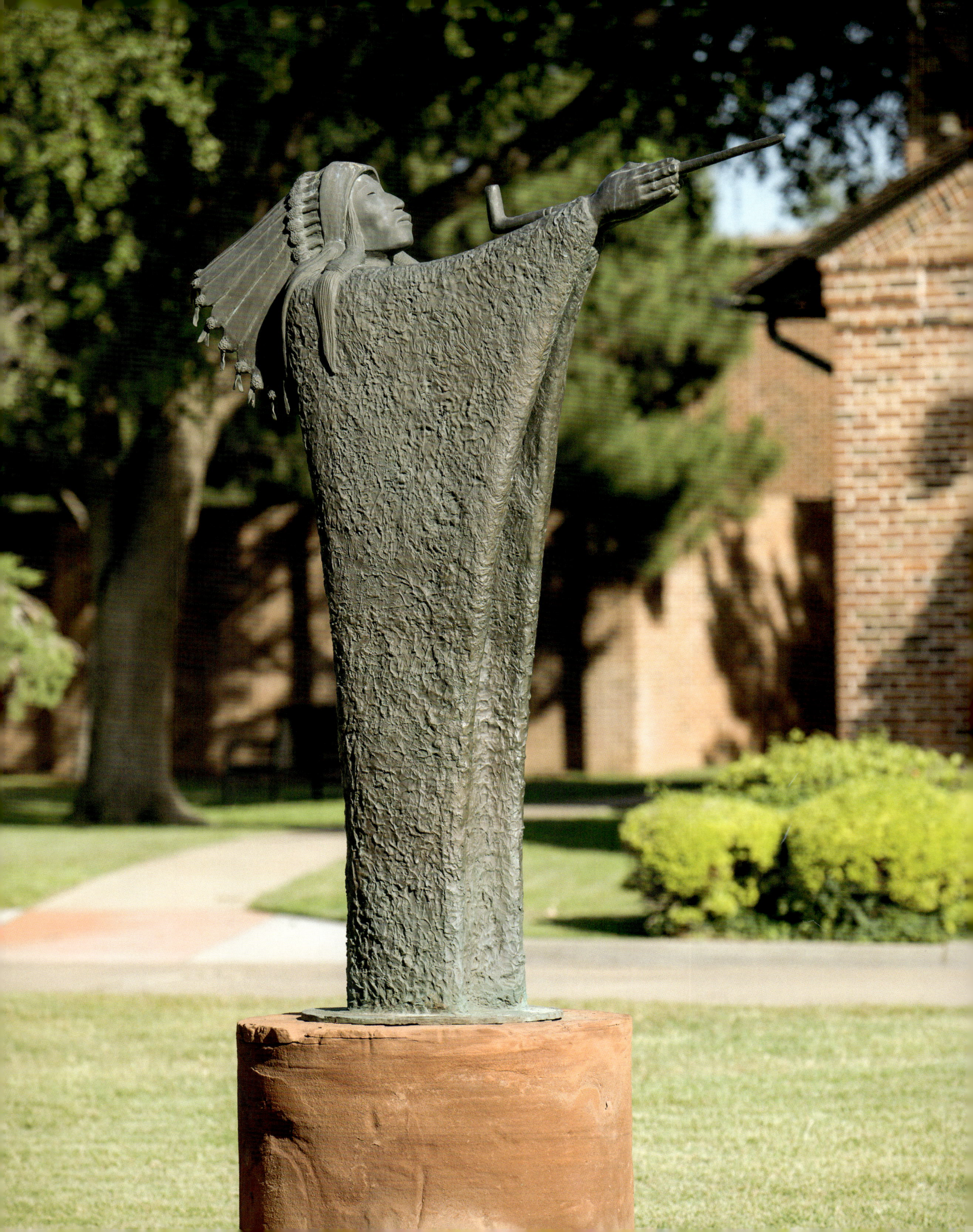

Museum of the Southwest

SELECTIONS FROM THE PERMANENT COLLECTION

FOREWORD

Brian Lee Whisenhunt

INTRODUCTION AND HISTORY OF THE MUSEUM OF THE SOUTHWEST

Wendy Earle

HENRY LUCE FOUNDATION

THIS PUBLICATION WAS MADE POSSIBLE
BY THE HENRY LUCE FOUNDATION

This book is dedicated to all of the patrons, donors and supporters of the Museum of the Southwest whose foresight and generosity have made this collection possible.

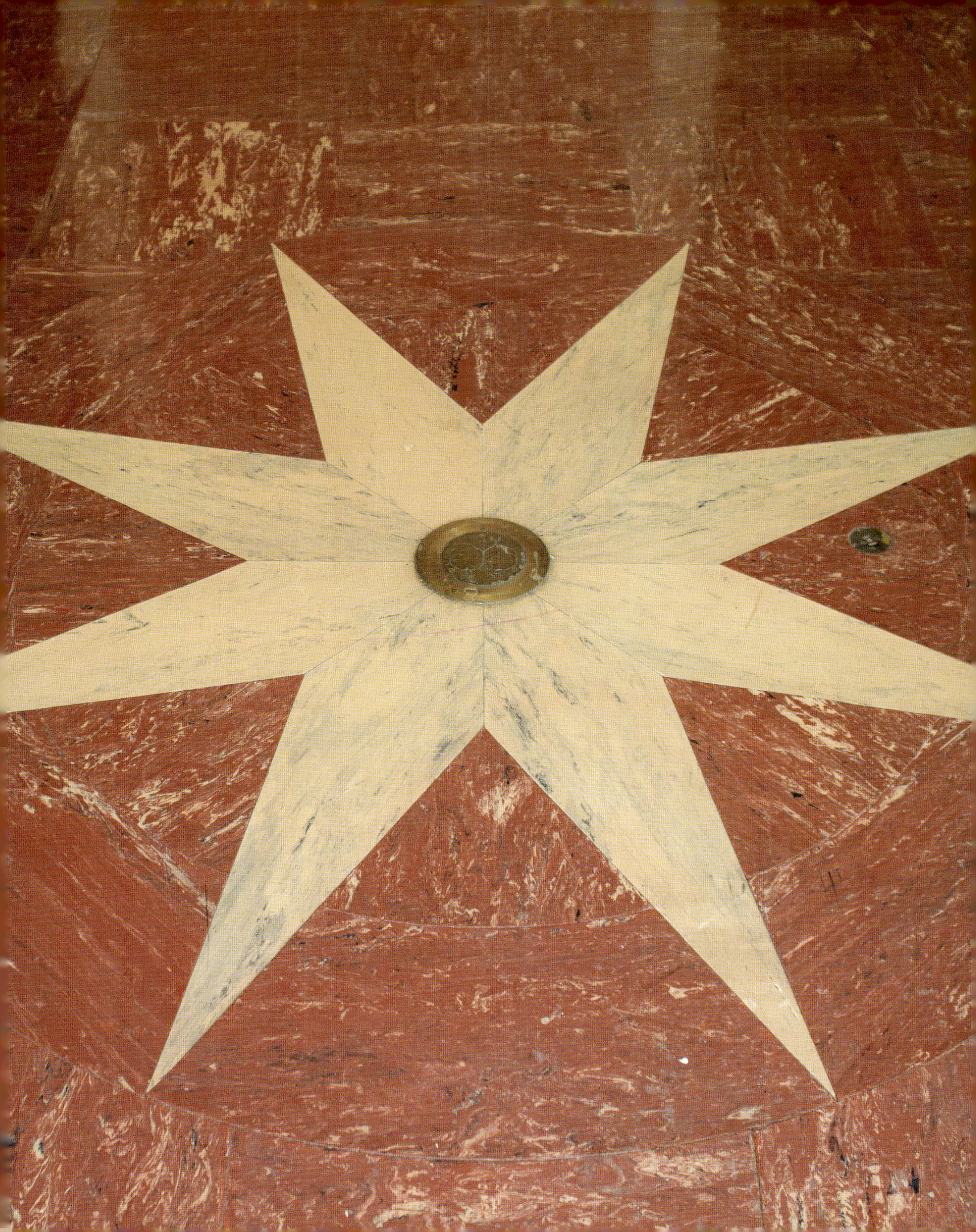

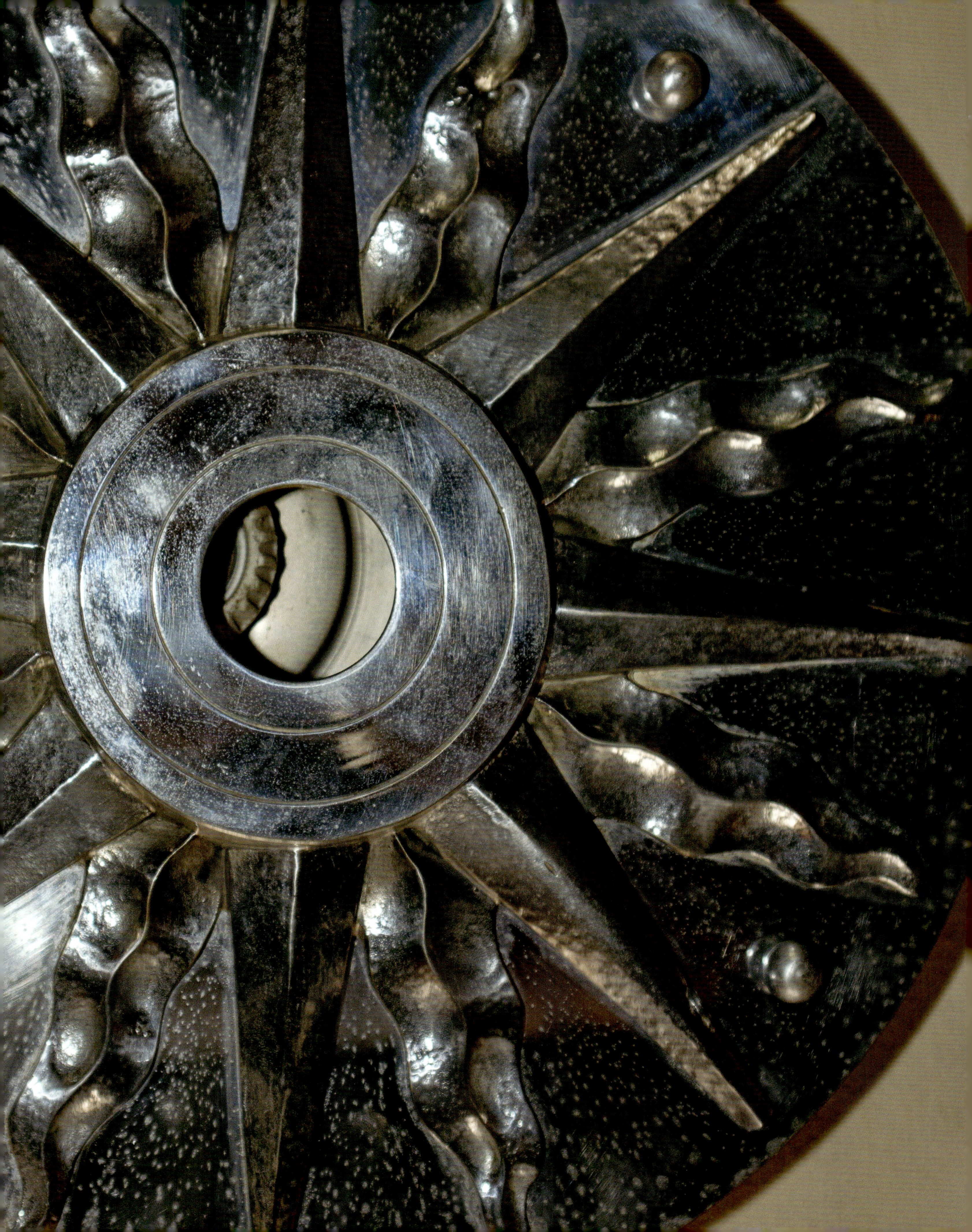

Foreword

This publication is more than simply a compilation of images of works of art and essays about them; it reflects the effort of so many board members, collectors, staff members and volunteers who have labored over the course of fifty years to build and grow this Museum from the idea of a committee to a campus of buildings dedicated to diverse artistic disciplines and experiences. The work of museums is twofold: The first is to gather, store and protect the material culture of the disciplines of its mission. In the case of the Museum of the Southwest, we collect not only works of art but also archaeological artifacts and historical objects from the American Southwest. Secondly, museums are obligated to interpret those collections, to bring them to life for audiences and communities through exhibitions, gallery tours and talks, and programs and experiences. The objects in our collections and the exhibitions organized to present them are the basis and inspiration of every aspect of our work.

Collections can be formed from a multitude of circumstances. In some cases, they are the gift of someone who has spent a lifetime amassing work of a group of artists, a time period or a culture. In other cases, collections begin with a gift of financial support that allows the institution to purchase objects that will serve the museum's mission and audiences. Over time, a collection is refined as important works are added and those that may not clearly suit the mission find homes elsewhere.

In the introduction, you will read about our origins in a committee of the Junior League of Midland who wanted a place for art and exhibitions for this city. From those humble beginnings, a collection began to grow as Texas artists and those who collected art in this community made donations to the institution. From there, a direction began to take shape to collect more broadly the art and cultural artifacts of the American Southwest—a collection that reflected the best of the world around West Texas. Luckily, important collectors such as Fred and Novadean Hogan believed in the organization, its mission and the work it was doing. The couple made major gifts of works of art by the Taos Society of Artists that solidified the direction of the art collection and became the bedrock of what now numbers over 1,600 works of art that the Museum holds in trust for the people of Midland. Innumerable others have made generous financial gifts that allowed the Museum to acquire objects for a collection that continues to grow. To tell the story of how our collection has grown and of the mission that has shaped it, we've chosen to present the seventy works of art included in this publication in the order of their acquisition.

It is a great honor for the current staff and leadership of the Museum of the Southwest to present the first-ever publication about the collection the Museum has been building for fifty years. It is our hope that it provides insight into the works of art that belong to this community; creates excitement about a collection that is still growing and developing; and becomes a resource for those wishing to share their love of art with students, children and friends. We therefore dedicate this publication to everyone who has been instrumental in the success of this Museum and the building of its collection for more than five decades. On behalf of the Museum of the Southwest, I extend our heartfelt thanks to each and every one of you.

Likewise, I would like to thank those who have worked so hard to make the idea of a guide to the collection a reality. Wendy Earle, the curator of collections and exhibitions for the Museum, undertook the majority of writing for this book as well as the coordination of its publication. She and Jenni Opalinski, manager of collections and exhibitions, worked on the photography with Dan Barsotti. Kristen Wagstrom, curator of education; Melissa Rowland, community outreach manager; and Dr. Marianne Woods, professor of art history at the University of Texas of the Permian Basin, all contributed to the writing process, along with myself and Ms. Opalinski. In addition, Audrie Palmer, director of development, captured a glimpse into the early history of the Museum in an interview with Mary R. Griffith. Our work was supported in many ways by the rest of the Museum of the Southwest staff, and we could not have completed this publication without them. In addition, we are indebted to David Skolkin for the design and production of this publication.

Finally and most of all, I hope that all of the work that went into creating this publication translates into a new way for you, the reader and visitor, to enjoy the collections of the Museum of the Southwest.

Brian Lee Whisenhunt
Executive Director

Introduction

Wendy Earle

LOCATED IN WEST TEXAS, MIDLAND might not be the obvious choice for a thriving museum campus, but that is exactly what the Museum of the Southwest has become. Celebrating its fifty-year anniversary in 2016, MSW has created a dynamic and versatile complex that anchors the diversity of its regional surroundings. West Texas is large enough to be its own state, a land mass encompassing roughly anywhere from the Texas Panhandle in the north, the Mexico border in the south, the Hill Country in the east and the New Mexico border in the west. With rugged landscapes ranging from extreme flatness to canyons and mountains, the semiarid country is hard to encapsulate. Art has long been vital to the region, from traditional depictions of the cowboy to conceptual and abstract art in places like Marfa. As the first publication on our permanent collection, this book has two purposes: to show the artistic legacy of this region and spotlight works and artists that may have received little attention and to contextualize the objects both within the scope of art history and for their place in the Museum.

Essays on art of the Southwest and Texas, France, Britain, America beyond our region and on several objects from the Kentucky Derby Collection allow us to trace the route that, for example, brought paintings by Norman Rockwell and Rosa Bonheur to a collection primarily of Southwestern art. This guide to the collections serves as an introduction but is by no means exhaustive. As the Museum continues to grow, subsequent publications will illustrate the scope and different facets of the collections.

The history of the Museum of the Southwest weaves its way through the Turner family, the construction of the Turner Mansion and the donation of the mansion to the newly formed Museum of the Southwest in 1968. The story of the Turners can be seen as a microcosm for the rise of West Texas and the oil booms that drastically changed—and continue to change—the landscape both physically and economically.

MIDLAND AND THE TURNER FAMILY

In the 1920s, the West Texas economic picture was dramatically altered by the discovery and production of vast oil reserves in the Permian Basin, a geologic region underlying much of West Texas and southeastern New Mexico. For thousands of years the area had been host to various native tribes, mostly nomadic and seminomadic, and over the past several centuries populations in the Permian Basin have included Jumano, Apache, Tonkawa, Kiowa, Wichita and Comanche tribes; Spanish conquistadors; and Anglo settlers.

In 1881 the Texas and Pacific Railway established Midway Station as the halfway point between Fort Worth and El Paso in what became the town of Midland. Populated mostly by ranchers and farmers making a hard living, the area developed slowly. In 1920 the population was less than 2,000, but the 1923 gushing of the Santa Rita #1 well in nearby Big Lake started an oil boom that brought thousands of workers and investors into the area.

This oil discovery drew the attention of larger oil companies and independent oilmen who started buying leases in the area. One of the most successful of these entrepreneurs was Fred Turner, Jr. Turner was born in 1896 into a pioneer West Texas family and in 1927 came to Midland as a scout for Marland Oil Company. In 1928, Turner filed a suit regarding several contested but ultimately unclaimed tracts of land in the Yates Field in Pecos County. The case was finally settled by the Texas Supreme Court in 1933 in favor of Turner, and as a result of the verdict, he became the owner of substantial acreage above the largest known oil reserve in the world. He made other discoveries in West Lovington Field, Shafter Lake San Andres Field, and the Parker Wolfcamp and Parker Pennsylvania Fields in Andrews County. He built on his success with other business endeavors, such as buying two large ranches in New Mexico in the 1950s and operating a pecan orchard in Brownwood.

Fred Turner, Jr., married Juliette Miller and they had two daughters: Fredda, born in 1922, and Dorothy, born in 1931. A family home on twelve lots in the neighborhood west of downtown Midland was completed in 1937. Both daughters married into families that were also involved in oil and ranching, with Fredda marrying Lynn Durham in 1943 and Dorothy marrying Clarence Scharbauer, Jr., in 1949. During the years of the Great Depression and shortages caused by World War II, Turner was among the few in Midland who managed to stay in business. As part of their interest in ranching, the Turners also purchased thoroughbred horses for racing. Their thoroughbred Tomy Lee won the Kentucky Derby in 1959.

In October 1963 Juliette Turner was tragically killed in the home by an intruder. Fred Turner died of natural causes four months later. The Turner heirs—the Durhams and Scharbauers—donated the family home in a public-private partnership with Midland County to the newly formed Museum of the Southwest to use for exhibitions, programs and activities for the people of Midland.

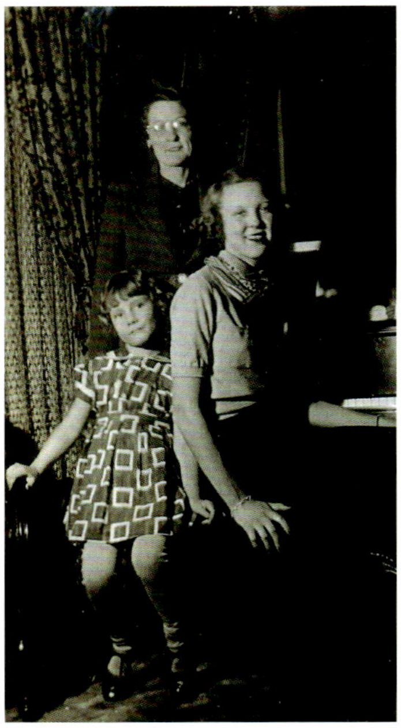

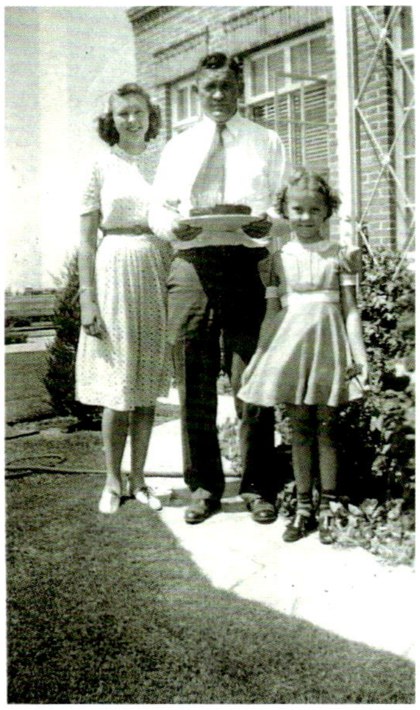

Above: Juliette Turner with daughters Dorothy and Fredda, 1936, photograph by Fred Turner. Below: Fred Turner with Fredda and Dorothy, c. 1937, photograph by Juliette Turner.

The Historic Turner Mansion

Dallas-based architect Anton Korn designed the Turner home in the Eclectic Style, combining elements of Tudor, Georgian, Art Deco, American Colonial, Mediterranean and other architectural styles, with details such as Mexican tilework. The first

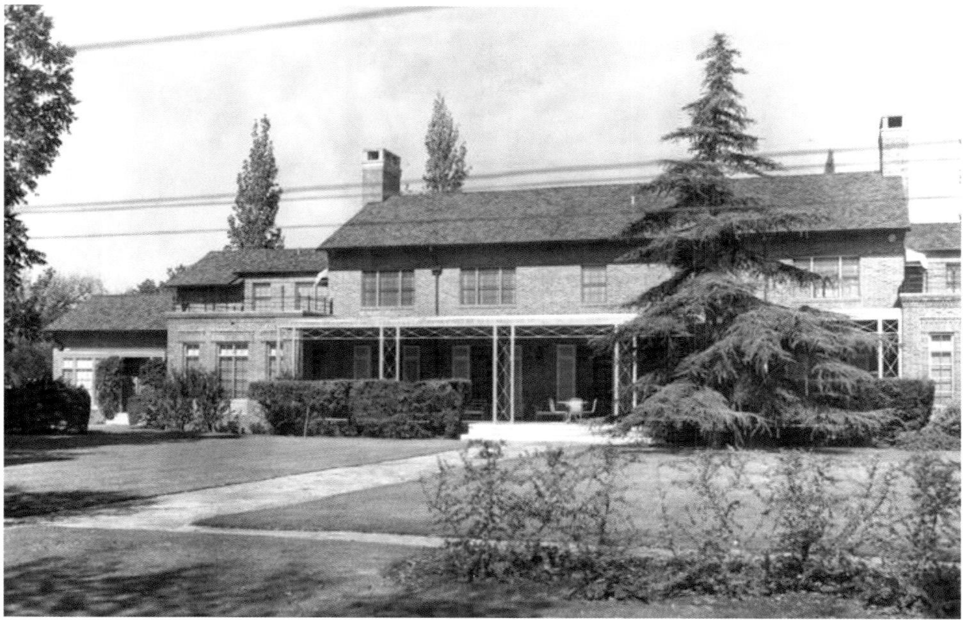

Turner Mansion back porch, c. 1963, photograph from public record.

floor was designed with entertaining in mind, with a dining room, living room, breakfast room, a powder room for visitors, large guest suite, wood-paneled library, solarium, and large front and back porches. The second floor of the home comprised a master suite, family bedrooms, baths and two terraces. Throughout the interior spaces is a repetition of a Texas star motif in both the architectural details and hardware; the library is paneled with wood from a single tree. The grounds included a garden, tennis court, stables for the Turner's horses and one of the first private swimming pools in the region.

The Turner family enjoyed twenty-six happy years in the home. In 1968 the mansion began its transformation from a private residence to a public museum, which has necessitated some changes. It became a registered National Historic Place in 1988 and much effort has been made to preserve the many details that illustrate the care and thought given to this home by its original owners. Much of the historic Turner Mansion today remains unchanged and in good condition, including most of the original tile work on the floors and walls, many original light fixtures and hand-carved plaster decorating the ceilings.

The Museum

The Museum of the Southwest was established in 1965 by a committee of the Junior League of Midland for the purpose of bringing art and exhibitions to the people of Midland. The Museum opened in 1966 in its first location, moving briefly before finally relocating permanently to the Turner Mansion in 1968. Since then, the Museum has expanded, adding additional gallery space in 1970 and

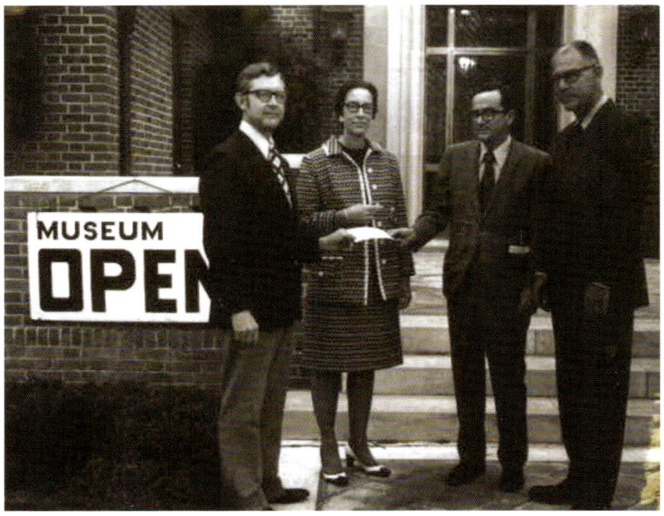

Museum of the Southwest volunteer organization Las Manos in front of the Turner Mansion, c. 1968, photograph by Museum of the Southwest.

the Lissa Noël Wagner Wing in 1987; building the Blakemore Planetarium in 1972, which was remodeled and expanded in 2009; and constructing the Durham Children's Museum in 1986. The Museum was accredited by the American Association of Museums (now the American Alliance of Museums) in 1992, with subsequent accreditation achieved in 2002. With the generosity of local and regional philanthropists, Museum members, area foundations, the City of Midland and Midland County, the Museum of the Southwest has grown and expanded during its years of service to the communities of West Texas.

Some changes have been made to features in the vicinity of the Turner property, most notably the repurposing of an area that was home to arts patron Naomi Lancaster, a neighbor of the Turner family. The Lancaster house had been donated to the Museum in 1970 and in a state of disrepair. It was leveled in 1984 to add a children's museum to the campus. Other changes include removal of the swimming pool and tennis courts to enable construction of the Wagner Wing in 1987.

Presently, the Museum of the Southwest's five-acre campus is comprised of the Juliette and Fred Turner, Jr. Memorial Art Museum, the Fredda Turner Durham Children's Museum, the Marian West and William Blanton Blakemore Planetarium, an outdoor Sculpture Garden and a collection comprised of more than 40,000 works of art and archaeological items. MSW is a vital resource for the West Texas and eastern New Mexico region. Over the last fifty years, Midland's population has grown exponentially, and the Museum has grown with it. Today the Museum of the Southwest inspires discovery, interaction and exploration of art, science, culture and history, enriching the lives of people of all ages.

The Permanent Collection

The Museum of the Southwest has a unique and exciting permanent collection of works ranging from ancient to contemporary. The archaeology collection consists of approximately 45,000 artifacts. The art collection comprises over 1,600 objects, including paintings, prints, sculptures, drawings, photographs, textiles, ceramics, basketry and mixed-media works.

The permanent collection began inauspiciously with the 1966 accession of a small U.S. Navy uniform button. The collection grew slowly with additional historical objects, including blacksmithing tools and Spanish conquistador armor and weapons. A focus emerged that centered on the art of Texas and the Greater Southwest, including New Mexico, Arizona, Nevada, Texas, Oklahoma, Utah and northern Mexico.

The archaeology collection began in 1976 with a large donation by Margaret and Cole E. "Bud" Bissell of 45,000 surface-collected artifacts, mostly lithics, or stone tools. Additional material in MSW's archaeology collection includes jewelry, grinding stones and pottery, which came to the Museum from various sources, with significant help from the Midland Archaeological Society. Some lithics have been tentatively identified as Clovis and Folsom points from approximately 12,000 years ago, while other material can be dated to the historic period of the last 200 years.

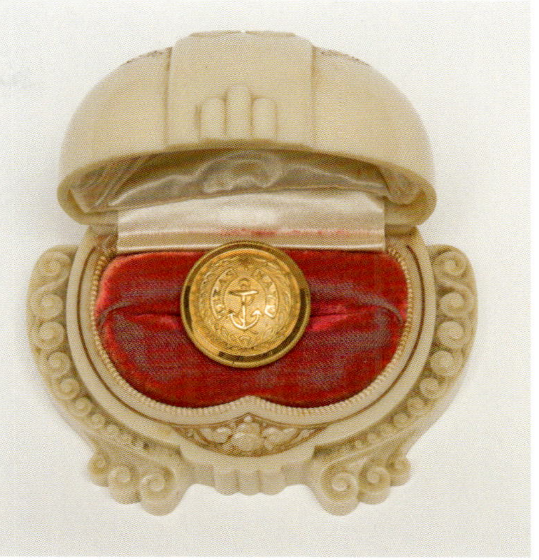

Texas Navy Uniform Button, 1840. Brass, 1" diameter. 1966.001.001. Gift of Mrs. Rosa Tod Hammer. The button was the first item accepted in the Museum's collection. It was originally part of Commander John Grant Tod's uniform in the Republic of Texas Navy.

Significant additions to the art collections include Edward Curtis photogravures (gift of Mary and William D. Kennedy), Woody Crumbo silkscreen prints (gift of Mr. and Mrs. Ed A. Vogler), Karl Bodmer acquatint engravings (Bodmer Acquisition Fund), Native Southwestern textiles and ceramics (gift of Adrian Randle), Casas Grandes ceramics (gift of Dr. Kirby Tarry), an almost complete suite of John James Audubon's *Viviparous Quadrupeds of North America* (Audubon Acquisition Fund), preparatory drawings by Joseph Imhof (gift of Bill and Mary Cheek) and many photographs by artists, including Esther Bubley and Burton Pritzker (gift of the artist).

There have been three transformative gifts to the art collection. The artist Merritt Mauzey donated the Texas Regionalist paintings and prints between 1967

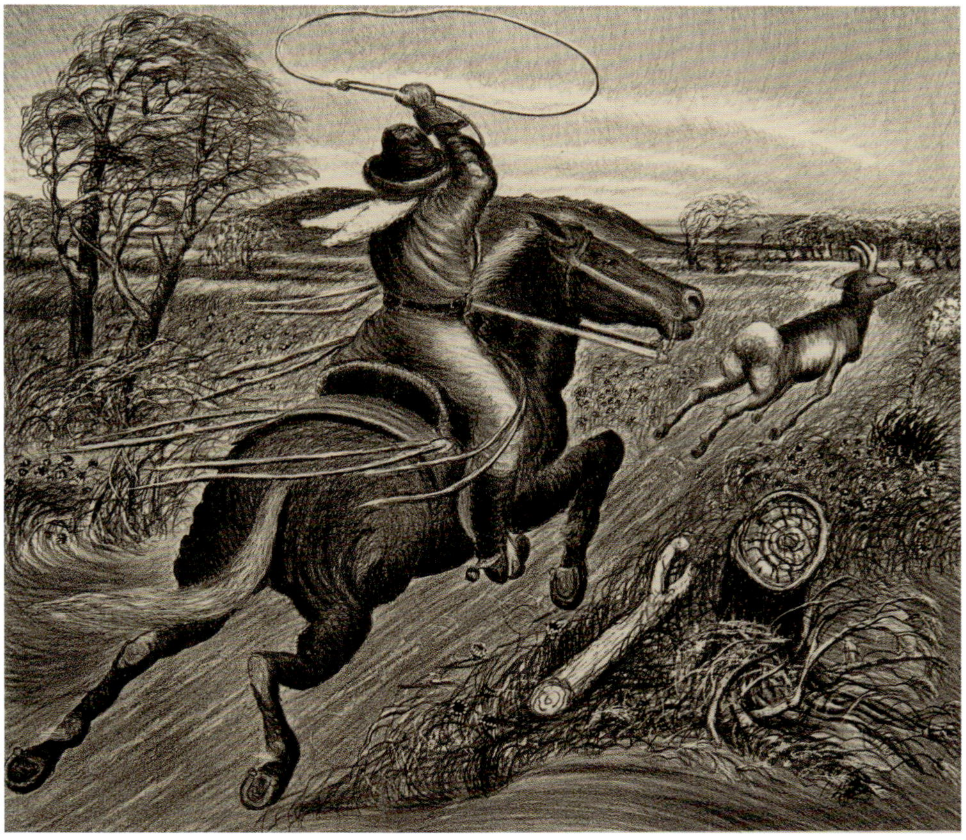

Merritt Mauzey. *Plainsman's Dream*, c. 1940. Lithograph, 19 15/16 x 14½. 1967.001.001. Gift of the Artist.

and 1970. Born in West Texas and working in Dallas, Mauzey was a prolific and gifted painter and lithographer documenting small-town life starting in the 1920s. While some of Mauzey's works were purchased by the Museum, the majority were donated and include a variety of artists from Mauzey's circle, including Jerry Bywaters, Alexandre Hogue and Thomas Hart Benton. Among the first acquisitions, this collection of over 200 works provides a basis for understanding Texas art and the Regionalist art movement.

In 1980, 1983 and 1996, Fred T. and Novadean Hogan donated paintings and sculptures from the Taos Society of Artists as well as later Taos artists and others, such as Norman Rockwell, Rosa Bonheur, Albert Bierstadt, Glenna Goodacre and Doug Hyde.

Finally in 2015 the Scharbauer family donated their equestrian collection of Kentucky Derby trophies, along with other horse-racing awards and cultural objects that were originally owned by Juliette and Fred Turner, Jr., and Dorothy Turner Scharbauer and Pamela Scharbauer, daughter and granddaughter of the Turners. Many of these items were originally displayed in the Turner Mansion, making this a homecoming.

"There is no culture here": An Account by Mary R. Griffith of the Museum's Beginnings

By Audrie Palmer

It is rare for museums to have direct links to the institutional founders; rarer still for those founders to be serving the museum through volunteer work fifty years later. Mrs. Mary R. Griffith was one of the key individuals who created the Museum of the Southwest, co-curated its first exhibition in 1966 (and many others since) and still sits on the Collection Committee and Board of Governors. Her deep institutional memory has been an important asset over the last five decades.

When Mary Griffith first moved to Midland in 1950, she was a new bride and a fourth-generation New Yorker. Her mother accompanied her on the trip to the Permian Basin and was absolutely horrified at what she found. The population of Midland was roughly 20,000—less than one-sixth of what it presently is—and for her mother it was lacking one thing. "She simply said, 'There is no culture here,'" Mrs. Griffith remembers. "And she was absolutely right. There was nothing here."

Mrs. Griffith and her late husband, Robert, were transferred from West Texas and then returned seven years later with children in tow. She joined the Junior League of Midland and was placed at the children's theater to volunteer. It was around that same time that the Junior League began looking at the needs of the community and decided that a museum would be a good idea for Midland. Mrs. Griffith was asked to join the founding placement group, and the League gave a start-up gift of $55,000 to the formation of the recently incorporated Museum.

"It was an adventure. A true adventure," Mrs. Griffith says fondly as she recalls the early years of the Museum of the Southwest. She and her friend Alice Tillett, another Junior League member, began to put together the first art exhibition for the Museum. The Museum had a building for lease on Highway 80 at the intersection of Bankhead Highway and Wall Street.

Mrs. Tillett was a native Texan and historian and one that Mrs. Griffith said she could learn from. The women roamed across the state of Texas together with their families looking for items and to gather art and artifacts for the exhibition. They borrowed from Texas Rangers, from the Fort Davis Historic Site and from the kin of Texas legend Stephen F. Austin.

"We did everything but steal," Mrs. Griffith says with a laugh. "We borrowed but we got enough stuff. It was a lot of fun and we did have a lot of fun putting it together."

Opening the doors for the first exhibition, they were nervous but excited; they didn't know how it would be received. Their group of volunteers was so relieved that they had put together their first show for the Museum. The reception from the community was a success. After the second exhibition in the Museum, the committee hired a director who helped to move the Museum of the Southwest to the Commercial State Bank. In 1968, almost five years after the deaths of Juliette and Fred Turner, Jr., the Museum was gifted the historic Turner mansion.

As she ponders the time she spent helping to get the Museum of the Southwest established and looks towards the future, Mrs. Griffith reflects on the individuals, businesses and foundations that have been the backbone of the city's institutions and made Midland what it is today. She looks at the culture and is reminded that it is now everywhere in the performing arts, ballet, theater and museums of Midland.

"It's amazing when I think back and it was sort of like a bare prairie," she says. "For me, it's been a fun run and then it started to grow and I'm still amazed at how it's done."

Mrs. Griffith still remembers the words of her mother, and yet, she would beg to differ: "There's plenty of culture here," she says. "All you have to do is look around and participate."

Museum of the Southwest Leadership

TERM	EXECUTIVE DIRECTORS
1968–70	John R. Vincent
1971–74	Ronald Deane
1975–78	Sam Grove
1979	Don Hedgpeth (acting)
1980–82	Joan E. Hellen
1983	Jerry C. Porter
1984	Dr. Mike Collins (acting)
1985	Jim Cox (acting)
1985–86	Sue E. Devine
1986–92	Jean Hagman
1992–94	Wendell Ott
1995	Denna McGuire (acting)
1996–2010	Thomas Jones
2010–11	Jim Byerlotzer (acting)
2011–present	Brian Lee Whisenhunt

TERM	BOARD OF TRUSTEES PRESIDENTS
1965–68	William Blakemore
1969	Harvey Herd
1970	William Marshall, Sr.
1971–72	Jim Hooker
1973	Leon G. Byerley, Jr.
1974	Betty Moss
1975–76	Dr. James Mailey
1977	Francis Stickney
1978	Bascom Mitchell
1979	Rosalind Redfern Grover
1980–81	Fredda Turner Durham
1982	Bruce Pearson
1983	Bruce Pearson
1983	Al W. Dillard, Jr.
1984	Al W. Dillard, Jr.
1985	Terry Wilkinson
1985	Jim Cox
1986	Jim Cox
1987–88	John Robert Lively
1988–89	Elizabeth Locker
1989–90	Jack D. Riggs
1990–91	Claire Woodcock
1991–92	Judith Devenport
1992–93	Cadell S. Liedtke
1993–94	Lissa Noël Wagner
1995	Denna McGuire
1996	A. J. Brune III
1997–98	Jeffrey Hewett
1999	Jay Reynolds
2000–01	Ginny Bailey
2002–03	Duke Edwards
2004	Stan Jacobs
2005–06	Chan Price
2007–08	Jim Byerlotzer
2009–10	Greg Dove
2011	Karmen Hendrix Bryant
2012	Karmen Hendrix Bryant
2013–14	Jaime Alexander
2015	James Small
2016	C. Dwight Alworth II

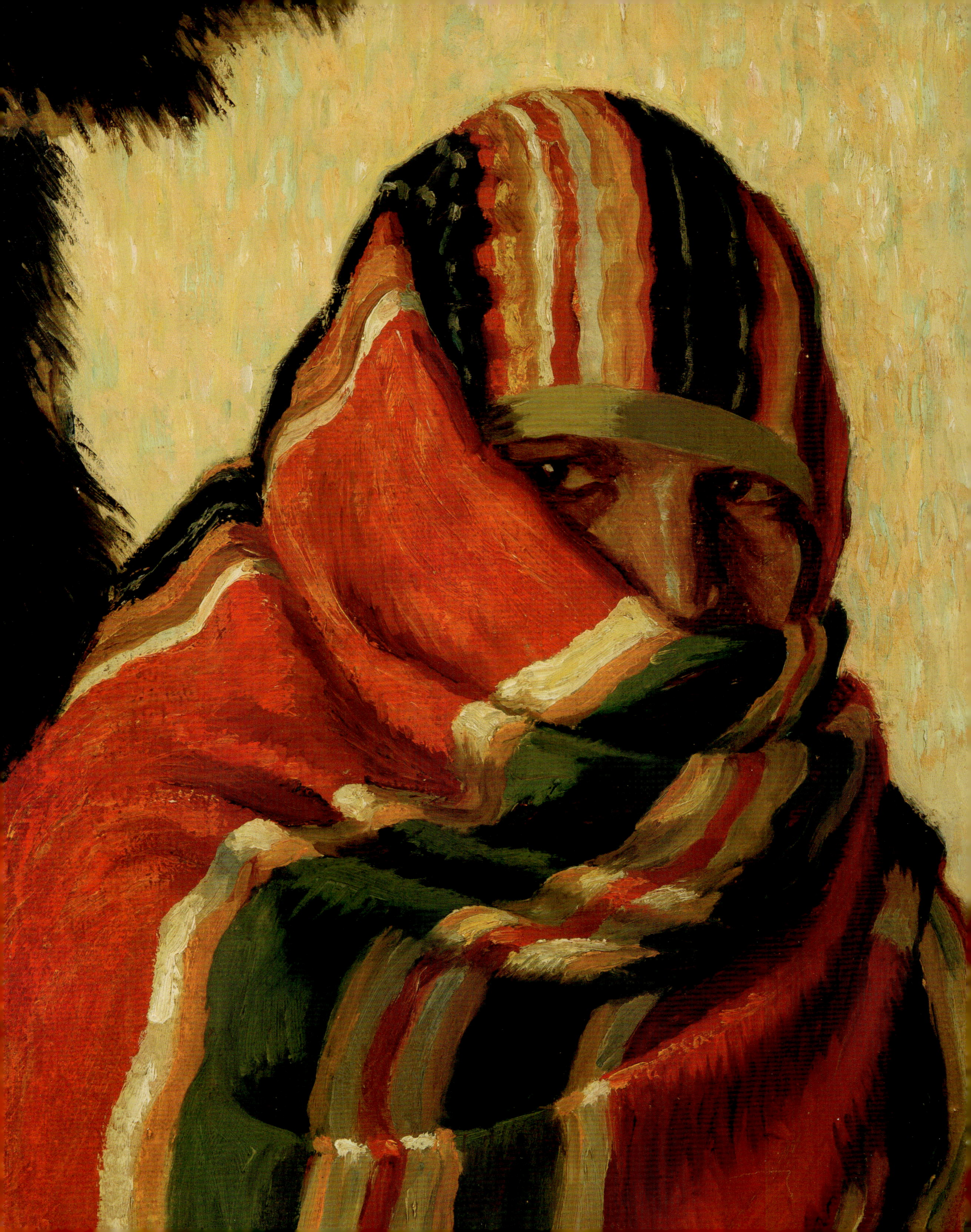

Museum of the Southwest

SELECTIONS FROM THE PERMANENT COLLECTION

The seventy plates presented here illuminate the highlights of the permanent collection of the Museum of the Southwest. Arranged in order of accession, these works allow readers to understand the building of a fine museum collection.

Gerald (Jerry) Bywaters

(1906–1989)

Election Day in Balmorhea, 1938

Lithograph, 11 x 16 in.

1967.002.012

Gift of Merritt Mauzey

One of the hotbeds of the American Regionalism movement in art was in Dallas, Texas, led by Jerry Bywaters. Bywaters grew up in Dallas at a time when little formal art instruction existed. He developed his own style through travels to major artistic centers, studying and meeting the important artists of the day. Bywaters was a tireless artist in a career spanning over sixty years. He worked in painting, printmaking and murals; was an active arts writer for the newspapers and magazines; taught for the entirety of his career; and served as one of the first directors for the Dallas Museum of Fine Arts, now called the Dallas Museum of Art.

Bywaters formed and led several important artist groups, including the Dallas Nine and the Lone Star Printmakers. The artists in these groups had individual styles but together they formed a cohesive body of work characterized by strong compositions, earthy color palettes, and, above all, a commitment to showing the people and lands of Texas. This style was a reaction against the Paris-inspired American Impressionism favored early in the twentieth century. By creating an "indigenous" art form, these artists could tell American stories instead of following European trends.

Bywaters' major influences include the Regionalist/American Scene paintings and prints of Grant Wood and Thomas Hart Benton, as well as the murals of Diego Rivera, seen in works like *Mexican Mother*. In *Election Day in Balmorhea,* Bywaters shows a scene from far West Texas, a favorite locale of his. Like most of the artist's paintings and prints, this 1938 lithograph provides glimpses of Texans engaged in the daily life of a small town.

WE

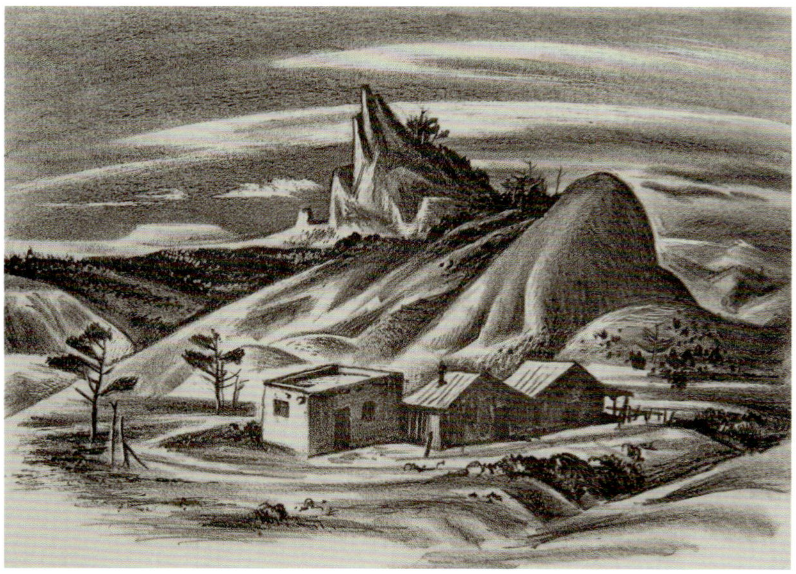

In the Mountains, 1942. Lithograph, 7¾ x 10¾ in. 1967.002.011. Gift of Merritt Mauzey.

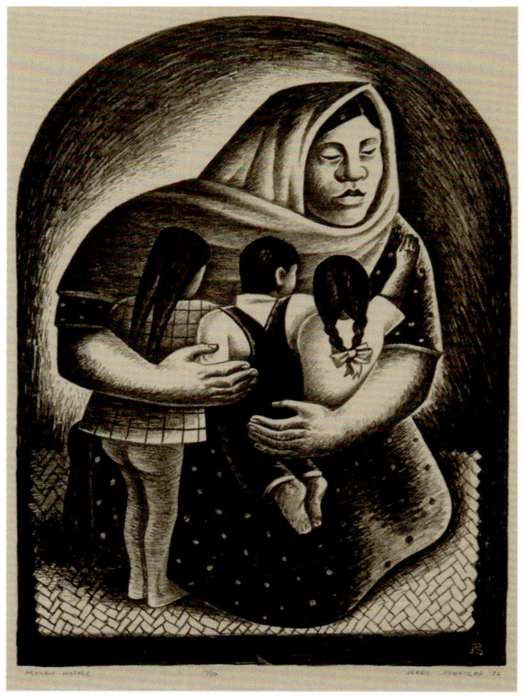

Mexican Mother, 1936. Lithograph, 16½ x 12½ in. 1969.002.012. Gift of Merritt Mauzey.

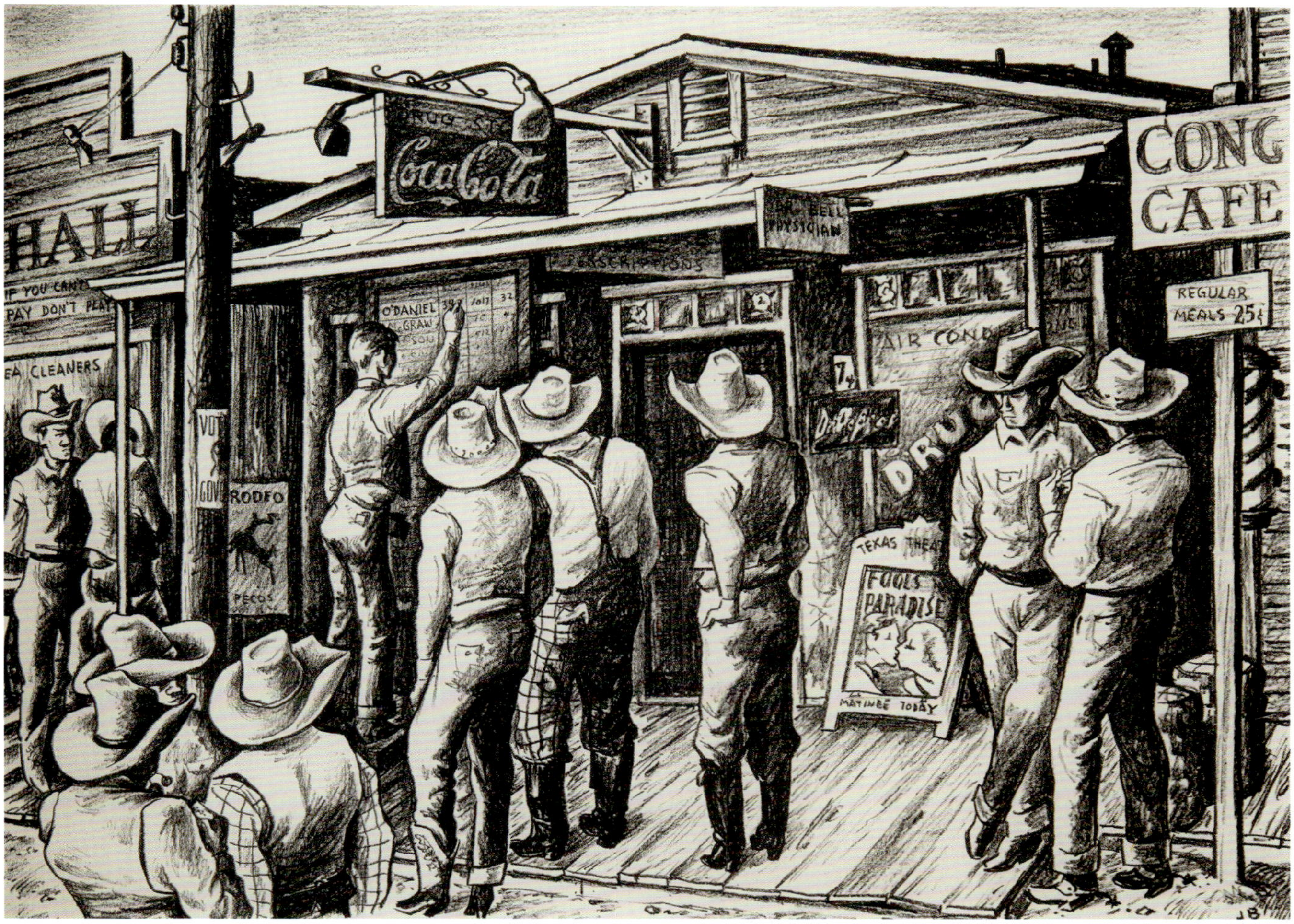
Coca-Cola
HALL
O'DANIEL
CLEANERS
DR. BELL PHYSICIAN
CONG
CAFE
REGULAR MEALS 25¢
PECOS
FOOLS PARADISE
MATINEE TODAY

Thomas Hart Benton

(1889–1975)

The Fence Mender, 1940

Lithograph, 10 x 14 in.

1967.002.032

Gift of Merritt Mauzey

Heir to a political dynasty in Missouri, Thomas Hart Benton broke from the legal and political aspirations of his family to follow his passion and study painting, first in Chicago and later in Paris, where Modernism influenced him to experiment with pure form, color and composition. While Benton quickly abandoned any pursuit of pure abstraction, he did merge Modernist ideas with his desire to create a uniquely American style of painting depicting the agrarian roots, rural environment and honest labor of its citizenry. With Grant Wood in Iowa and John Steuart Curry in Kansas, Benton formed the triad of Regionalism that worked in direct opposition to American artists pursuing abstraction in the first half of the twentieth century.

The Fence Mender is one of many lithographs produced by Benton, occasionally from the subjects of his paintings and sometimes from the many drawings he made on his travels across the Midwest, South and Western United States. This image is similar to the subject matter of a painting gifted to Winston Churchill on the occasion of his Iron Curtain speech in 1946 at Westminster College in Fulton, Missouri. Here, a man is repairing a barbed wire fence while his horse and a cottonwood tree stand in silhouette against the undulating rhythm of passing clouds in a broad vista of western sky. A large stone at the bottom of the picture plane solidly balances the dancing clouds and tree. With a great economy of composition and subject, Benton encapsulates the development of the American West as settlers fenced off the land to bring order, used horses to navigate the vast spaces as well as to manage cattle and farmlands, and planted fast-growing cottonwoods to bring a sense of stability and place to the broad, open plains. In many of his paintings, murals and prints, Benton sought to express not only the local and personal but also the broader universal change settlement brought to the West.

BLW

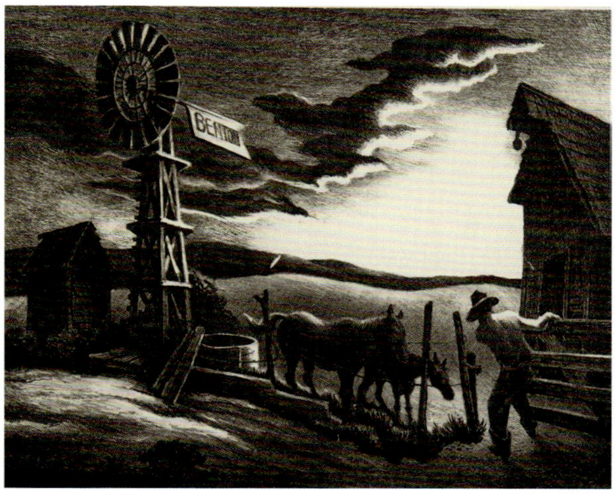

Nebraska Evening, 1941. Lithograph, 10 x 13 in. 1984.003.001. Gift of Mr. and Mrs. Zeb Conely, Jr.

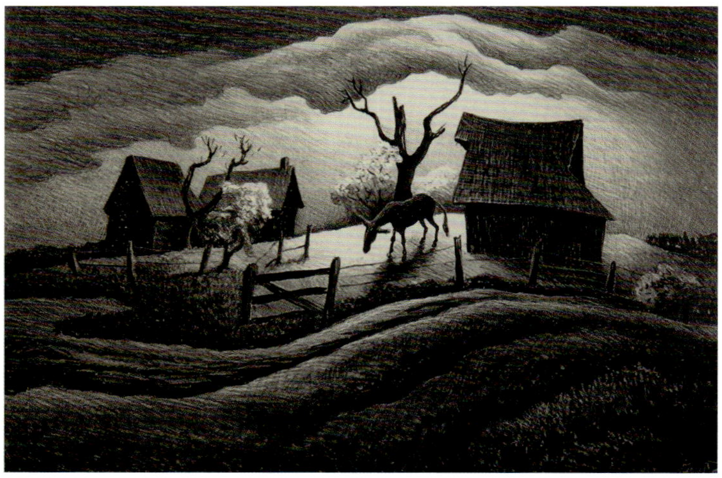

Rainy Day, 1938. Lithograph, 8½ x 13½ in. 1996.002.020. Gift of Fred T. and Novadean Hogan.

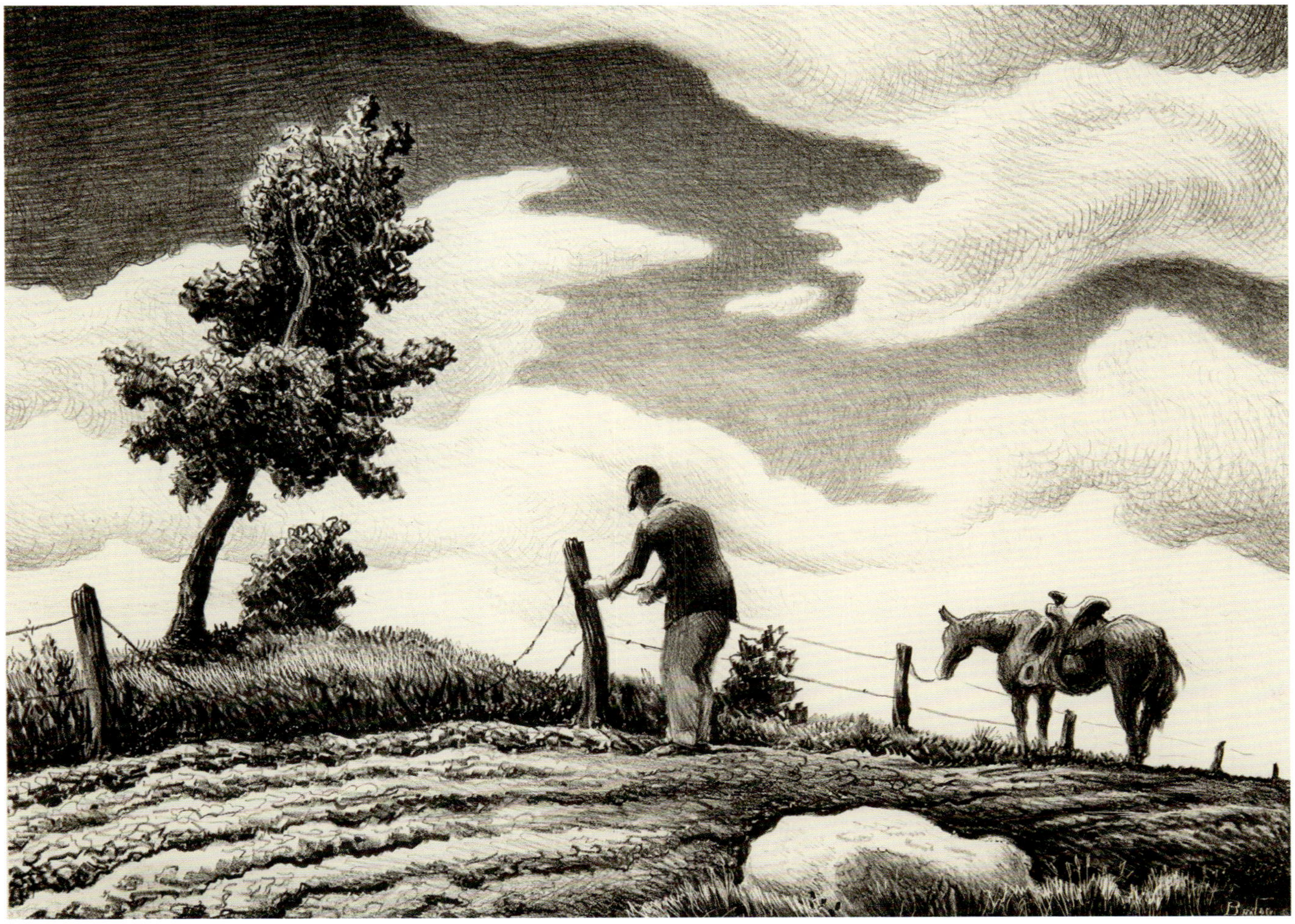

William Lewis Lester

(1910–1991)

Yucca and Prickly Pear, 1941

Lithograph, 9¼ x 13 in.

1969.002.007

Gift of Merritt Mauzey

Like many of the Texas Regionalists, William Lester was born in a small town (Graham), moved to Dallas in the 1920s and studied with Olin Travis and Thomas Stell. Lester was part of the Dallas Nine, an active member of the Dallas Artists League and one of the founding members of the Lone Star Printmakers. Like all of his associated artists in Dallas in the 1930s and '40s, he used scenes of everyday life in Texas as the inspiration for his paintings and prints. Lester was able to support himself through the Great Depression with several art-related government jobs, including as a staff artist for the Civilian Conservation Corps, working in Palo Duro Canyon and Oklahoma. His story closely parallels with that of Everett Spruce, an Arkansan who moved to Dallas to study with Olin Travis and created *Wild Place*. Both artists taught at the University of Texas at Austin.

The lithographs owned by the Museum of the Southwest reflect two distinct parts of Lester's life. *Yucca and Prickly Pear,* from 1941, shows a timeless landscape that can still be found today in many parts of Texas. These would have been produced when Lester was living in Dallas but making frequent trips to West Texas to sketch the land. *A Store in Austin* was created in 1942, and would be totally unrecognizable to denizens of that city today. Lester experimented with different styles throughout his career, moving from strong outlines and distinct forms to looser and more abstract compositions.

WE

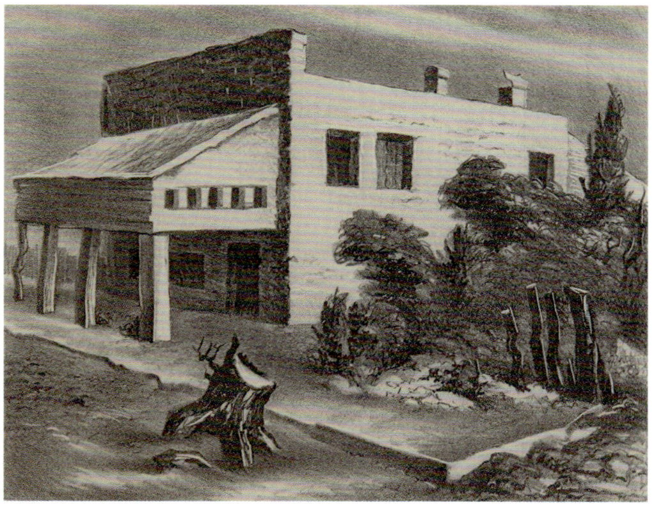

A Store in Austin, 1942. Lithograph, 8½ x 11 in. 1967.002 004. Gift of Merritt Mauzey.

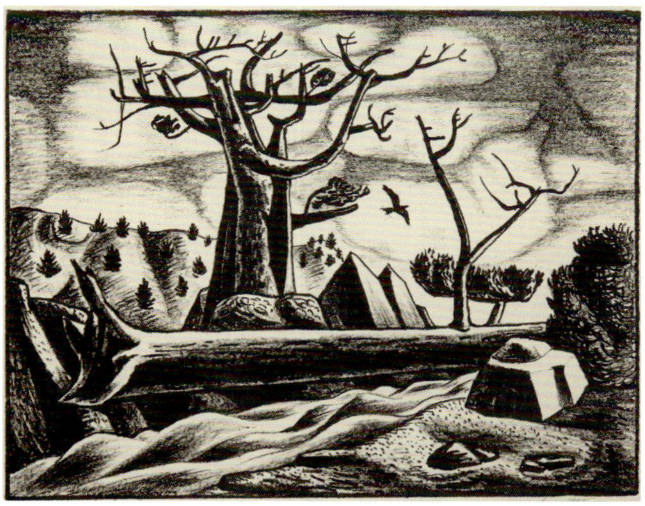

Everett Spruce. *Wild Place*, c. 1940. Lithograph, 9¼ x 12¼ in. 1970.015.012. Gift of Merritt Mauzey.

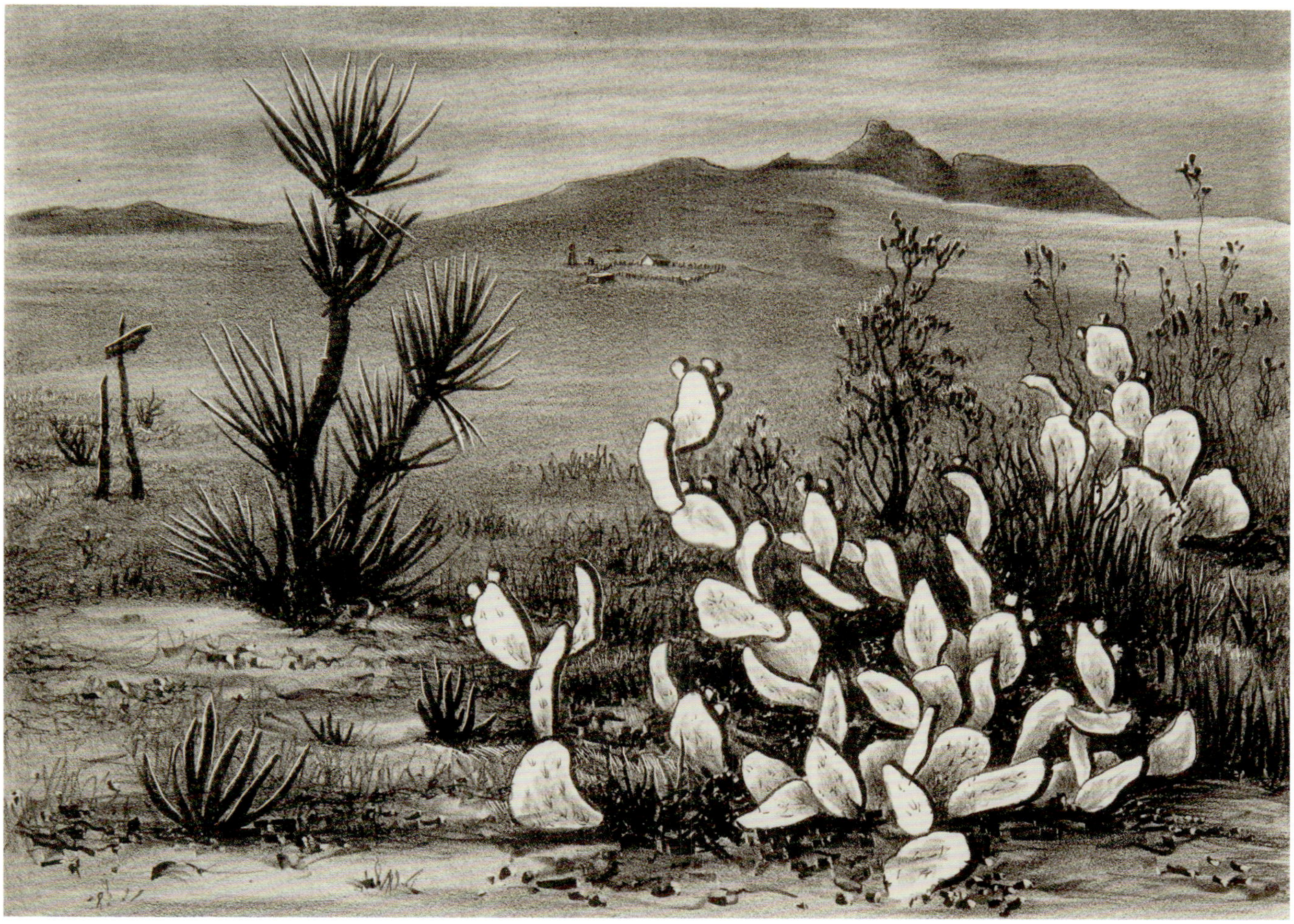

Charles T. Bowling

(1891–1985)

Industrial Encroachment, 1939

Lithograph, 9¾ x 12 in.

1969.012.005

Gift of Merritt Mauzey

Charles Bowling's nine prints in the collection of the Museum of the Southwest reveal an artist with many similarities to other members of the Texas Regionalist circle. Like many artists in Dallas at the time, he studied with Olin Travis at the Dallas Art Institute and later independently with Frank Klepper and Alexandre Hogue. He worked as a draftsman and civil engineer for the Texas Power and Light Company where he was able to get Otis Dozier and William Lester drafting jobs.

His greatest impact on the Dallas art scene was founding and serving as president for the Lone Star Printmakers, which ran a print circuit to promote and sell the work of local artists from 1938 to 1942. Bowling and Merritt Mauzey achieved success with this printmaking group, each man eventually purchasing his own lithography stone for use by others in the community of artists. Bowling's prolific body of lithographs showcase his strong compositions and textures in scenes of rural and lonely landscapes in works such as *Deep Woods* and *Wet Road*. In others, such as *Industrial Encroachment,* the artist's affinity with Alexandre Hogue is evident in the theme of man's intrusion upon the natural world. In this 1939 work the typical signs of progress—cars, factories, telephone lines—are seen intruding onto the edges of the city where before there had been only nature.

WE

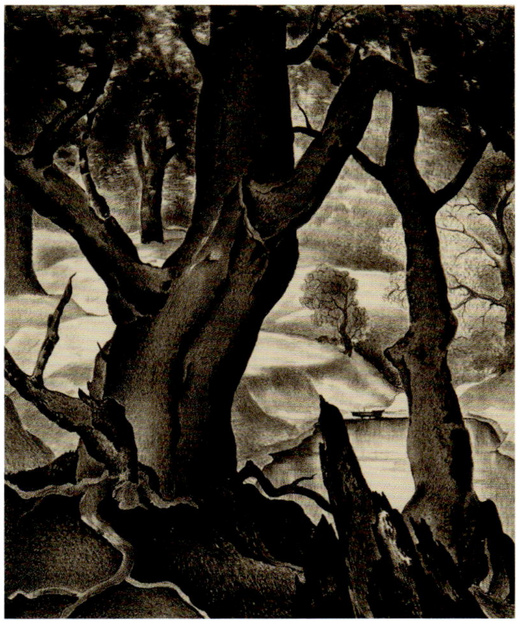

Deep Woods, 1940. Lithograph, 11¼ x 9½ in. 1969.012.002. Gift of Merritt Mauzey.

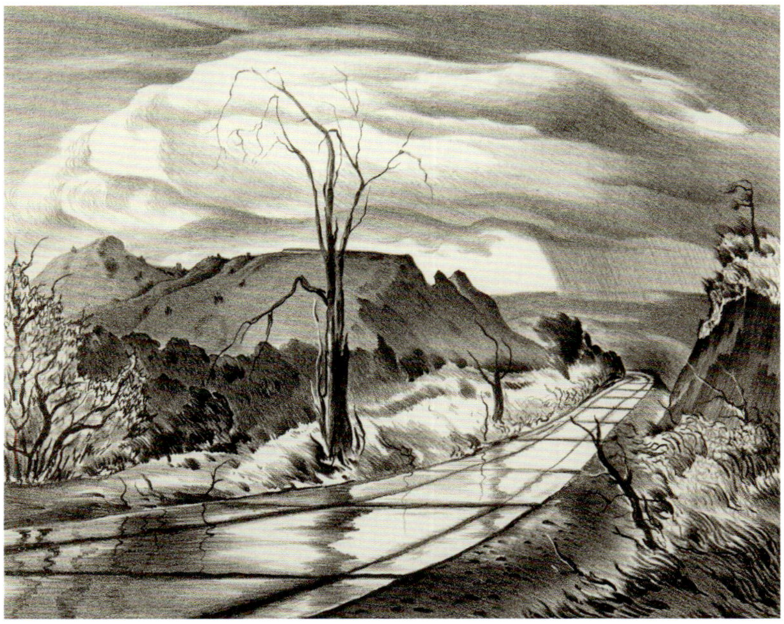

Wet Road, c. 1939–1942. Lithograph, 9 x 12 in. 1967.002.009. Gift of Merritt Mauzey.

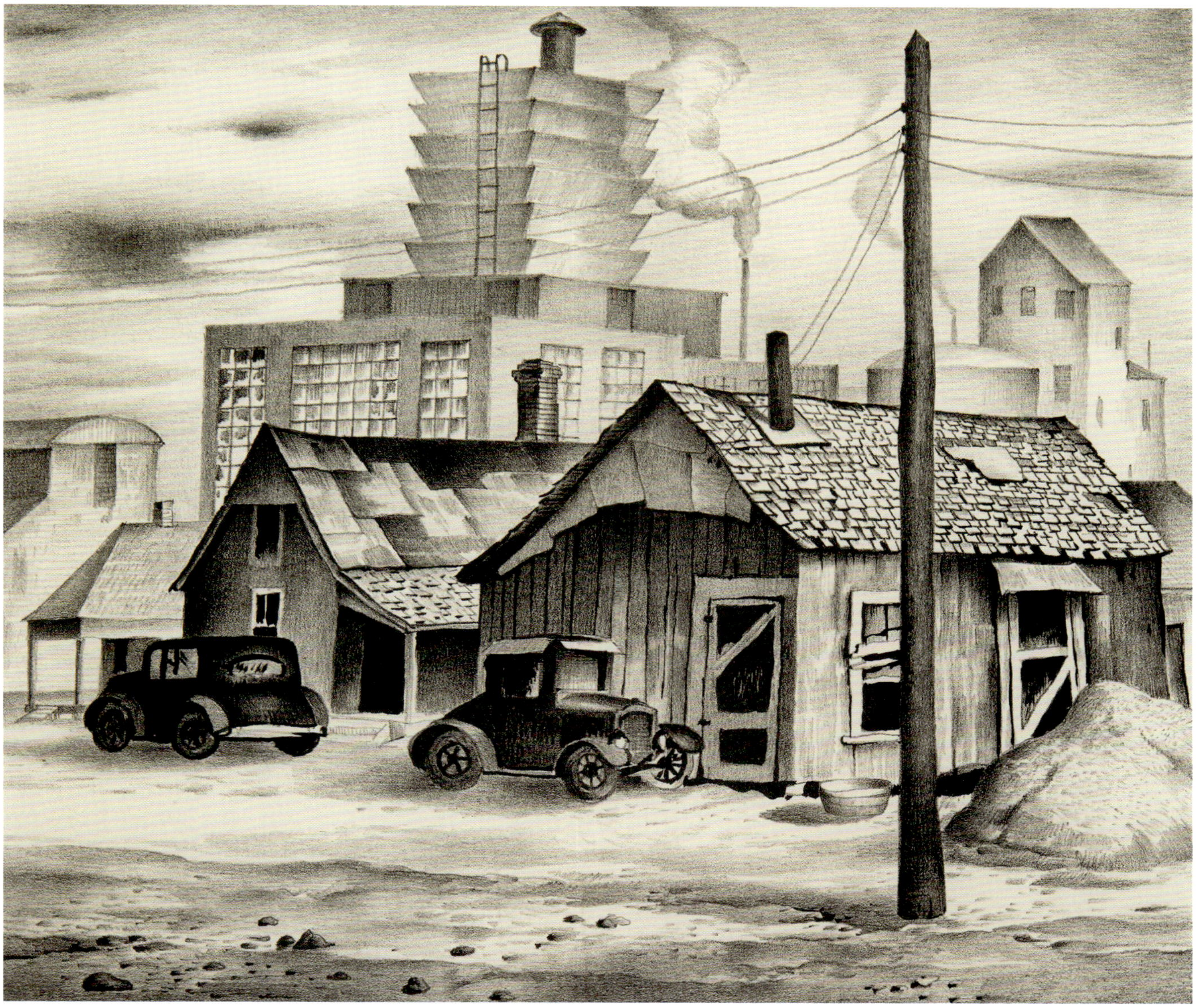

Merritt Mauzey
(1898–1973)

Nugent's Homestead, c. 1941

Oil on Masonite, 22 x 36⅛ in.

1969.013.001

Gift of Mr. and Mrs. William S. Marshall

MERRITT MAUZEY'S ARTWORK WAS VITAL to the early formation of the permanent collection of the Museum of the Southwest. Mauzey's lithographs were among the first accessioned works, and the artist donated some of his most important works on paper to the collection. His lithographs and paintings comprise 161 objects, a large body of work that illustrates the depth of his interest in exploring rural life in West Texas.

Mauzey was born to a cotton-farming family in Clifton, Texas, and worked as a cotton farmer in Sweetwater during the early part of his life. In 1927 he moved to Dallas and started exploring his passion for art, taking classes and producing art while maintaining a day job at a cotton company. He eventually became part of the Texas Regionalist group and the Lone Star Printmakers. In 1946 he was awarded a Guggenheim Foundation fellowship in fine arts, the first ever given to a Texan. The subject of cotton appears in almost every work, but he also documented architecture, weather and rural towns such as Shiner and Leander.

Mauzey preferred what he called the "strength and vital qualities" of lithography over other black-and-white media but he also painted. In *Nugent's Homestead* Mauzey documents an old wooden cabin remembered from his youth in Nolan County. The home stands windblown and likely forgotten, a homestead like so many others from the Depression era. In *Self-Portrait* his only worldly possession is a cotton plant. *Neighbors* is a lithograph from the Cotton series, where Mauzey depicts a poor and a rich farmer working their respective cotton fields. On the left are poor fields and rudimentary equipment, with a church in the distance. On the right the richer fields are tilled with mechanized equipment; in the distance is a schoolhouse.

WE

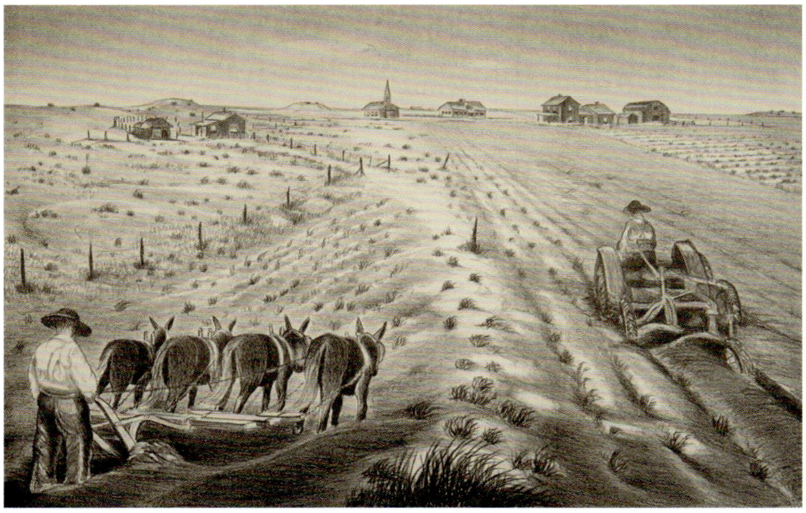

Neighbors, c. 1938. Lithograph, 10¾ x 17 in. 1967.001.031. Museum Acquisition Fund.

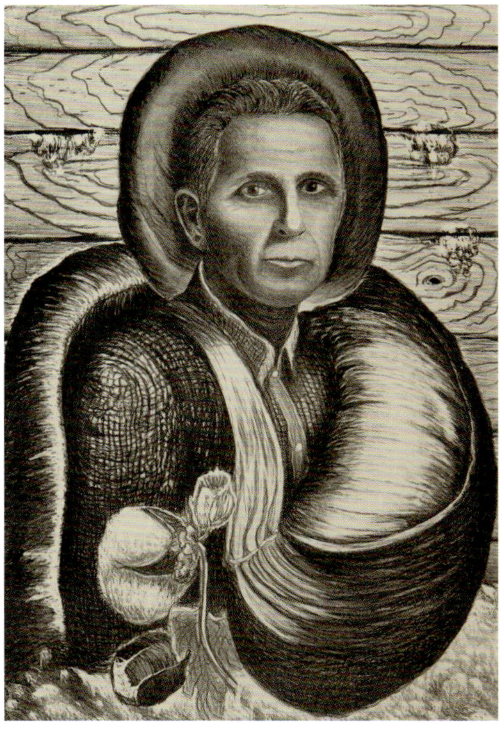

Self-Portrait, c. 1943. Lithograph, 15¼ x 10¾ in. 1970.004.063. Museum Acquisition Fund.

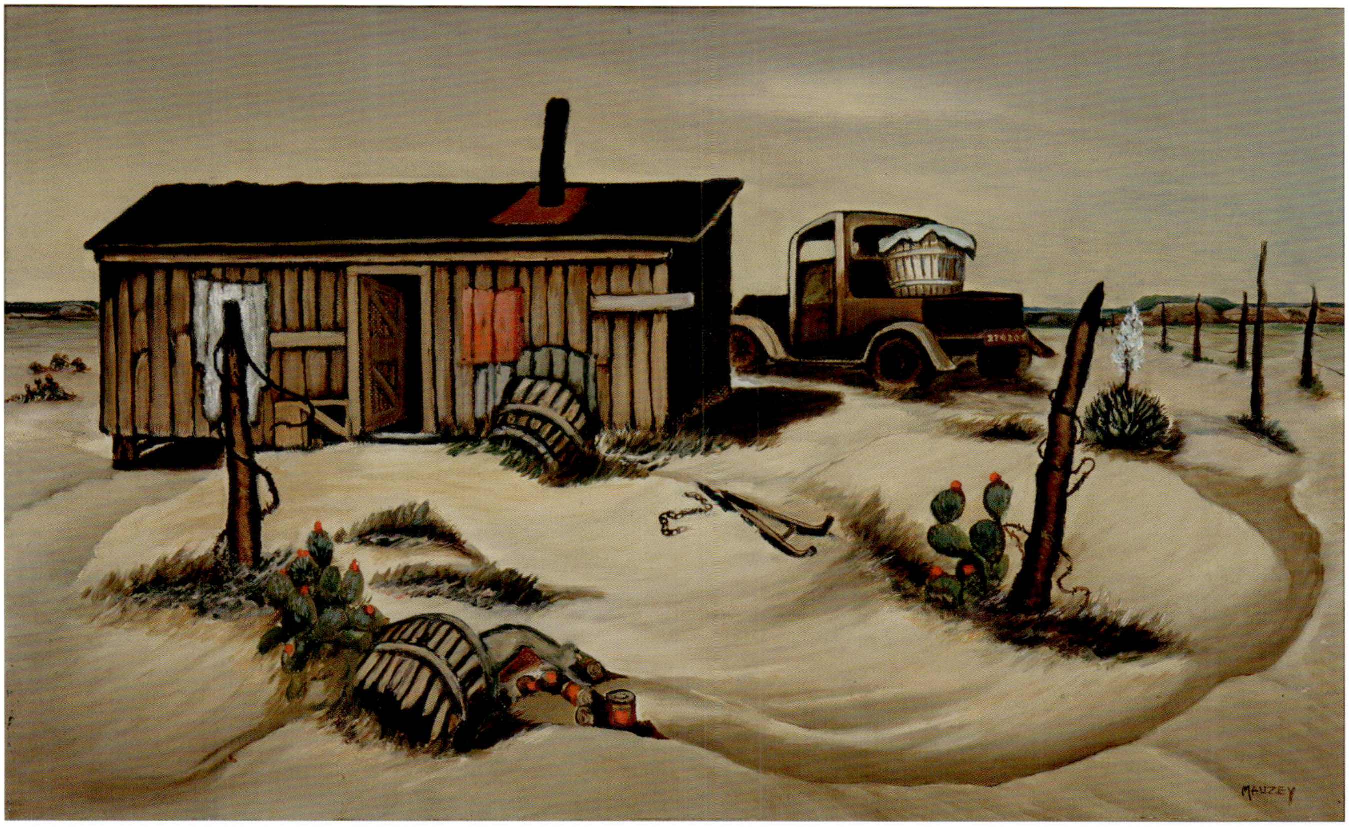
MAUZEY

Alexandre Hogue

(1898–1994)

Ranchos Mountains from Talpa, 1931

Oil on canvas, 5½ x 7½ in.

1970.001.003

Gift of Merritt Mauzey

Alexandre Hogue was one of the best-known artists to emerge from the Texas Regionalist group, and his ecological perspectives on landscapes give his work a unique quality that still resonates with viewers today. Raised in Denton, Texas, he studied at the Minneapolis College of Art and Design and worked at advertising agencies in New York before moving to Dallas in 1925. In the 1920s and '30s he spent a lot of time traveling around Texas, including the Big Bend area of West Texas, and Taos, New Mexico. In Taos he befriended other artists, including Joseph Imhof, Ernest Blumenschein and Buck Dunton, as well as the Taos Pueblo Indians. His interest in the Pueblos and their ethics of land use would inform his work and how he investigated the environment in the Southwest. His paintings from this period include *Ranchos Mountains from Talpa*, a small landscape imbued with characteristic vast, almost geometric mountains that show the large Taos Valley below. *Five Crosses*, printed on Imhof's lithographic press, shows the famous San Francisco de Asis Church in Ranchos de Taos, well documented by many artists, and here slightly abstracted by Hogue.

As the Great Depression and the Dust Bowl unfolded in the 1930s, many artists, including those associated with the Texas Regionalists, depicted the toll taken on the people and communities. Hogue is best known for depicting the effect that the Dust Bowl took on the land itself, with paintings showing the earth stripped bare, revealing the vulnerable female form underneath. With such works he differentiated himself from his contemporaries, but he also was an important part of the art scene in Dallas with such works as *Prairie Dog,* with its affinities to artists such as Jerry Bywaters and Merritt Mauzey.

WE

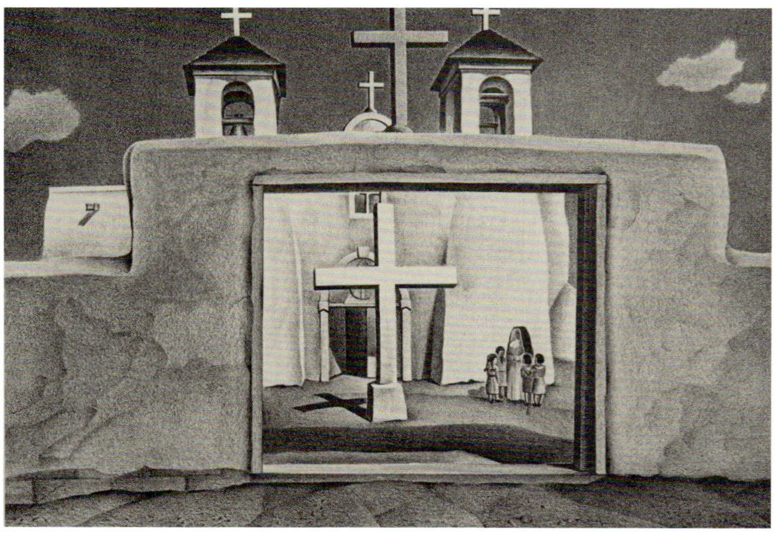

Five Crosses, 1938. Lithograph, 8½ x 12½ in. 1970.015.003. Gift of Merritt Mauzey.

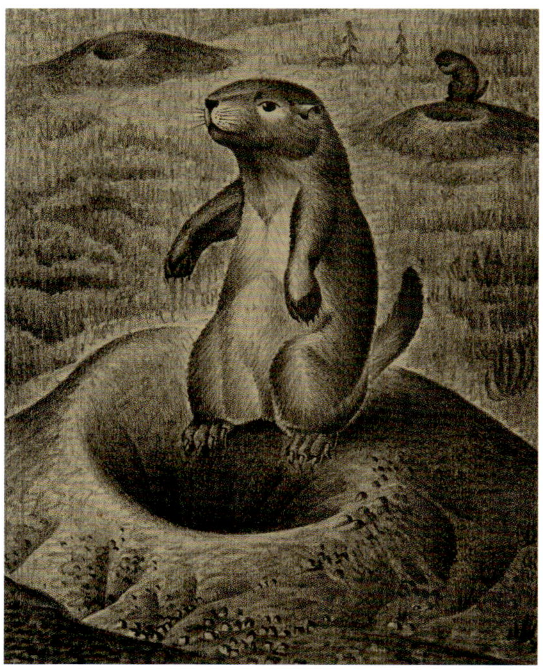

Prairie Dog, 1938. Lithograph, 6½ x 5½ in. 1969.002.013. Gift of Merritt Mauzey.

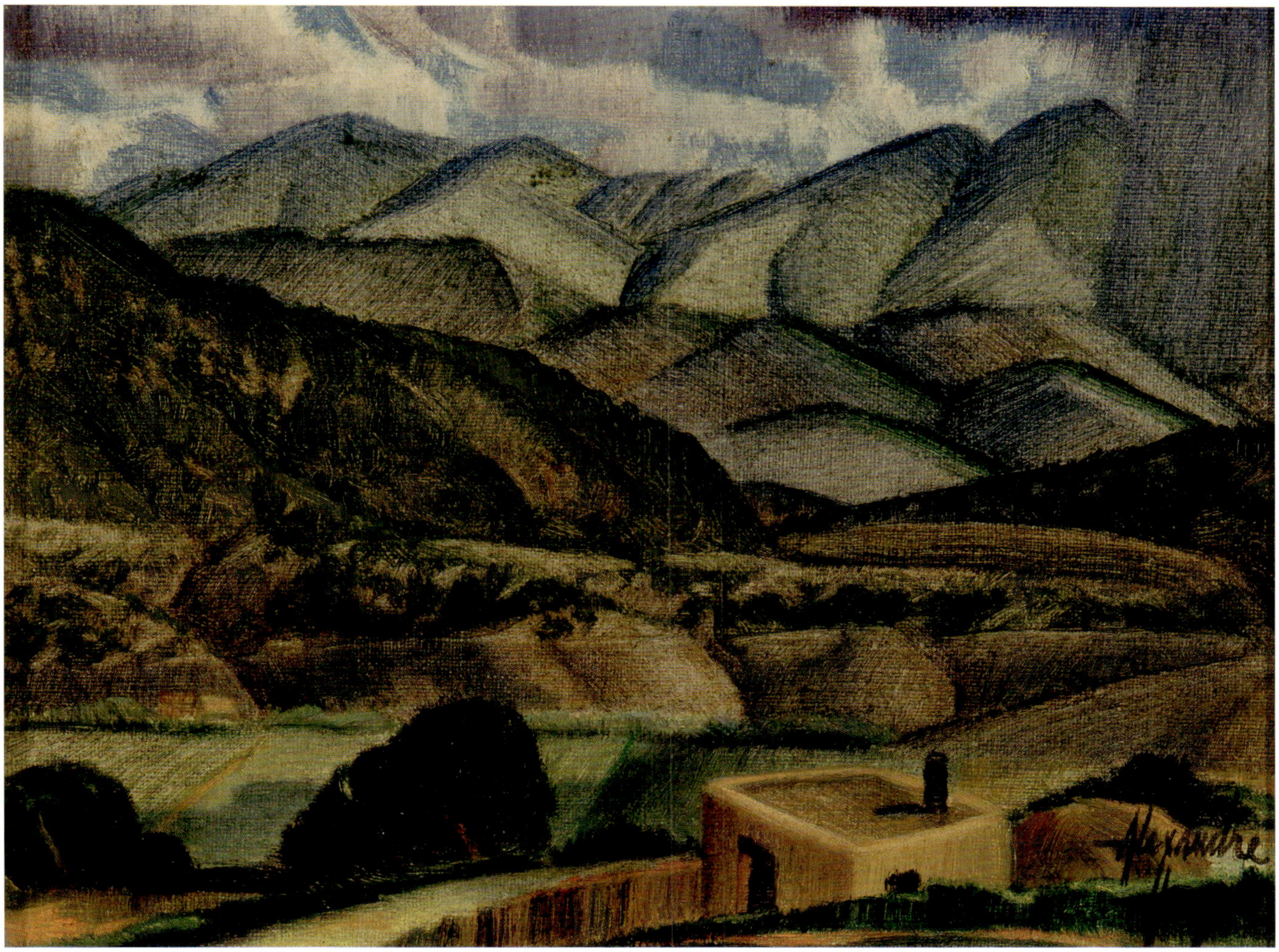
Alexandre

E. Martin Hennings

(1886–1956)

Evening Solitude, c. 1925

Oil on canvas, 23¼ x 29½ in.

1970.007.001

Gift of Mrs. Naomi A. Lancaster

One of the later arrivals to the core group that formed the Taos Society of Artists, E. Martin Hennings visited the town in 1917 before permanently moving in 1921. Raised in Chicago to a family of German immigrants, he graduated from the Art Institute of Chicago in 1904 and would continue his studies there for several years. Hennings found work as a commercial artist, working as an illustrator and painting murals and portraits in the area before seeking more art education in Europe. He studied at the Academy of Fine Arts in Munich, where he would meet future Taos artists Victor Higgins and Walter Ufer. These three artists were also connected with arts patron Carter Harrison, who would eventually send all of them to Taos on painting trips. When the Taos Society of Artists disbanded in 1927, Hennings was still in the prime of his career and continued to find commercial success as well as winning numerous art prizes. His works were included in the Venice Biennale of 1924 and the Paris Salon of 1927.

All three of Hennings' paintings in the Museum of the Southwest collection feature his academic style of solid, unwavering brushwork, evenly applied color palettes, and an emphasis on patterns. *Evening Solitude* shows a rare nighttime landscape, with a lone man walking towards a well-lit home under the Taos night sky. Because of his academic training he had a strong interest in portrait painting and sought out Indian models in works such as *Taos Pueblo Indians*. He was also able to explore *plein air* painting with works including *Around the Campfire—On the Trail to Blue Lake*. This work integrates native subjects, each rendered in interestingly patterned textiles, with a larger natural landscape of rocks and trees.

WE

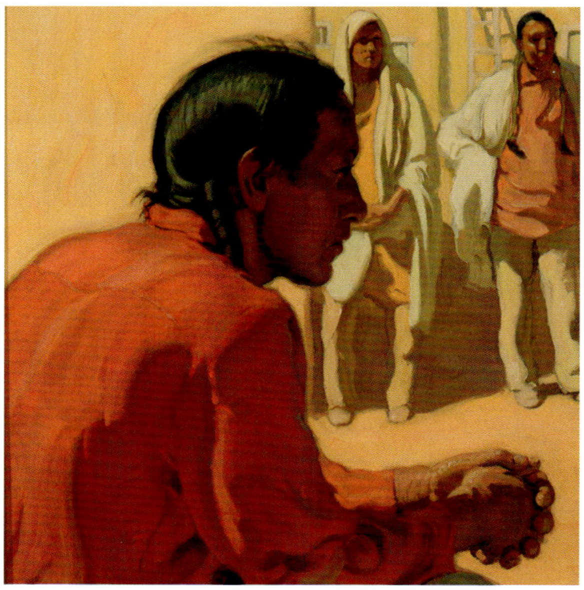

Around the Campfire—On the Trail to Blue Lake, c. 1925. Oil on linen, 25 x 30 in. 1980.009.009. Gift of Fred T. and Novadean Hogan.

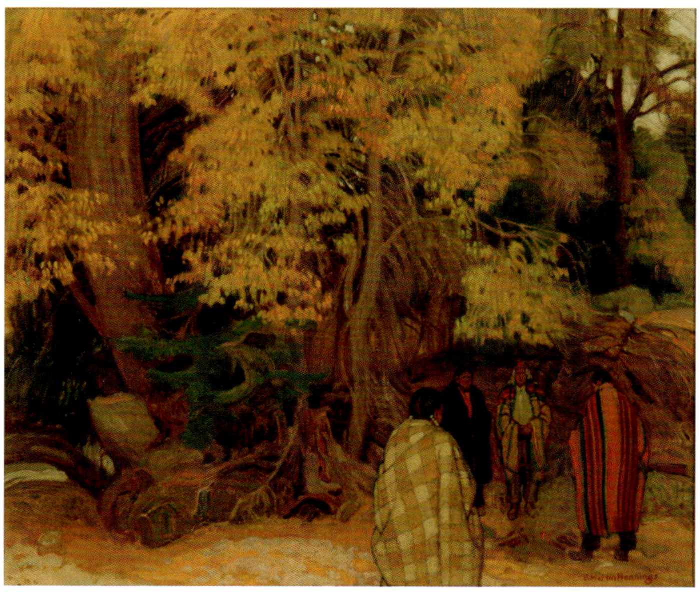

Taos Pueblo Indians, c. 1925. Oil on canvas, 14⅛ x 14 in. 1980.009.008. Gift of Fred T. and Novadean Hogan.

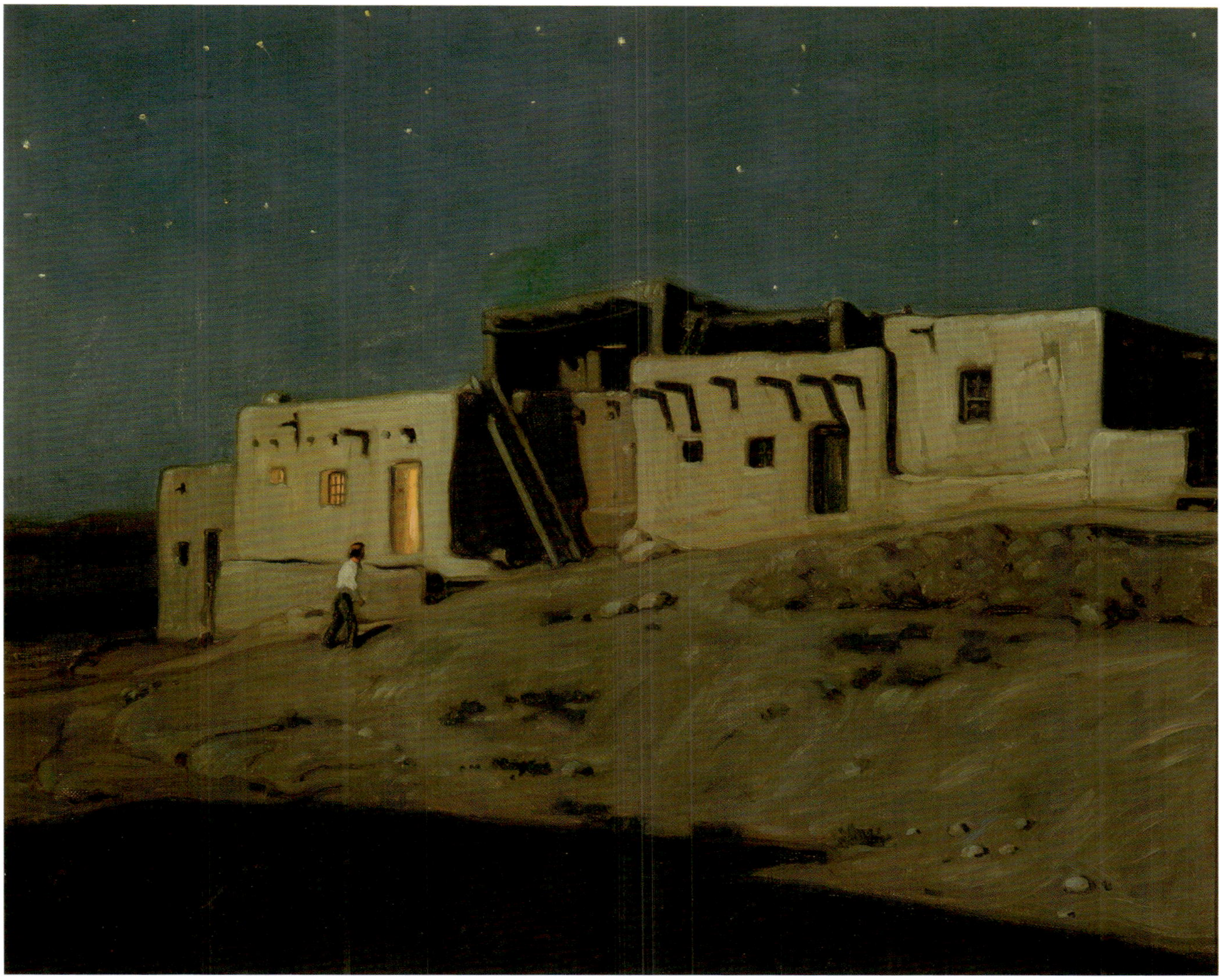

Peter Hurd

(1904–1984)

Early Autumn, 1969

Watercolor, 14¼ x 21 in.

1970.009.001

Gift of Mr. and Mrs. Carlton Beal

Peter Hurd was a prolific artist who worked in a variety of media: painting in egg tempera, oil and watercolor; designing and painting fresco murals; drawing in charcoal, pen and inkwash; and printing in lithography. In the narrative of Hurd's life and art, great emphasis is placed on his relationship with the dynastic Wyeth family. Born in Roswell, New Mexico, and studying at the New Mexico Military Institute and the United States Military Academy, West Point, he renounced a career in the military in favor of art. For five years he apprenticed with the painter and illustrator N. C. Wyeth at Chadds Ford, Pennsylvania, and worked closely with other artists in the Wyeth family, including Andrew Wyeth. He married N. C. Wyeth's daughter, fellow painter Henriette, and their children include the artist Carol Hurd, whose husband, Peter Rogers, is also in the collection of the Museum of the Southwest.

He worked as a professional artist in Pennsylvania for several years, but in 1934 he purchased a ranch in San Patricio, moving his family there in 1940. He drew great inspiration from the landscape of southwestern New Mexico. During World War II he served as a war correspondent for *Life* magazine. Hurd is well known in West Texas for his murals in several post offices and at the Museum of Texas Tech, and his paintings are in many museums in the region. His New Mexican paintings highlight his artistic focus on sun and light, often showing exact moments in time, as seen in *Early Autumn* and *The Dam at Dusk*. In his many landscapes he depicts the earth and sky of the Southwest imbued with the various effects of light. With his lithographs such as *Sermon from Revelations* Hurd also creates striking contrasts of light and dark filling the scene.

WE

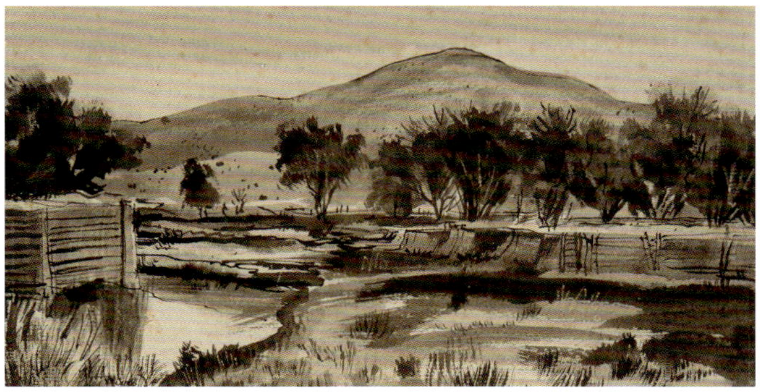

The Dam at Dusk, 1952. Inkwash drawing, 6 x 11½ in. 1980.012.001. Gift of Marshall and Winston, Inc.

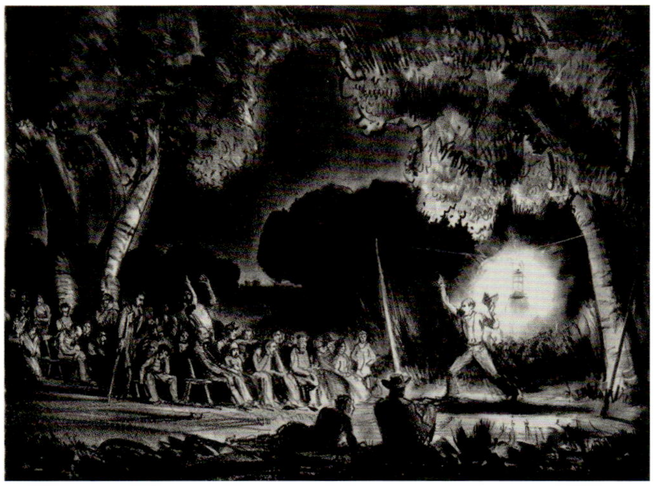

Sermon from Revelations, 1937. Lithograph, 10½ x 13¼ in. 1996.002.019. Gift of Fred T. and Novadean Hogan.

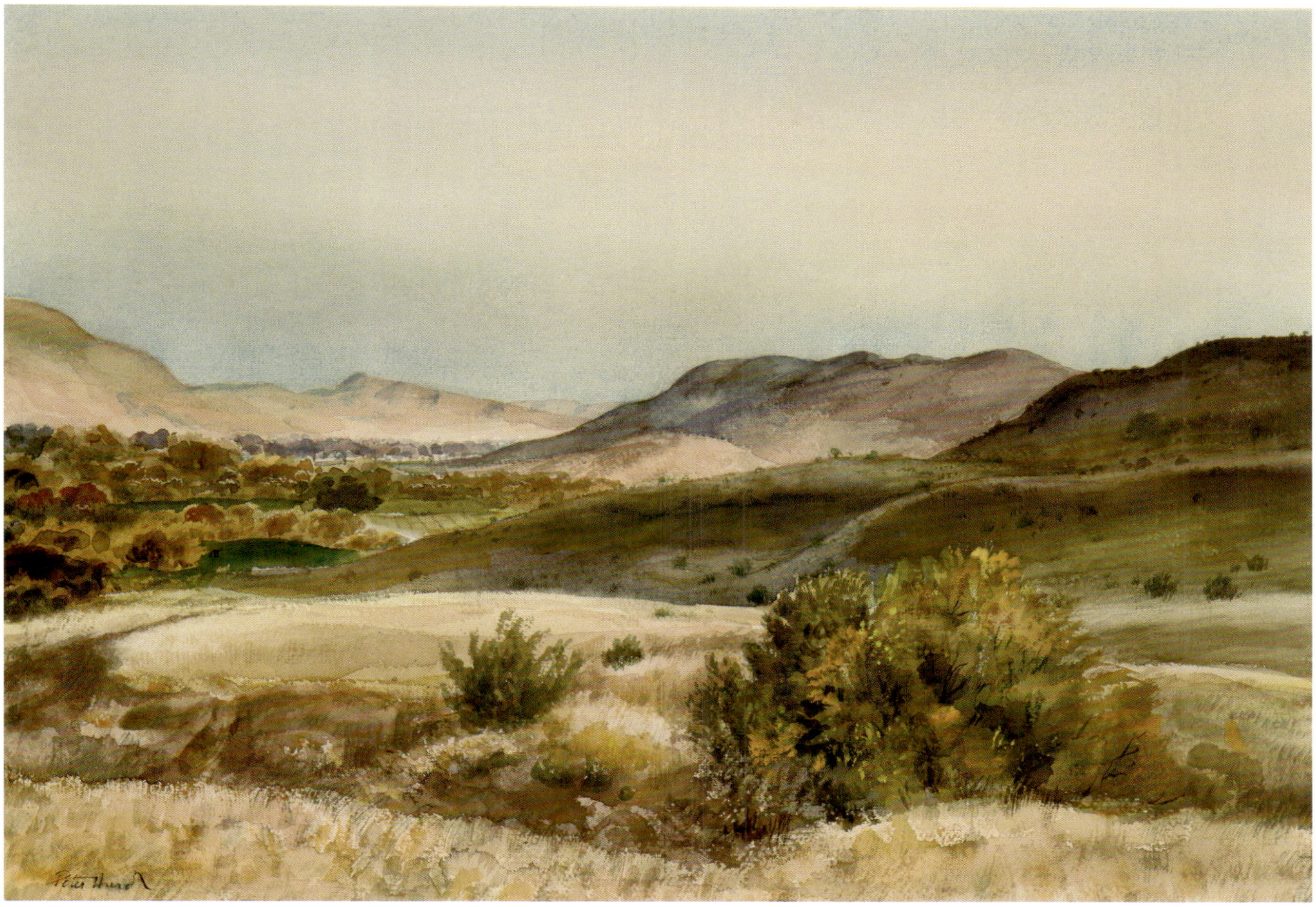

Thomas Wayne (T. C.) Cannon

(1946–1978)

Untitled #22
(Young Man with Scarf), c. 1977

Charcoal and lamp black on paper, 47 x 31 in.

1980.003.001

Museum Acquisition Fund

One of the most prevalent narratives about T. C. Cannon emphasizes the relatively short length of artistic production due to his early death at the age of thirty-one. Cannon became an influential figure while still a student at the Institute of American Indian Arts in Santa Fe, influencing his fellow students and instructors alike, most famously his teacher Fritz Scholder, only nine years his senior.

Cannon, of Caddo and Kiowa ethnicity, enrolled in the IAIA at the age of seventeen, having grown up in a small town in Oklahoma. His experimentation and exchange were deepened in Santa Fe, followed by a brief period of study at the San Francisco Art Institute and service in Vietnam in the 101st Air Cavalry. After his tour of duty he returned to Santa Fe to continue his artistic endeavors, painting and writing poetry.

With Cannon's work there is often a starkness that confronts the viewer. Like his other works on paper, *Untitled #22 (Young Man with Scarf)* has no background, but is simply a figure looking into the distance. The man's face, hair and scarf are beautifully rendered with precise details and shading, but his body is somewhat amorphous. Although Cannon is best known for vividly colored Pop Art paintings, his simple expressionist figures in both painting and drawing were the true focus, and instantly recognizable.

A poem he wrote in 1968, which appeared in the catalog for his 1972 exhibition with Fritz Scholder, *Two American Painters*, at the Smithsonian's National Collection of Fine Arts, provides insight into such works as *Untitled #22:*

> art. . . being the fiend that it is
> wraps me in a bundle
> and sends me off
> to the house of myself.

WE

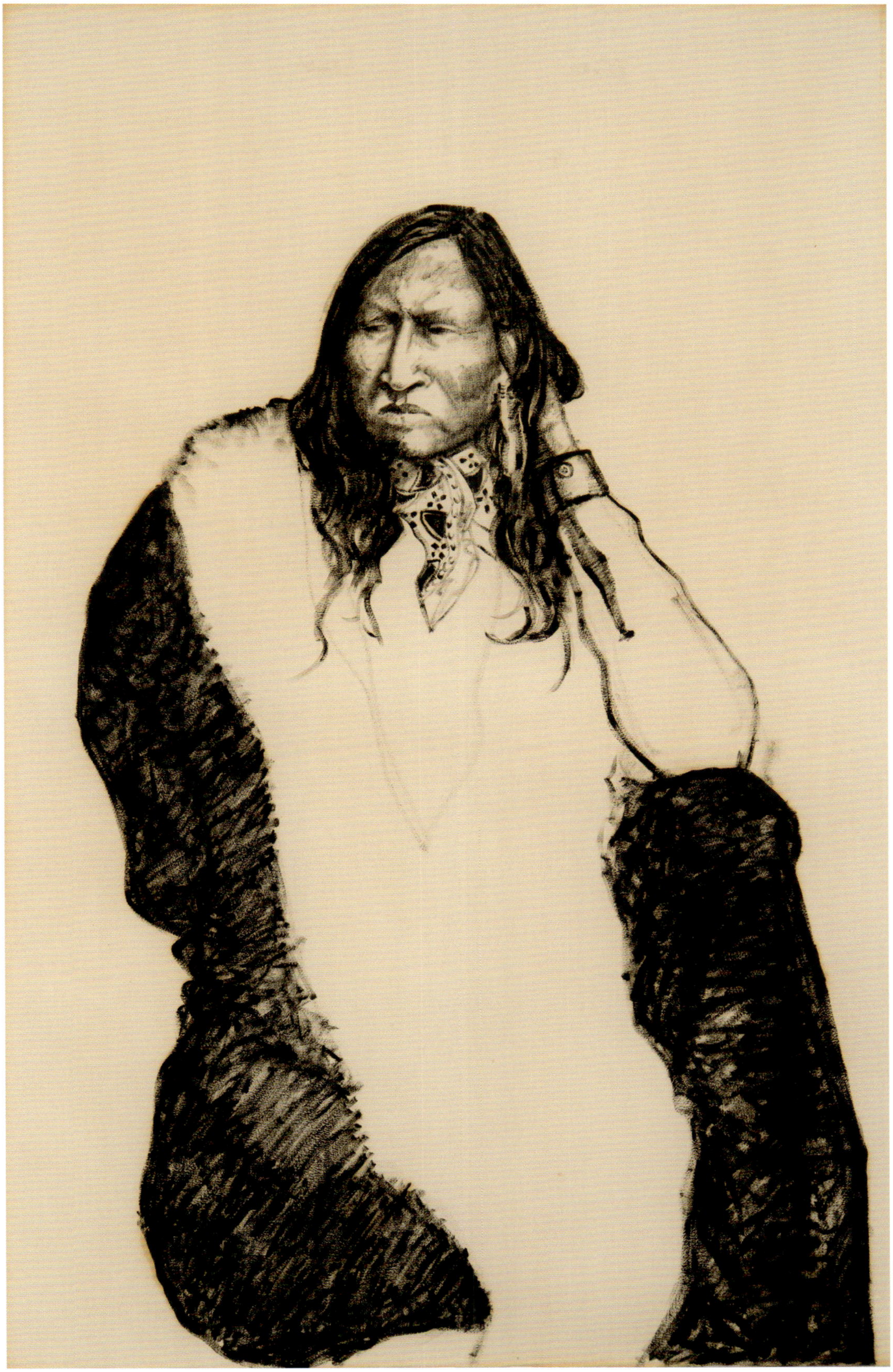

Fritz Scholder

(1937–2005)

My House in Taos, 1979

Acrylic on canvas, 68 x 80 in.

1980.004.001

Gift of Marshall & Winston, Inc.

Fritz Scholder is best known for his depictions of American Indians, but his landscapes, such as *My House in Taos,* show an important component of the artist's career. The lion's share of scholarship on Fritz Scholder focuses on his portraits of Indians, his identity as an American Indian artist and how that identity informs his work. His family is a mix of German and Indian on his father's side. His father, Fritz the elder, was half Luiseño, part of the California Mission tribes, and worked as an administrator for the Bureau of Indian Affairs. Scholder is officially on the rolls of the California Mission tribes but never considered himself a full Indian. As a young man he studied with several prominent Indian artists in both South Dakota and at the University of Arizona, where he obtained his MFA.

In 1964 Scholder moved to Santa Fe to accept a teaching position at the Institute of American Indian Arts, one of the first institutions of its kind in the country. His early output was very abstract and highly experimental, synthesizing the different styles and influences he had been exposed to. Before he arrived in Santa Fe he showed no interest in the American Indian as a subject, but by 1967 he started painting his most iconic works, including the Indian series of paintings and prints. His Indian works were strongly influenced by the artists Wayne Thiebaud, Francis Bacon and Nathan Oliveira, and by his own students, especially T. C. Cannon.

Through these Indian paintings, Scholder became a huge figure in contemporary art. His later work in Taos, Galisteo, and other smaller towns in New Mexico, as well as in Arizona, showed a more abstract, experimental and often contemplative side to his work. It was during this period that he created *My House in Taos.* There is a strong resonance between Scholder's Southwestern landscapes and Richard Diebenkorn's landscape-inspired California abstractions. Scholder's mid-career output illustrates his profound and striking color sense mixed with Pop Art compositional style and Abstract Expressionist drip-painting techniques.

WE

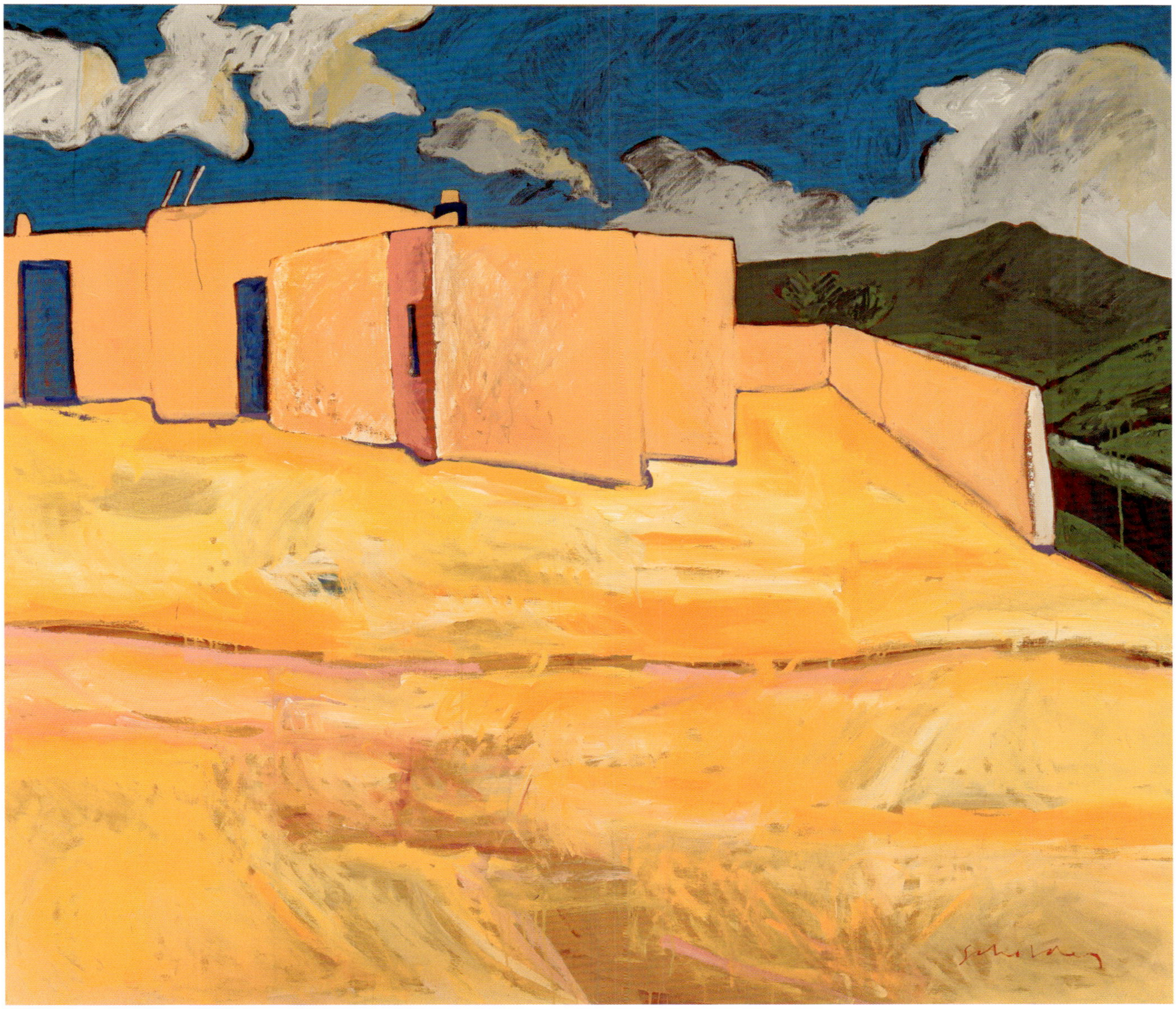

Allan Houser

(1914–1994)

Offering of the Sacred Pipe, 1979

Bronze, 79 x 64 x 19 in.

1980.007.001

Gift of Mary and William D. Kennedy

ALLAN HOUSER'S *Offering of the Sacred Pipe* was one of the first sculptures added to the Museum of the Southwest, and the nearly seven-foot bronze has always held a prominent—now iconic—place in front of the historic Turner Mansion on the campus lawn. This reverential figure stands tall and imposing, his long robe rippling with texture, and holding in his outstretched arms a sacred pipe, with viewers able to provide their own interpretation as to whom exactly he is offering it. Another casting of this sculpture stands outside the United States Mission to the United Nations in New York City, conveying the universal sentiments that Houser so ably evoked in his work. An indoor Houser sculpture, *Watching for Dancing Partners,* is carved from pink Tennessee marble, showcasing Houser's versatility in almost any material.

Houser (born Haozous) was Warm Springs Chiricahua Apache and created American Indian figures throughout his career as a painter and sculptor, while determined not to be defined simply as an "Indian artist." Born on a farm in Apache, Oklahoma, and attending Indian boarding schools, he went on to graduate from the Studio at the Santa Fe Indian School in 1938. The school was led by Dorothy Dunn, well known for teaching the "studio style" with Native figures engaged in traditional activities in a flat, outlined style. Houser started his art career as a painter, but through several teaching positions that afforded him the opportunity to experiment, he moved into sculpture. He was a professor and later head of the sculpture department at the newly formed Institute of American Indian Arts in Santa Fe from 1962 until 1975. He received many honors and awards throughout his lifetime. Working in stone, wood and bronze, he created sculptures on a continuum between realistic human figures and fully abstract forms.

WE

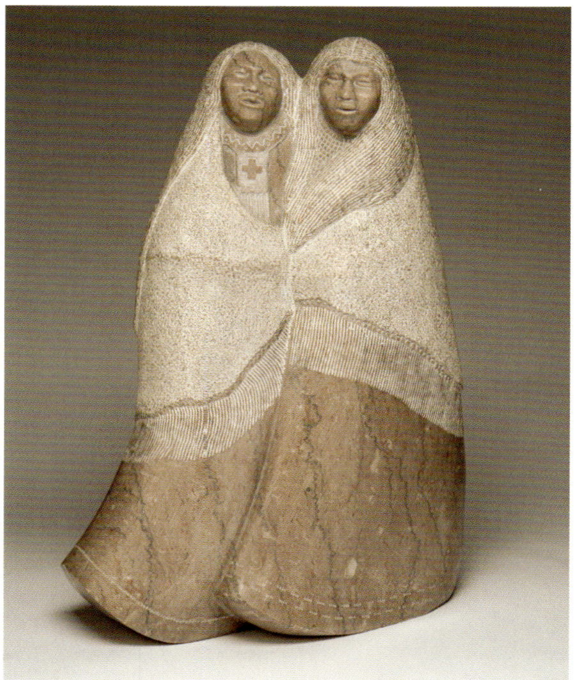

Watching for Dancing Partners, 1978. Pink Tennessee marble, 31 x 22 x 12 in. 1980.006.001. Gift of Mr. and Mrs. Lynn Durham.

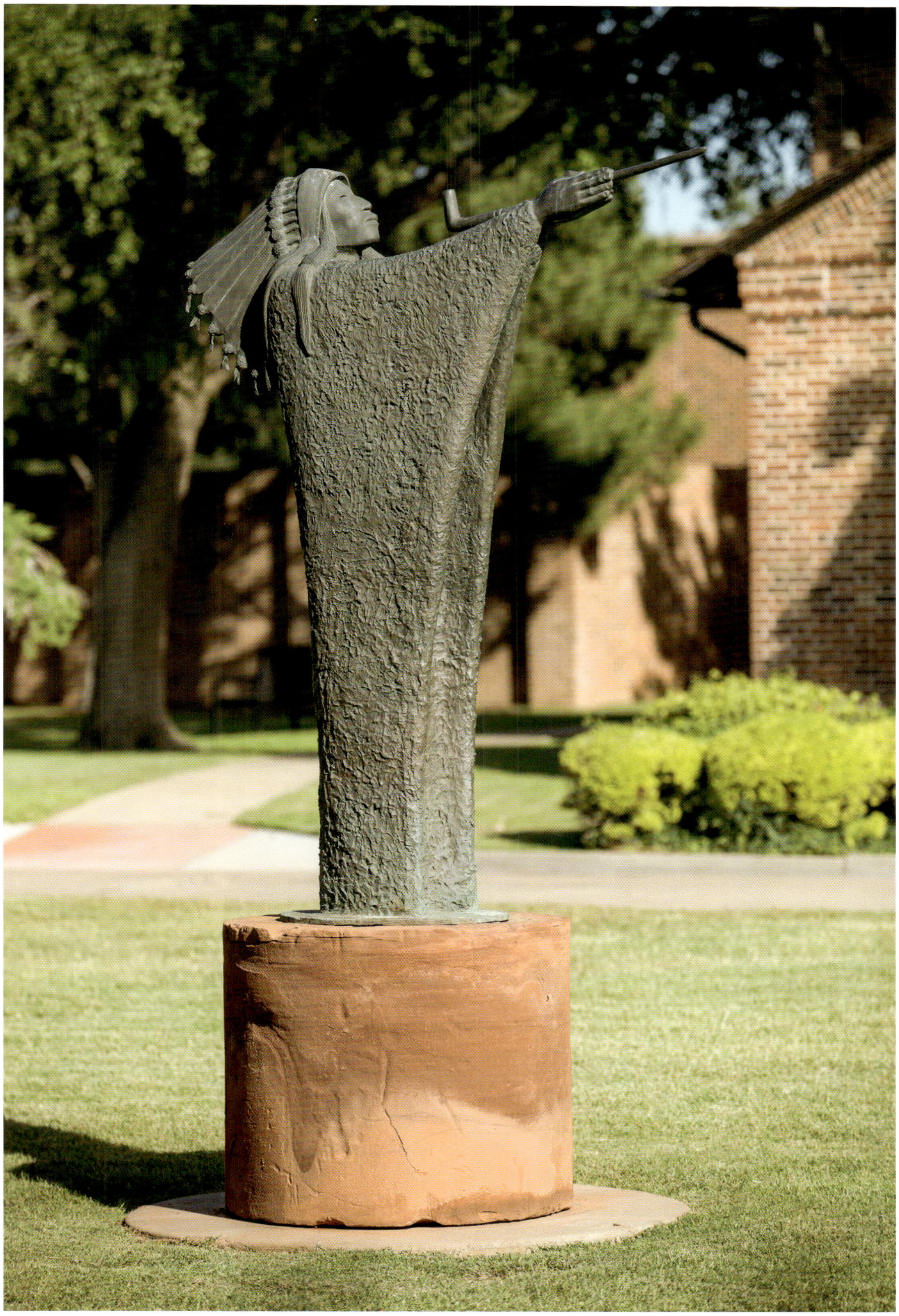

Eric Sloane

(1905–1985)

Sky Cathedral, 1979

Oil on Masonite, 43½ x 38½ in.

1980.008.001

Gift of Fred T. and
Novadean Hogan

It should come as no surprise to anyone who takes even a cursory glance at a painting by Eric Sloane that the artist was a passionate meteorologist. Born Everard Jean Hinrichs in New York City, he lived near the distinguished printer and type designer Frederic W. Goudy and studied art with Goudy and at the Art Students League. At an early age he ran away from home and made his way across the country, working as a sign painter and developing a distinctive style that served him well. During his travels he discovered the Taos Pueblo, where he would return on a regular basis. In 1975, he built a house in La Tierra, near Santa Fe, called "Casa de las Nubes" (House of Clouds). Fascinated by the sky, clouds and weather, he painted those subjects prolifically and went on to illustrate works on meteorology and forecasting. He also created the first televised weather-reporting network and painted commissions for the U.S. Air Force. His large skyscape mural *Earth Flight Environment* is on display in the lobby of the Smithsonian's Air and Space Museum.

His large skyscape *Sky Cathedral*, in the collection of the Museum of the Southwest, illustrates many of Sloane's passions. Although depicting a New England landscape, the vastness and primacy of the sky compared to the small trees and buildings in the foreground are likely a result of his many trips to Taos, where the sky overtakes everything. The buildings shown are painted in oil, but several features are redrawn with an ink pen, a part of Sloane's distinct style and most likely the result of his early work as a pen-and-ink artist and sign painter. The title *Sky Cathedral* alludes to the church spire, which in turn is a representation of Sloane's interest in New England architecture, the subject of several of his books.

WE

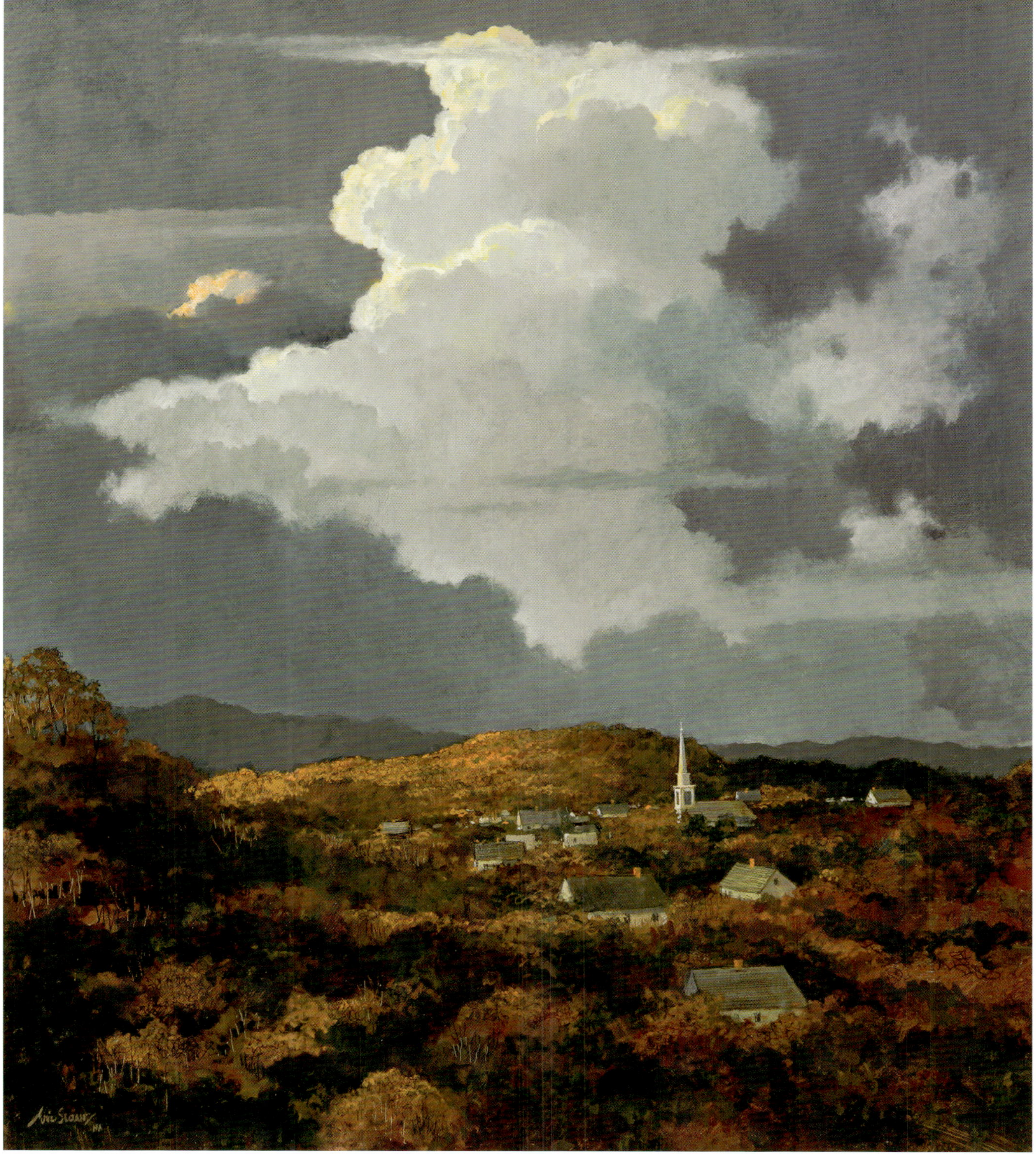

Kenneth Adams

(1897–1966)

Red Zinnias, c. 1950s

Oil on Masonite, 16 x 12 in.

1980.009.001

Gift of Fred T. and Novadean Hogan

The painting and print by Kenneth Adams in the Museum of the Southwest collection provide a different lens from that associated with other members of the Taos Society of Artists. Adams was the youngest member of the TSA and the last artist voted in, arriving in 1924 and staying until 1937. Born in Topeka, Kansas, in 1897, he received little artistic exposure until moving to Chicago in 1916 and studying at the Art Institute before moving on to the Art Students League in New York. He studied with Andrew Dasburg, a proponent of Modernism who introduced Adams to Cubism, and then continued his studies in France. In 1924 he accompanied Dasburg on one of his yearly trips to New Mexico, first traveling to Santa Fe but ultimately staying in Taos. He was particularly interested in painting portraits of the Hispanic people in the area.

During the 1930s Adams found work painting murals and creating prints as part of the Works Progress Administration before accepting a position as artist-in-residence and later faculty member at the University of New Mexico in Albuquerque. His lithograph *Card Players*, printed in 1957, features his characteristically strong and expressive lines. *Red Zinnias* was likely painted in the 1950s. During this period he taught in Albuquerque and devoted himself to the study of flowers, creating still lifes based on the flowers he grew in his garden. One of the few still lifes in the collection of the Museum of the Southwest, it showcases his artistic skill in a subject apart from his better-known portraits.

WE

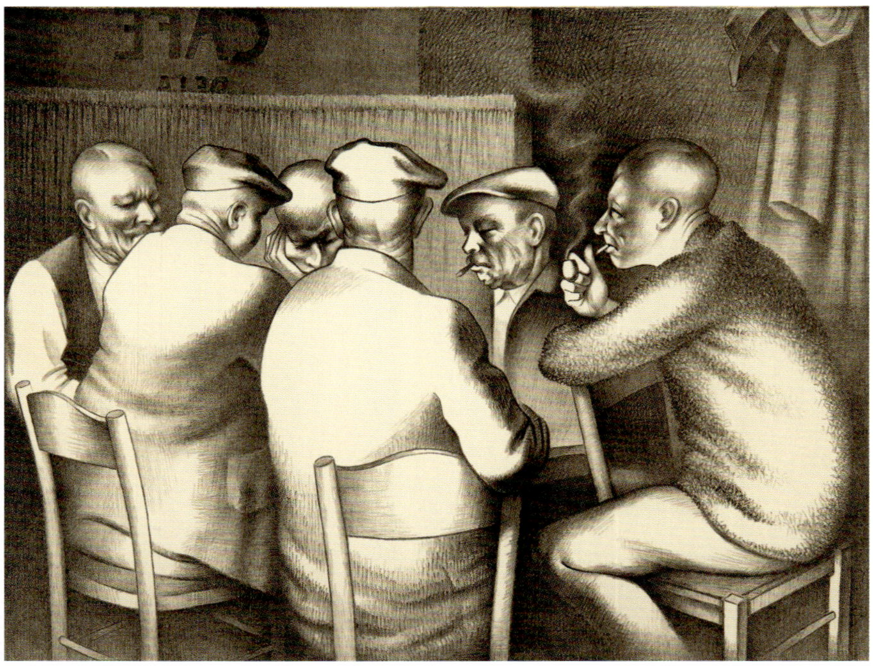

Card Players, 1957. Lithograph, 17¼ x 23 in. 1969.003.001. Gift of Mr. and Mrs. John Miller.

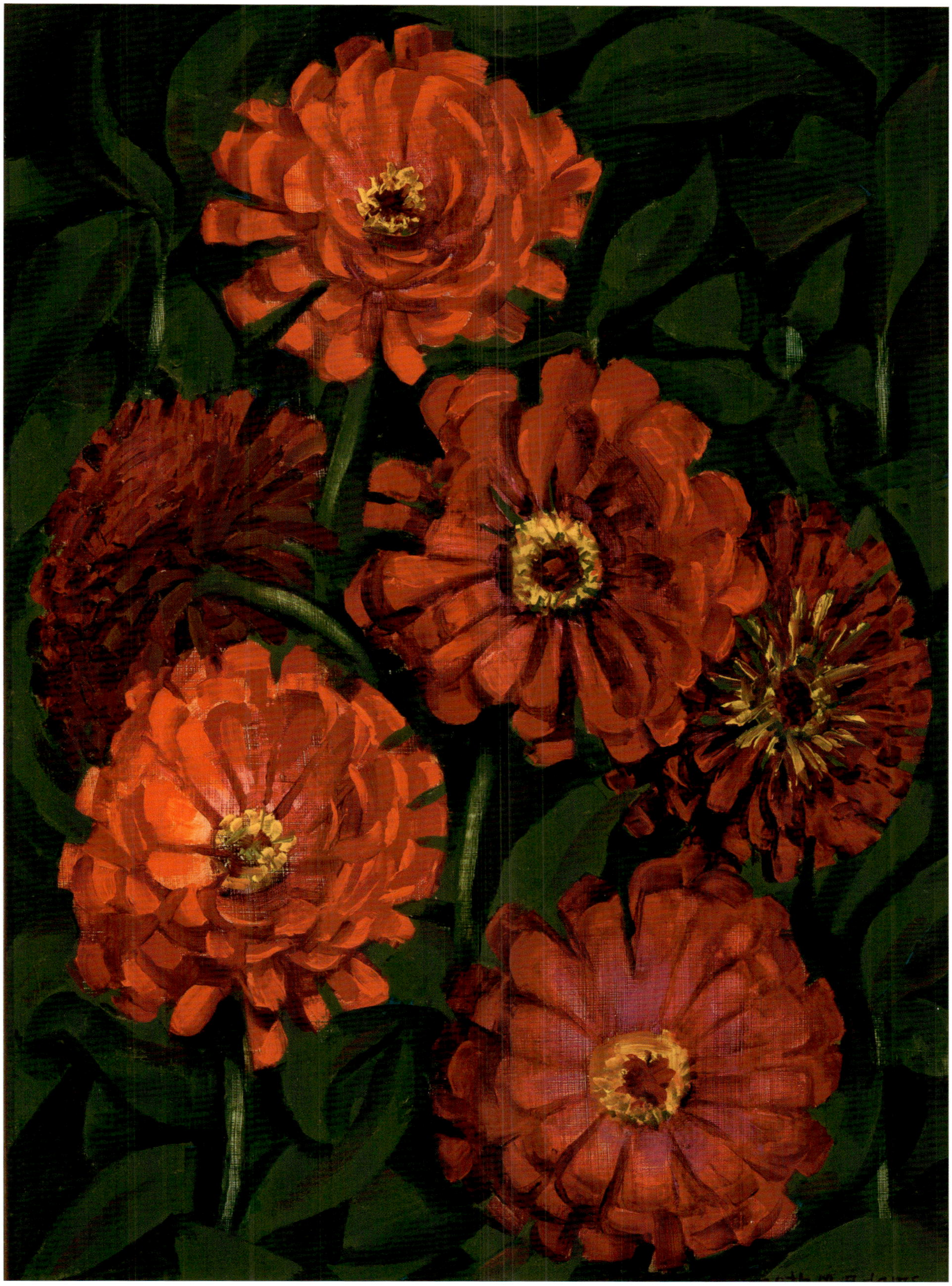

Oscar E. Berninghaus

(1874–1952)

Taos Landscape, c. 1910–1930

Oil on linen, 16 x 20 in.

1980.009.002

Gift of Fred T. and Novadean Hogan

Oscar E. Berninghaus was born in 1874 in St. Louis, Missouri, to German immigrants and was influenced to pursue a career as an artist from an early age by looking at the lithographs produced in his father's shop. As a child, he drew constantly and was fascinated by the stories of the Western frontier. He ended his formal education at the age of sixteen to become a commercial artist by pursuing an apprenticeship in a printing studio but continued his studies with evening classes at the School of Fine Arts at Washington University. Berninghaus' strict early education led him to become a disciplined and determined artist who went to the studio in a suit and hat and eschewed the bohemian stereotype often associated with his profession.

Everything changed in 1899 when Berninghaus was hired by the Denver and Rio Grande Railroad to sketch and produce watercolors of the Western landscape as part of an advertising campaign to attract people from the East Coast. It was on this trip that he first encountered Taos and the landscape and culture that would become the inspiration for his paintings for the rest of his life. In *Taos Landscape*, Berninghaus captured the quintessential elements of the area, including an adobe home inhabited by local people, chile ristras drying against a wall, a domed clay oven, the changing of the aspens, the mountains that surround the town and the clear, crisp mountain sky. Most of all, he infuses the entire scene with the special quality of light so attractive to the many artists who made Taos their home.

BLW

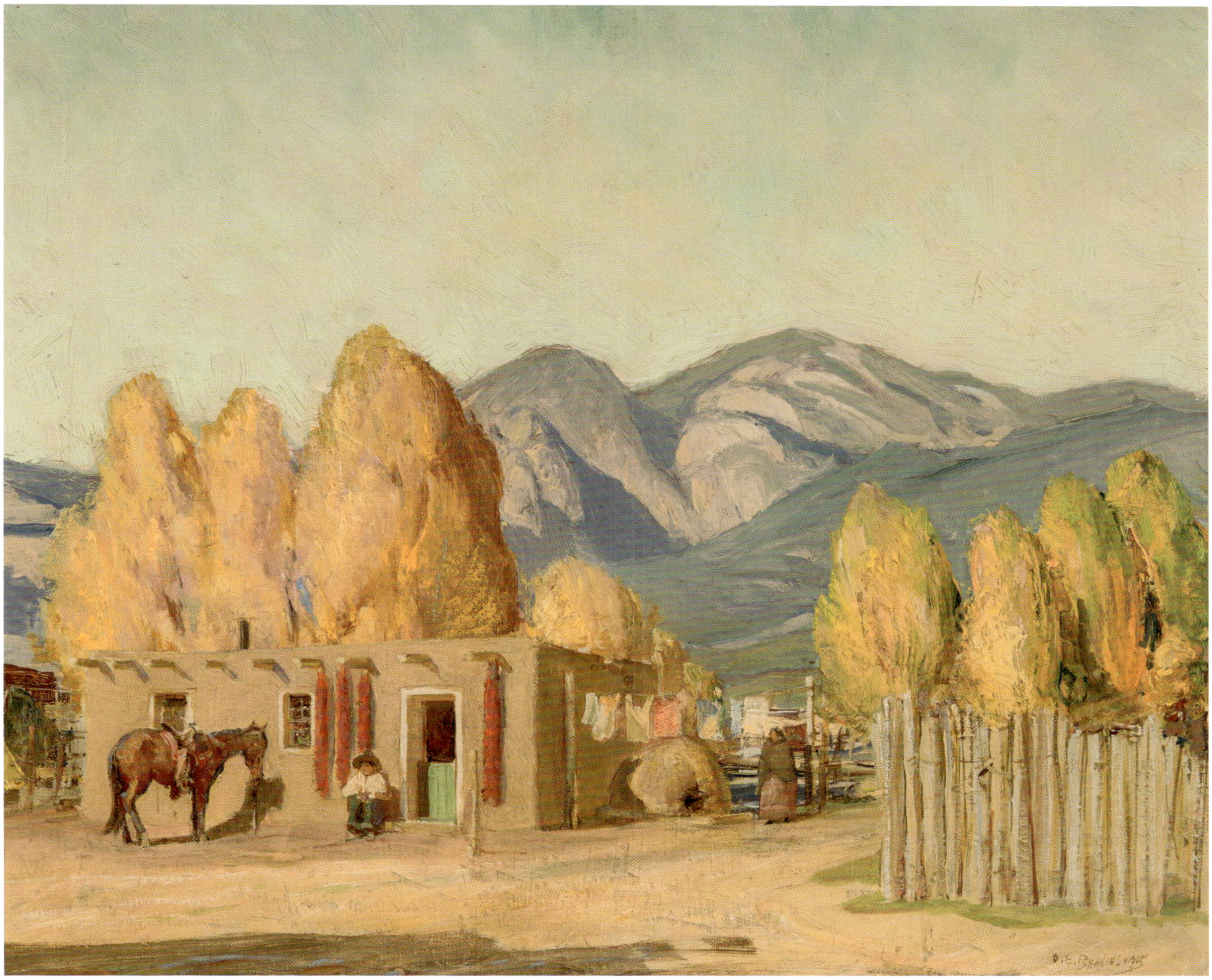

Ernest L. Blumenschein

(1874–1960)

Portrait of Indian with Hair Ornament, Early twentieth century

Oil on linen, 23 x 15 in.

1980.009.003

Gift of Fred T. and Novadean Hogan

THE BOLD COLORS ON DISPLAY in Ernest L. Blumenschein's *Portrait of Indian with Hair Ornament* might be the feature that draws the viewer initially, but the artist's skill in rendering the emotions of his subject is what makes viewers stay and contemplate. A master portraitist, Blumenschein was one of the most highly regarded members of the Taos Society of Artists in terms of sheer artistic talent. This oil-on-linen work features a composition with just a slice of landscape, brilliant blue peeking out of the window or doorway on the far right side, with a small structure off in the distance shaded an even deeper blue. The unnamed man is framed against an adobe wall, looking down and wearing a large gray textile filled with expertly rendered shadows and creases. The hair ornament of the title is detailed and intricate, illustrating the artist's appreciation of Indian craftsmanship, but far more captivating is the contemplative expression of the man. Blumenschein was strongly influenced by the Post-Impressionists, evidenced through his use of large blocks of color delineating sections of the canvas.

Blumenschein first ventured to Taos in 1898 on a painting trip with Bert Phillips, with whom he shared a studio in New York. He began spending his summers there starting in 1910 before a permanent move in 1919. Born in Pittsburgh and raised in Dayton, Ohio, Blumenschein was initially interested in music and briefly attended the Cincinnati College of Music. After taking an illustration class he switched to fine art and received his training at the Art Students League in New York and the Académie Julian in Paris. Before moving to Taos he worked as an illustrator in New York. He was a highly awarded and successful artist, elected a full member of the National Academy of Design. Due to his strict standards he would often repaint or destroy unsatisfactory canvases, making it difficult to date his work.

WE

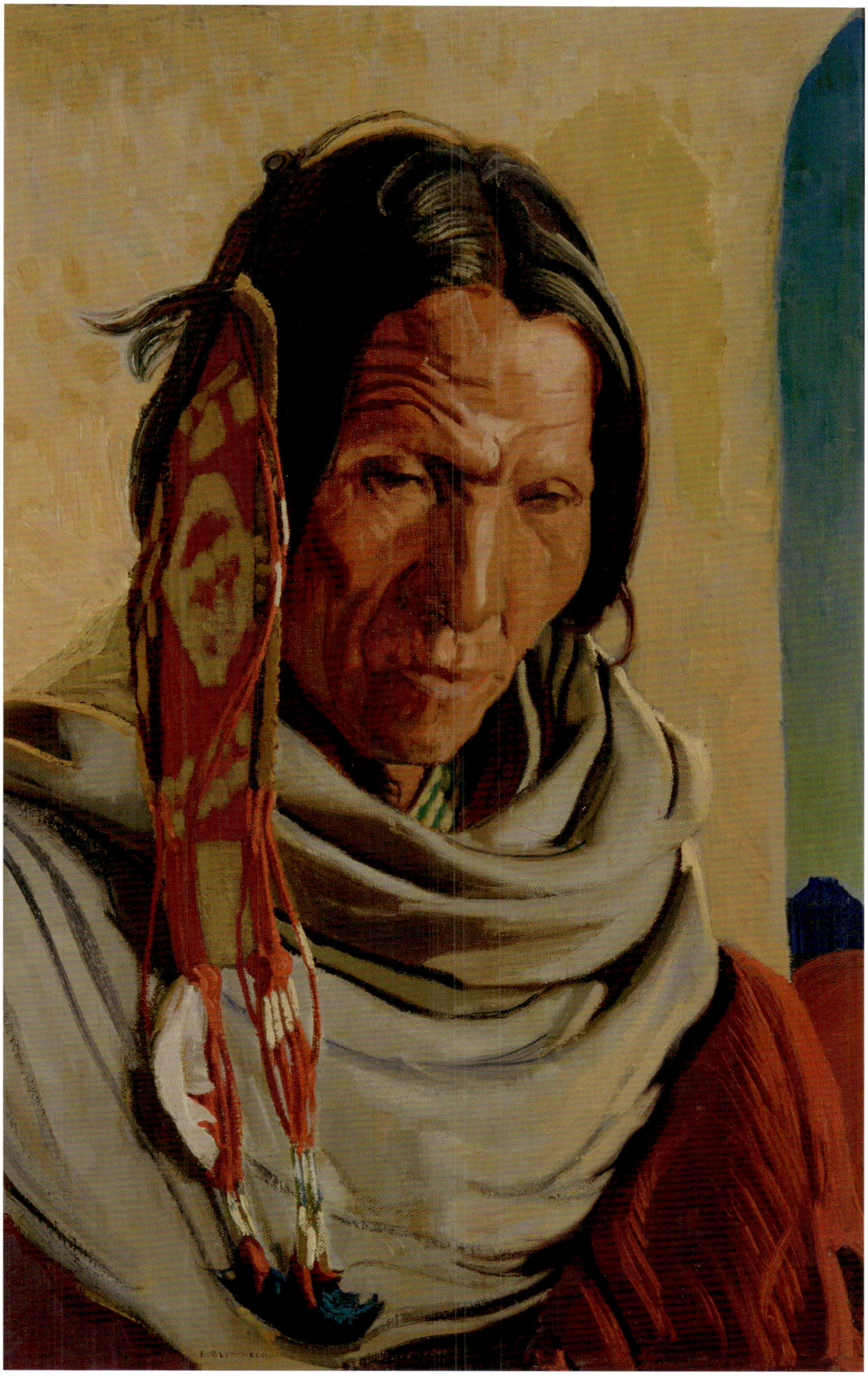

William Herbert (Buck) Dunton

(1878–1936)

Riders of the Purple Sage, c. 1921

Oil on linen, 26 x 20 in.

1980.009.006

Gift of Fred T. and Novadean Hogan

Buck Dunton's passion for the outdoors and sporting is evident in all of his paintings. Born in Augusta, Maine, he was interested in art and mostly self-taught, which led to a successful career in illustration at a very early age. He took several classes at the Cowles Art School in Boston and the Art Students League, but even before any formal artistic education he was earning illustration commissions at sixteen. He produced illustrations for many of the leading magazines of the day, including *Harper's Weekly* and *Cosmopolitan*. Dunton also found success in book illustration, producing work for Jack London and Western author Zane Grey. Starting in 1896 he spent each summer traveling in the American West to find inspiration and solitude.

Dunton settled in Taos around 1912, joined the Taos Society of Artists and began his painting career. Known for his precise painting style, he created dramatic scenes of typical Western subjects. *Fall in the Aspens* shows his impressionistic brushwork and a color sense that captures a real moment of solitude in the New Mexico high country. *Riders of the Purple Sage* is an oil painting that served as the basis for one of Dunton's several illustrations in the novel of the same name by Zane Grey. First published in 1912, it became one of the most popular Western novels of all time. The 1921 edition features several of Dunton's illustrations, based on paintings he created around that time. The hazy painting style gives a sense of timelessness that allows the painting to be appreciated without knowledge of the book. The central figure turns away from the viewer to engage with another group further in the background, framed by foreboding weather over the dramatic mountain range.

WE

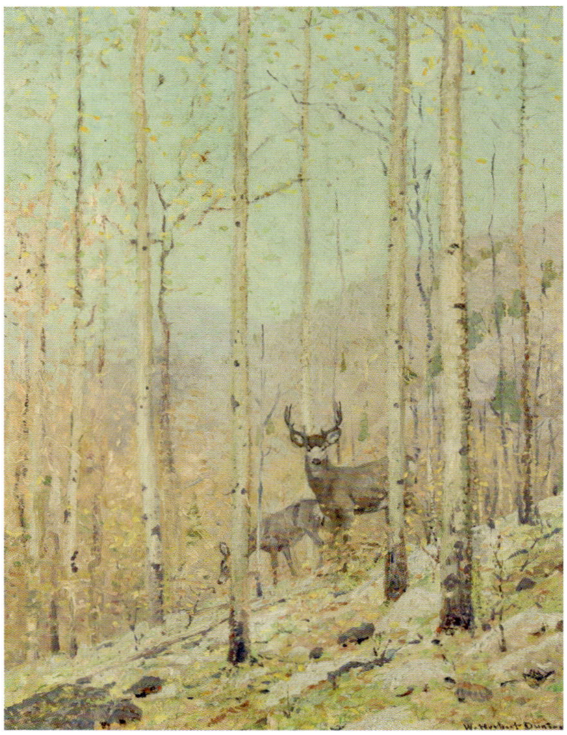

Fall in the Aspens, c. 1918. Oil on linen, 20 x 16 in. 1980.009.007. Gift of Fred T. and Novadean Hogan.

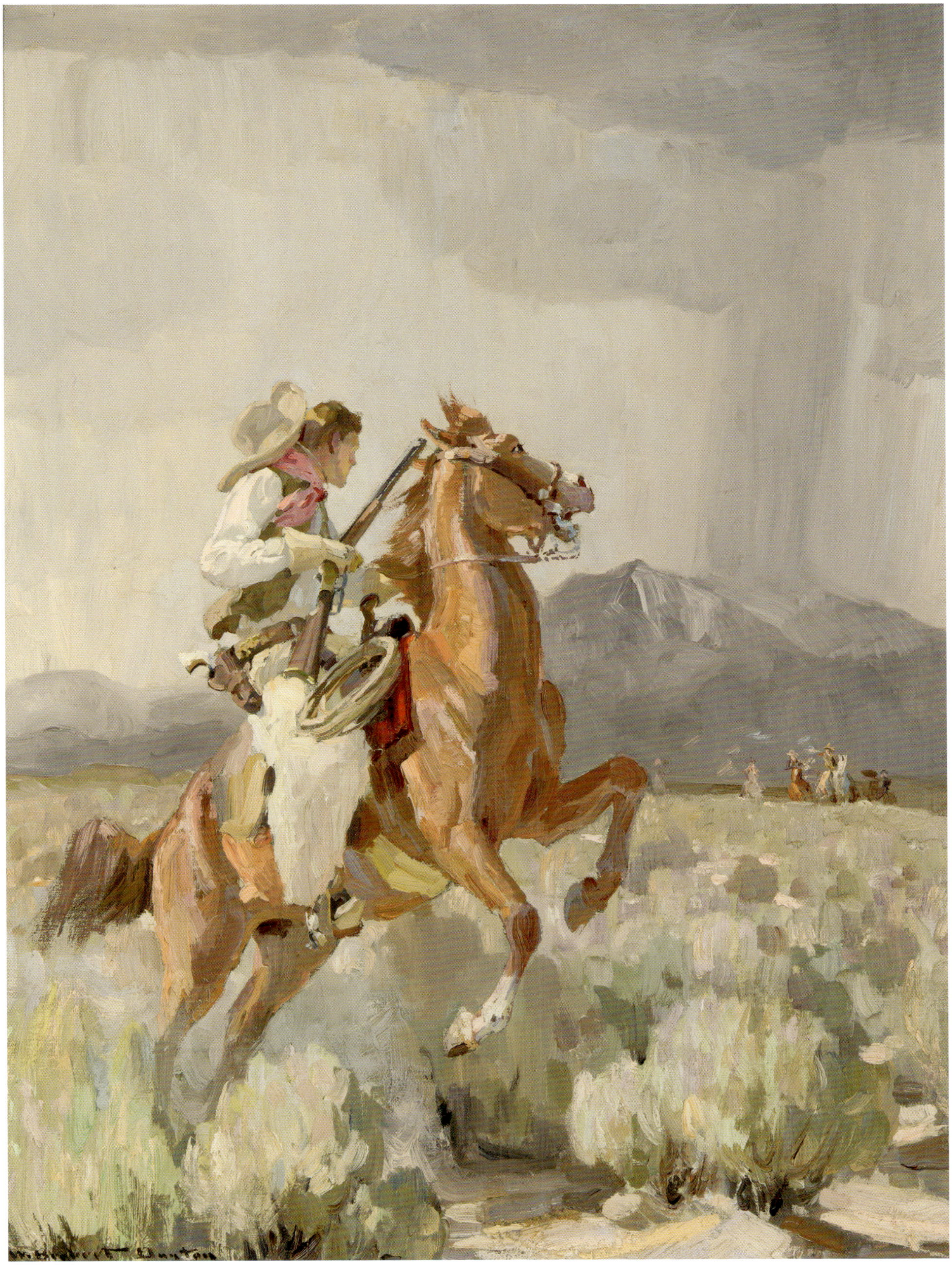

William Victor Higgins

(1884–1949)

Taos in Winter, c. 1910–1930

Oil on linen, 24 x 27 in.

1980.009.010

Gift of Fred T. and Novadean Hogan

A COMMON SUBJECT IN VICTOR HIGGINS' PAINTINGS IS ARCHITECTURE and its place in the landscape of New Mexico. Both *Kit Carson Street* and *Taos in Winter* show the houses and other buildings of Taos, with some human figures engaged in daily life but a focus on the forms of the man-made structures contrasted with the mountains in the background. His thickly applied brushstrokes have some Impressionist qualities, especially evident in the snowy tracks found in *Taos in Winter*.

Born in Shelbyville, Indiana, to a poor rural family, Higgins saved his allowance to pay for his art education at the Art Institute of Chicago where he began his studies when he was fifteen years old. In Chicago he found a patron in former mayor and art collector Carter Harrison, who financed Higgins' additional art study in Paris and Munich and eventually sent him and fellow artist Walter Ufer to Taos on a commission. Higgins found camaraderie and success through joining the Taos Society of Artists and lived in Taos from 1914 until his death in 1949. The artist exhibited his work internationally and was elected to the National Academy, while also maintaining many connections in Chicago, where he was able to win numerous prizes. Higgins was briefly married to San Antonio arts supporter Marion Koogler McNay.

Most members of the Taos Society of Artists found success through depicting the landscapes and peoples of New Mexico in a traditional, realist style rarely deviated from throughout their long careers. Higgins is one of the few exceptions. Starting in the late 1920s, he started to assimilate some Modernist tendencies, in part due to the influence of other New Mexico transplants like Andrew Dasburg. This resulted in a move toward Cubism, with the use of multipoint perspective and interlocking planes. The seeds of this path are evident in his treatment of buildings in such works as *Kit Carson Street*.

WE

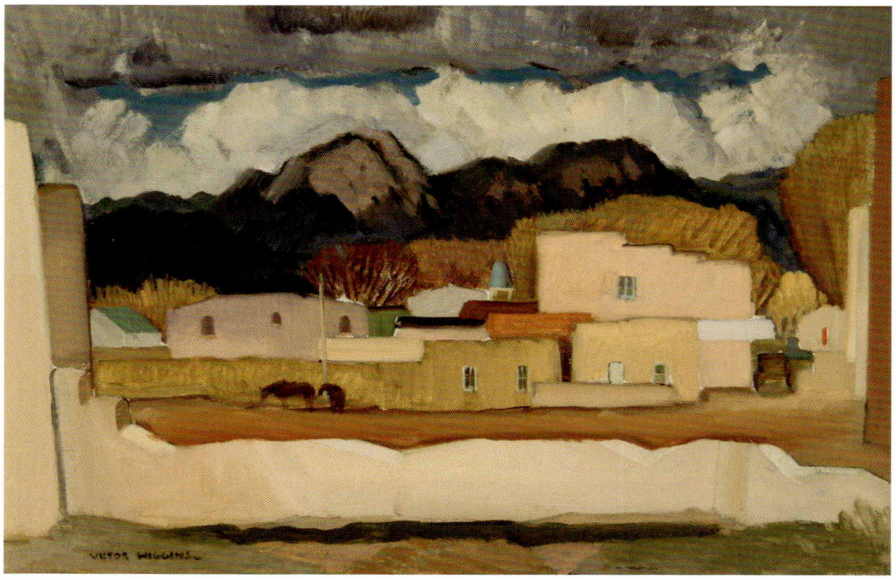

Kit Carson Street, early twentieth century. Oil on linen, 17 x 27 in.1980.009.011. Gift of Fred T. and Novadean Hogan.

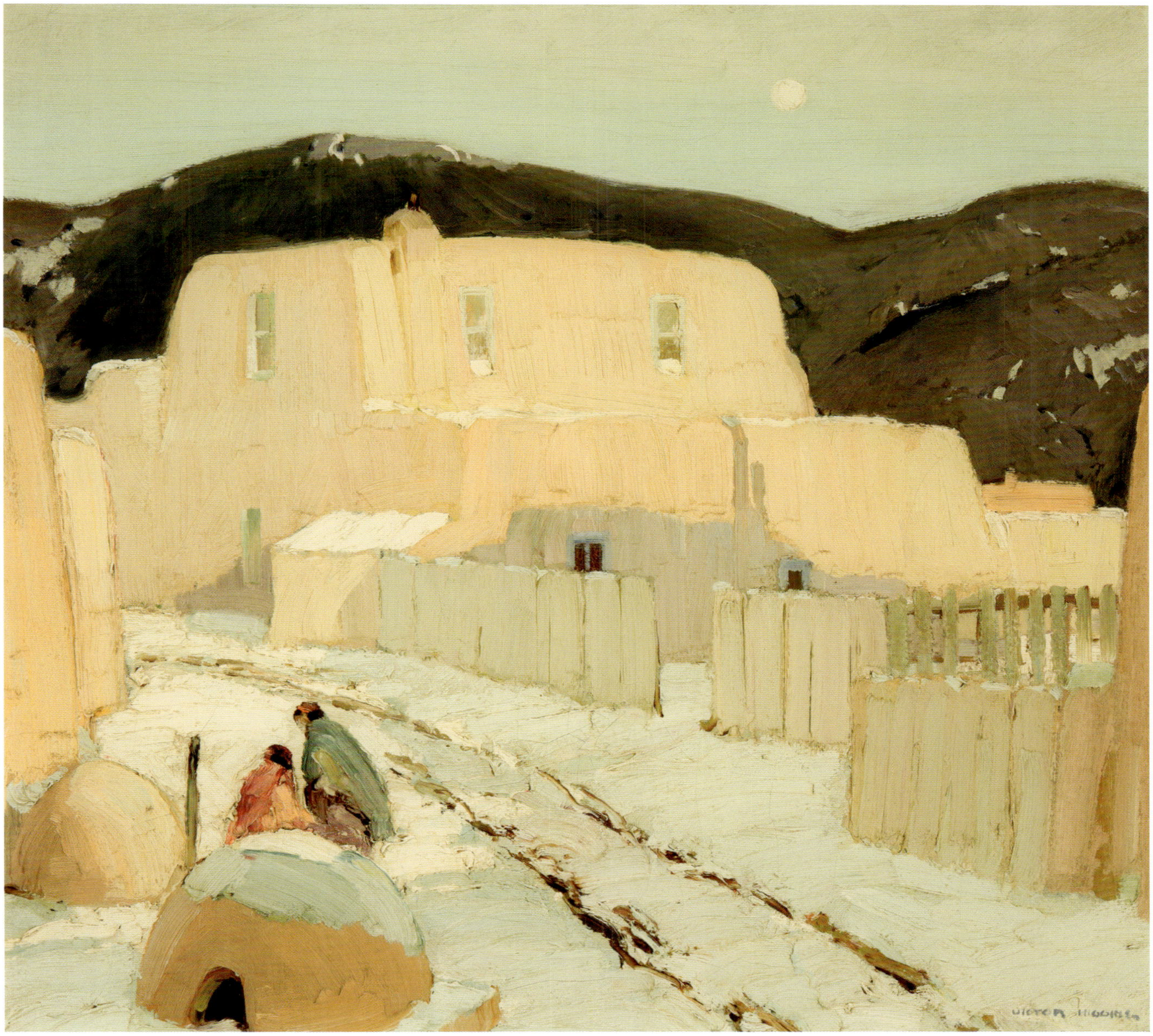

Bert Geer Phillips

(1868–1956)

A Daughter of the Water Clan, c. 1911

Oil on linen, 30 x 25 in.

1980.009.012

Gift of Fred T. and Novadean Hogan

Bert G. Phillips was the first Anglo artist to move to Taos permanently, establishing his home there in 1898 after a painting trip with Ernest Blumenschein. Born in Hudson, New York, in 1868, as a child Phillips idolized the American West and figures like Kit Carson and the characters from James Fenimore Cooper's novels. He studied art at the Art Students League and the National Academy of Design and was able to set up a studio in New York City in the 1890s. He went on to study at the Académie Julian, where he met Blumenschein and Joseph Henry Sharp, who encouraged the two artists to visit Taos. Living in Taos until shortly before his death in 1956, Phillips was instrumental in founding the art colony, encouraging other artists to visit or stay, and establishing the Taos Society of Artists.

Phillips developed long-standing relationships with the Taos Pueblo Indians, who served as his models. His canvases depicted them as wholly separate from white culture, characterizing them as peaceful and in a natural, pristine state. *A Daughter of the Water Clan* is an exemplary painting by Phillips and was exhibited at the National Academy of Design's Winter Exhibition in 1911. The work is imbued with Phillips' typical romanticism when painting Pueblo subjects, characterized by figures devoid of expression, their stoic and dignified postures enveloped in an atmosphere of darkness and solitude. Like many Anglo artists at the time, Phillips "dressed up" his models by adding textiles, basketry and pottery not necessarily pertinent to the tribe being portrayed. Women carrying water vessels or associated with water clans were a popular subject for Phillips. The sense of timelessness and dignity demonstrates Phillips' artistic talent, his striking light and shadow depicting the details of the woman and her surroundings.

WE

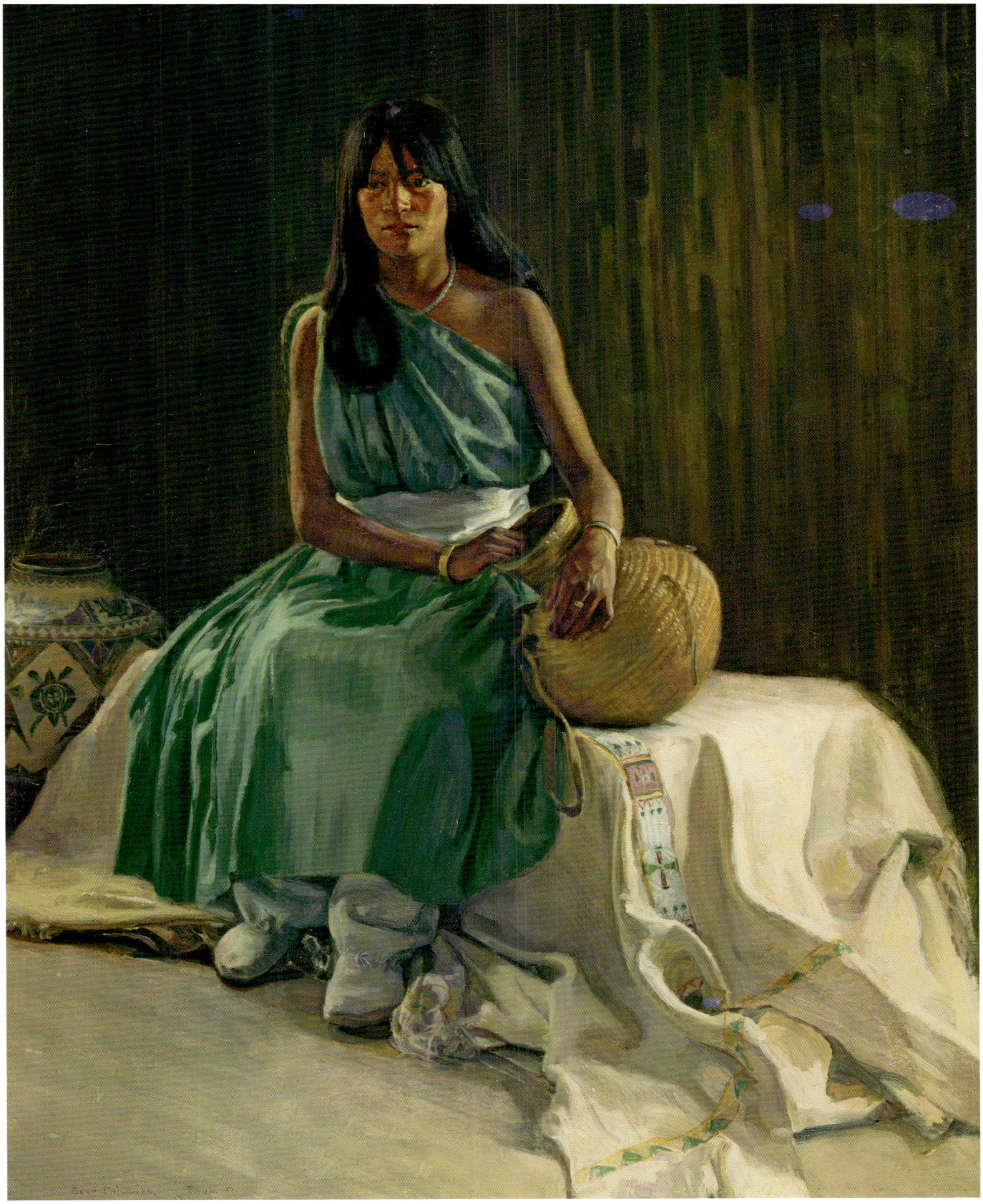

Joseph Henry Sharp

(1859–1953)

Chant to the Redstone Pipe, Early twentieth century

Oil on linen, 20¼ x 16⅛ in.

1980.009.014

Gift of Fred T. and Novadean Hogan

An incredibly prolific painter, Joseph Henry Sharp produced over 10,000 canvases in his lifetime, most of which featured American Indians. He was born in Bridgeport, Ohio, in 1859 and started his art education at the age of fourteen at the Art Academy of Cincinnati. Sharp traveled widely throughout his life, initially for his art education, which took him throughout Europe, and later to find subjects for his extensive artistic output. In between his many years of study he explored the American West, starting in 1883. It was Sharp who first found Taos, visiting briefly to illustrate a commission for *Harper's Weekly,* and after returning he encouraged Bert Phillips and Ernest Blumenschein to take a painting trip there. Sharp settled in Taos permanently in 1912, usually staying for the summer and traveling in winter. One of the places to which he frequently returned in winter was Hawaii, where he painted landscapes like *Moonlight, Marine Koko Crater.*

Because of his prolific output, he rarely dated works and often reused titles. There are at least six canvases that share the name *Chant to the Redstone Pipe*, and at least three *Visions of the Past. Chant to the Redstone Pipe* features one of Sharp's favorite subjects, a fire-lit scene of Pueblo Indians in beautiful dress, one figure beating a drum and the other holding the titular red pipe. The figure on the left is Jerry Mirabel, a Taos Indian and frequent model for both Sharp and E. Irving Couse who also appears in *Visions of the Past.* On the back of the painting Sharp scrawled a series of notes: "Fire light and twilight—interior of lodge or tepee Indian painted elk skin back of figures, war bonnet was in Custer battle." Although prolific, Sharp was never hurried, putting uncommon detail and finely rendered color and texture into each composition.

WE

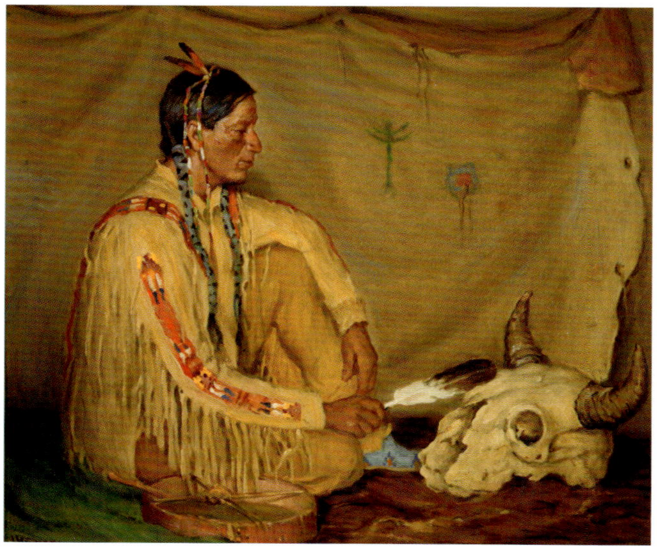

Visions of the Past, early twentieth century. Oil on linen, 20 x 24 in. 1980.009.013. Gift of Fred T. and Novadean Hogan.

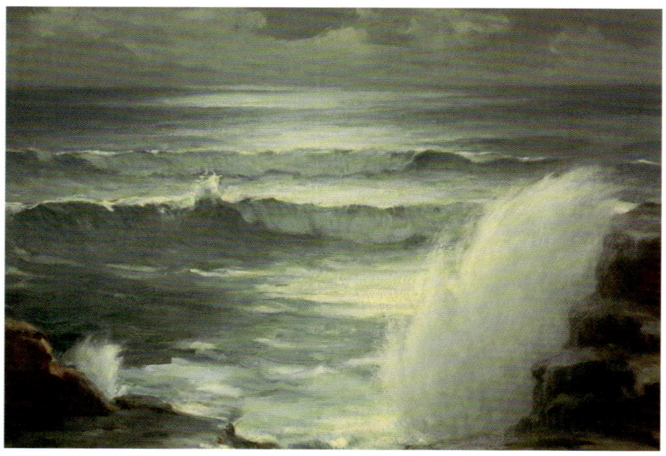

Moonlight, Marine Koko Crater, early twentieth century. Oil on canvas, 28¼ x 38½ in. 1996.002.014. Gift of Fred T. and Novadean Hogan.

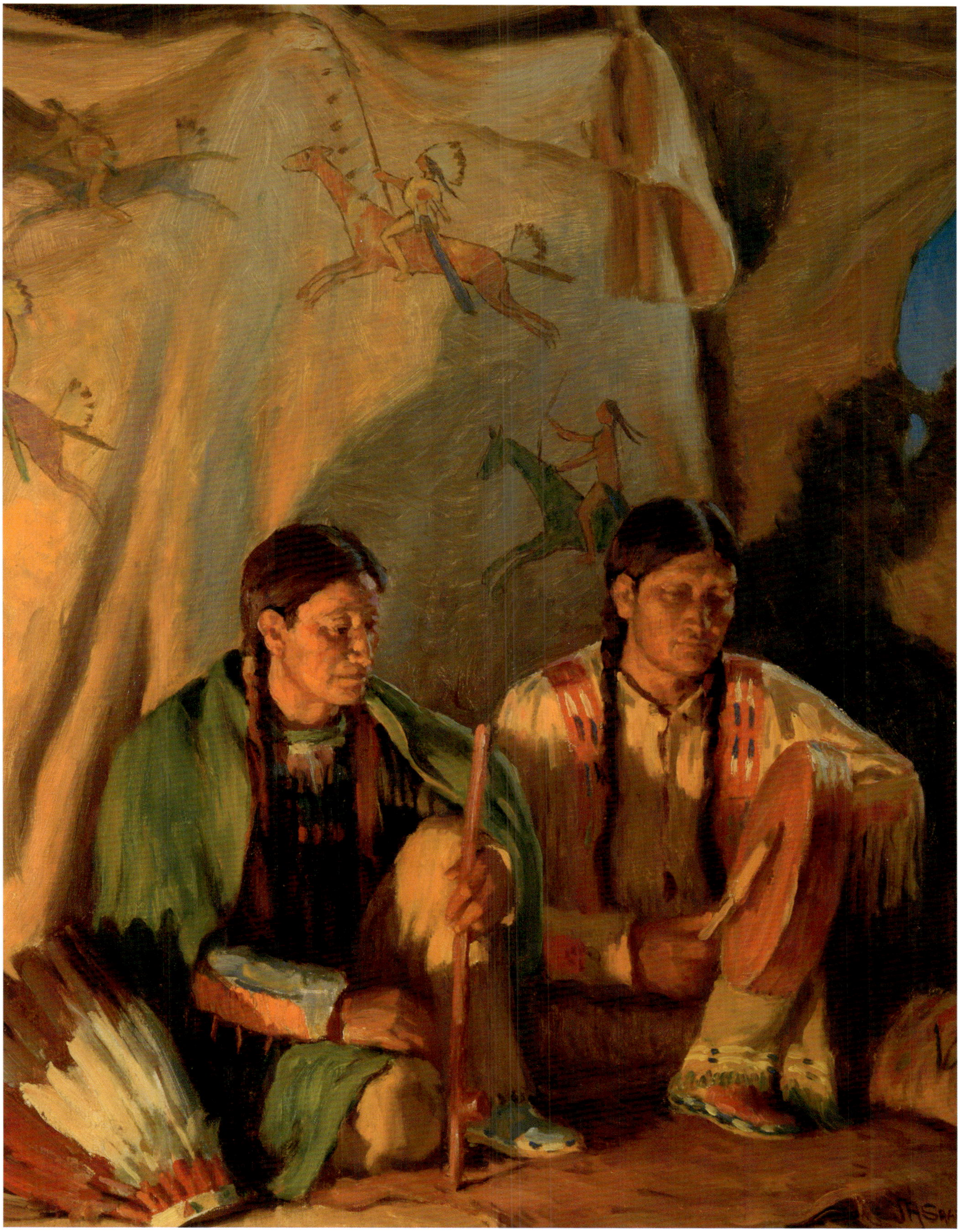

Walter Ufer

(1876–1936)

Storming the Foothills, Early twentieth century

Oil on linen, 24 x 30⅛ in.

1980.009.015

Gift of Fred T. and Novadean Hogan

Walter Ufer was born in 1876 in Louisville, Kentucky, to parents who had recently emigrated from Germany. His father, a master engraver, provided his son his earliest artistic and informal education at home. As a young man, Ufer pursued more formal artistic training at the Royal Academy of Fine Arts in Dresden, as well as at schools in Hamburg and Munich. When he returned to the United States, Ufer discarded this academic training that emphasized posed or contrived compositions and situations in favor of direct observation of natural subjects and people in their daily lives. He also rejected the dark palette associated with the German schools for the bright, clear colors of the American Southwest that he first encountered on a trip in 1914. Well known for his personal sense of drama and the many feuds he loved with fellow artists, Ufer had the word "Dynamite" emblazoned across his studio door as an inspiration for himself and a warning to those who would enter.

Storming the Foothills depicts two mules traversing the landscape with a single rider pushing them forward on a cold morning in New Mexico—the light diminished by the clouds in the distance. Like his fellow Taos painters, Ufer sought to capture the magic of this world so different from the cities and countryside in the eastern United States. Like many of his counterparts in the Taos Society of Artists, Ufer painted the great variations in both landscape and seasons but favored simple, quotidian moments like this one to invoke the quiet poetry and unique sense of place that Taos offered.

BLW

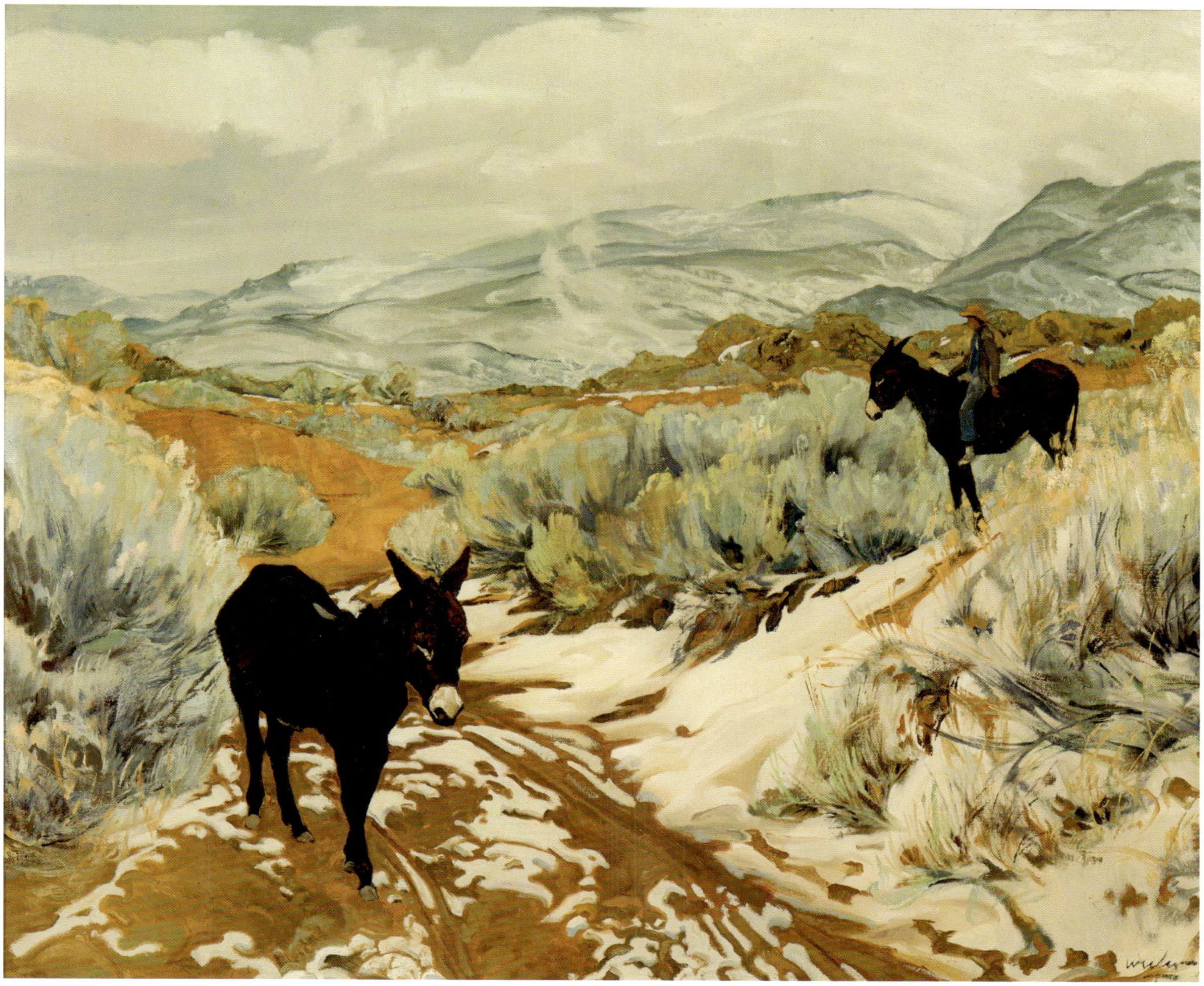

Blanche Chloe Grant

(1874–1948)

Indian Eyes,
Early twentieth century

Oil on canvas, 20 x 15½ in.

1981.003.001

Museum Acquisition Fund

What would make a young woman want to hide all but her nose and eyes, as seen in *Indian Eyes* by artist Blanche Chloe Grant? The answer may lie in *The Taos Indians,* written by the artist in 1925. In describing the way Native women ground meal, Grant first noted the Pueblo's separate room or space that was devoted to the process: "Three women go in here, each one having a stone, with which one of them breaks the corn, the next grinds it and the third grinds it again. They take off their shoes, do up their hair, shake their clothes and cover their heads before they enter the door." It is likely the anonymous young woman in this portrait had recently engaged in the grinding ritual Grant described. Both of Grant's paintings in the collections of the Museum of the Southwest feature native people cloaked in fabric shielding their faces and looking away from the viewer.

The portraits Grant painted were primarily of Native Americans from Taos Pueblo, but Grant wrote several historical accounts of life in the Southwest. Born in Leavenworth, Kansas, she graduated from high school in Indianapolis, Indiana, and then matriculated to Vassar College, where she graduated in 1896. From there she went on to study art at the Museum School of the Boston Museum of Fine Arts, the Pennsylvania Academy of Art and the Art Students League in New York. Until 1920 she lived and worked in Wilmington, Delaware, and then moved to Taos, where she authored and illustrated many books and chronicled the local life on canvas.

MBW

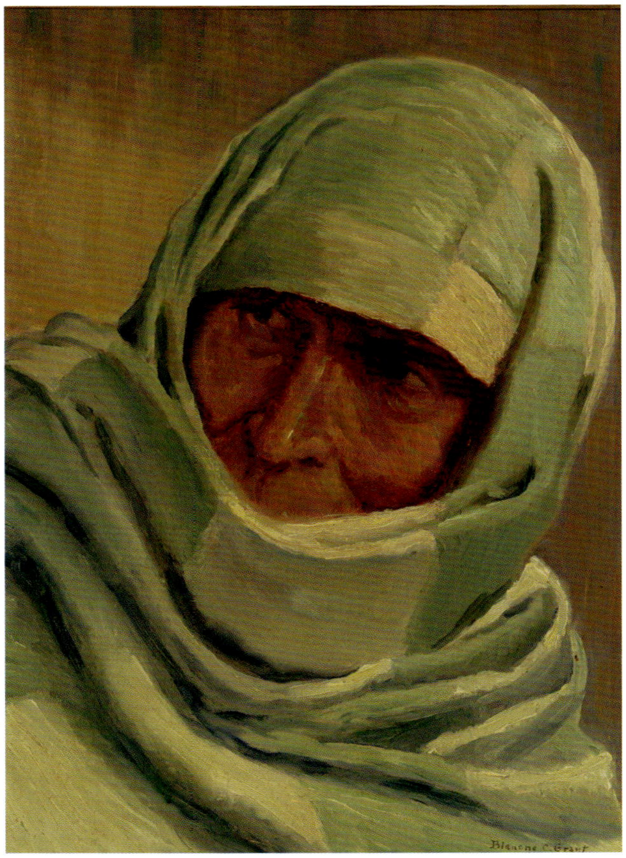

Indian Eyes, early twentieth century. Oil on canvas, 15¼ x 11½ in. 1980.009.016. Gift of Fred T. and Novadean Hogan.

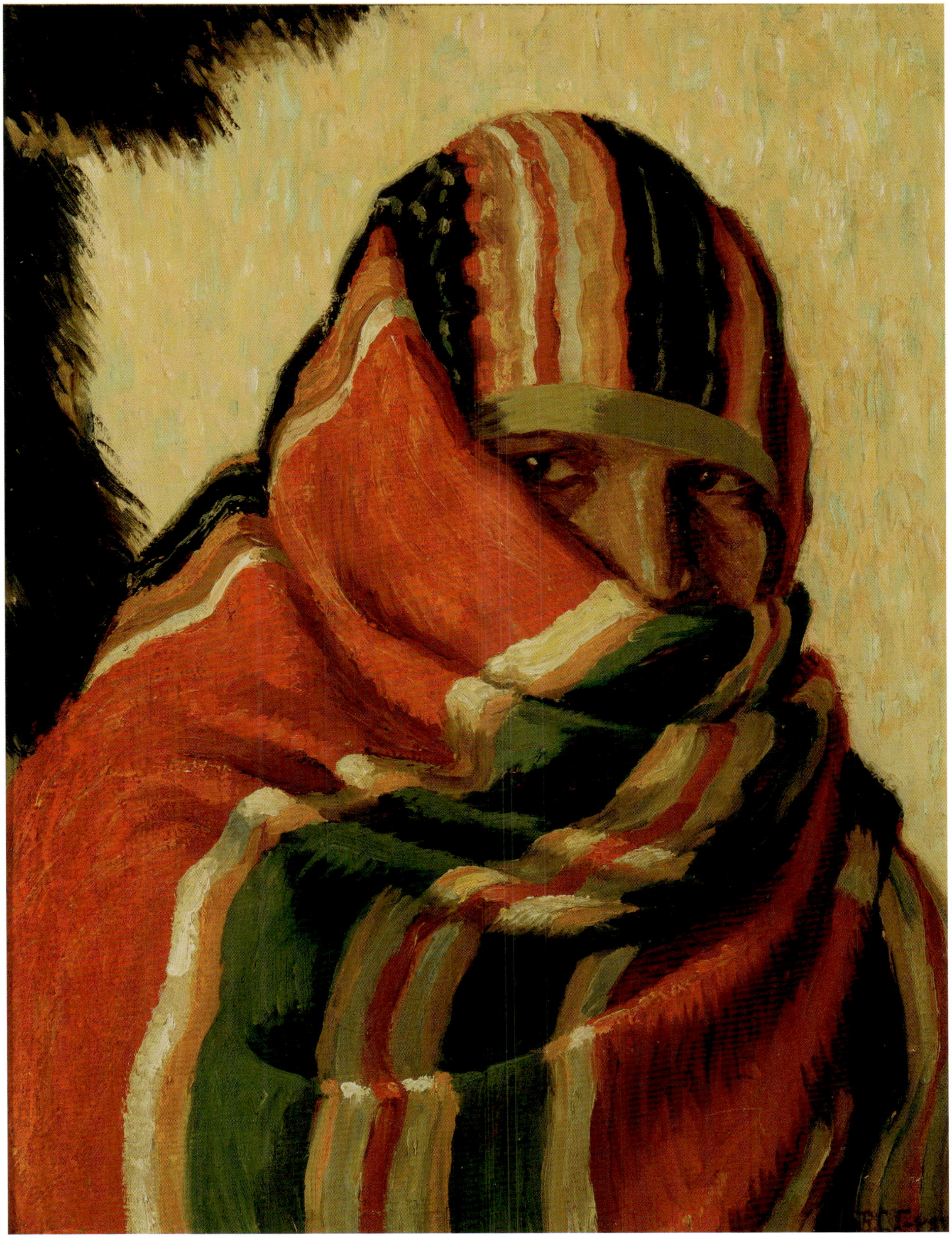

Joseph Amadeus Fleck

(1892–1977)

Untitled (Landscape with Horses and Trees), Mid-twentieth century

Oil on wood, 28¾ x 34¾ in.

1980.010.001

Gift of Glenn Stehle

The simplicity of Joseph Fleck's untitled landscape lies in its composition—a scene of a pasture with horses and trees enveloped by a big sky. It's a scene many viewers have encountered countless times. The true skill shown here is evident in the color palette, with the brilliant blue of the sky and rich greens in the grass and trees, both filled with underlayers of additional color that add a rich texture to the painting. Simple and effective, it invites and rewards repeat viewing.

Born in a small village in Austria in 1892, Fleck displayed strong artistic talent from an early age. As a teenager he worked as an apprentice to an ornamental engraver, then began his studies at the Vienna Royal Academy of Fine Arts. His academic career was interrupted by World War I, when he was drafted into the Austro-Hungarian army. He later became an official government artist in Vienna, painting war scenes and portraits of government officials. The postwar economy in Vienna caused Fleck to travel to America in 1922. He immigrated to Kansas City, Missouri, and shortly found work at a stained-glass window workshop and was able to start a successful career as a portrait painter.

In 1925 Fleck moved to Taos, where he took inspiration from the landscape and people, as well as his many friendships with the Taos Society of Artists and other artists like Leon Gaspard. Fleck spent most of the rest of his life in Taos, except for the years 1942 through 1946, when he worked as artist-in-residence at the University of Kansas City and spent extensive time with Thomas Hart Benton. The landscape shown was almost certainly painted after he returned to Taos in 1946, when he began a highly productive period of painting nature in a more expressionist style.

WE

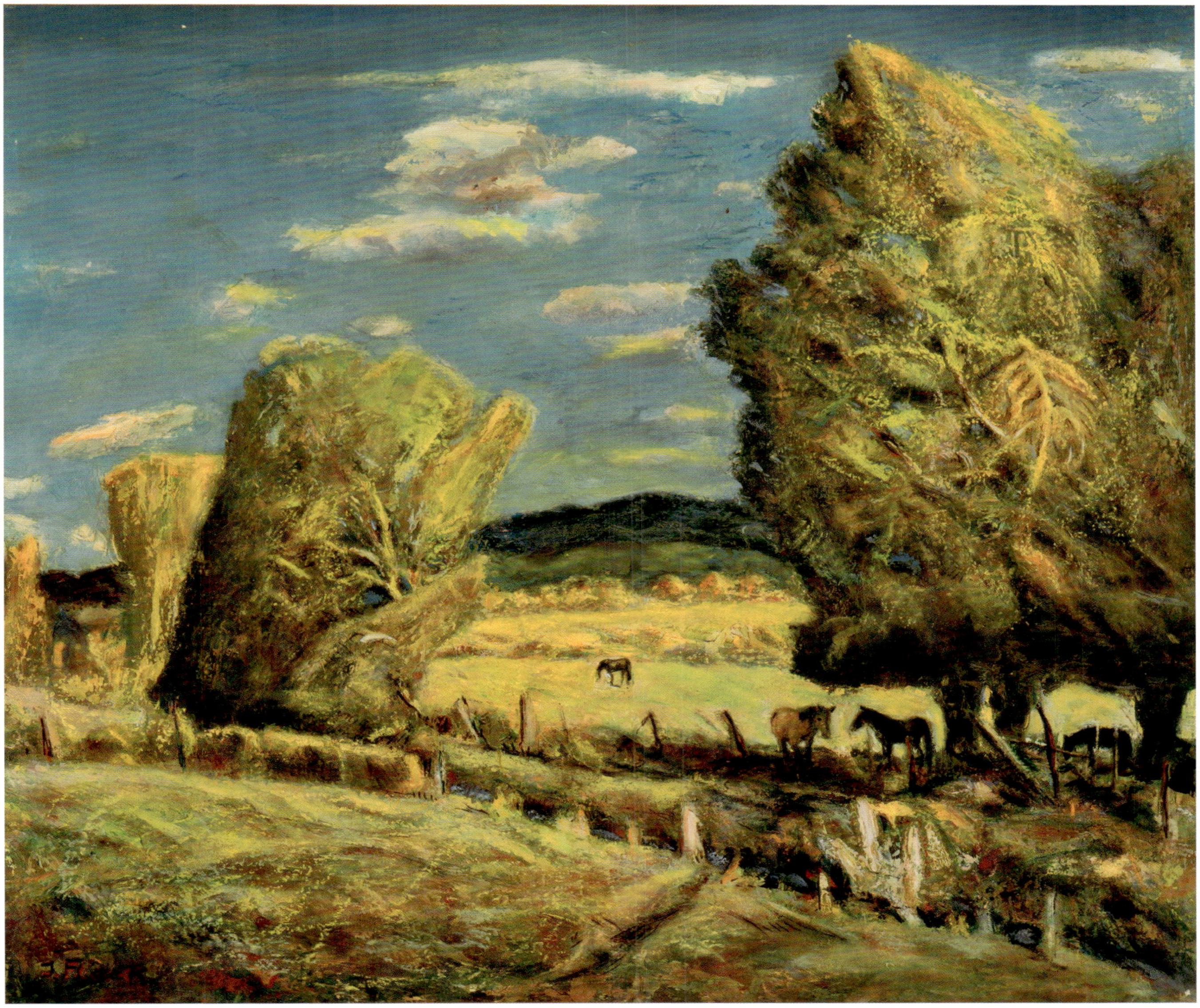

Alice Geneva (Gene) Kloss

(1903–1996)

Land of the Osier Willow People, c. 1950

Oil on linen, 30 x 40 in.

1981.004.001

Museum Acquisition Fund

It may have been an advantage in the male-dominated art world of the first half of the twentieth century for Gene Kloss to adopt a masculine nickname. Although Kloss is perhaps best known as a skilled etcher—she executed over 600 copperplate etchings—she also worked in the paint media of oil and watercolor. Her virtuosity in creating contrasting lights and darks is especially apparent in the prints she created during her long career. In a 1935 *San Francisco Chronicle* article, critic Alfred Frankenstein quoted Kloss, indicating her preference when capturing the likenesses of the Native peoples, "The art of etching seems most fitting to express the values of Indian culture by its very sheerness and limited values of black and white."

Gene and her husband, Phillips, became good friends with Native Americans in Taos, where they resided several months each year. While Kloss never sketched the Native American ceremonies they were invited to attend, she was able to recall through visual memory what she had seen. Many of these images became a part of her large output of prints. The history of the conquest and Christianization of Native peoples is lengthy and complex, and the artist became interested in the Indian dances and ceremony that combined tradition with elements of the two. This can be seen in the etchings *Processional—Taos* and *Morning Worship*. The *reredos,* or altar screen, in *Morning Worship* is a carryover from the Spanish Baroque, whereas the depiction of angels, other religious figures and the multitude of worshippers takes on a more Modernist appearance.

The monochromatic palette Kloss used in *Land of the Osier Willow People* indicates movement in the trees, mountain and clouds. Only the two horses appear still, with heads down, grazing. The curved roadway leads the viewer's eye to the middle ground and, while there is no evidence of human habitation, one has a sense that the horses belong to someone.

MBW

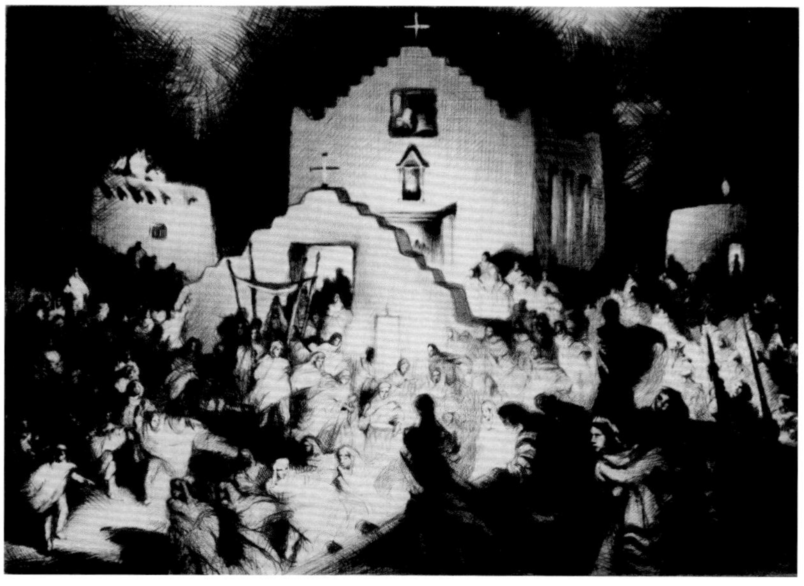

Processional—Taos, 1948. Etching, 9¾ x 14 in.
1972.006.004. Museum Acquisition Fund.

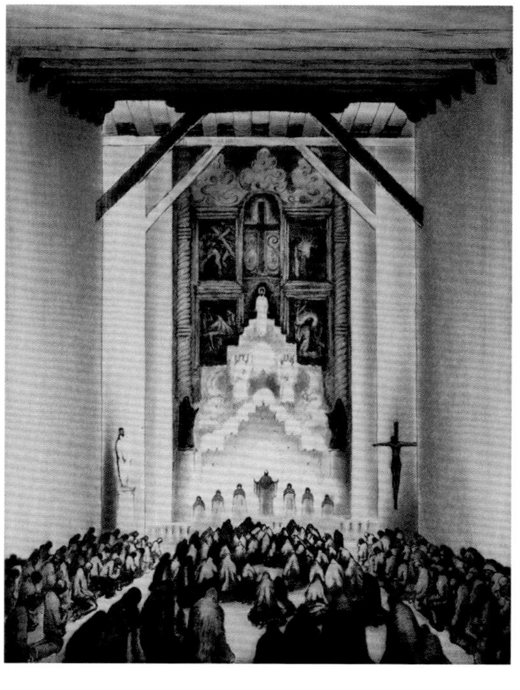

Morning Worship, 1939. Etching, 14 x 10¾ in.
1972.006.005. Museum Acquisition Fund.

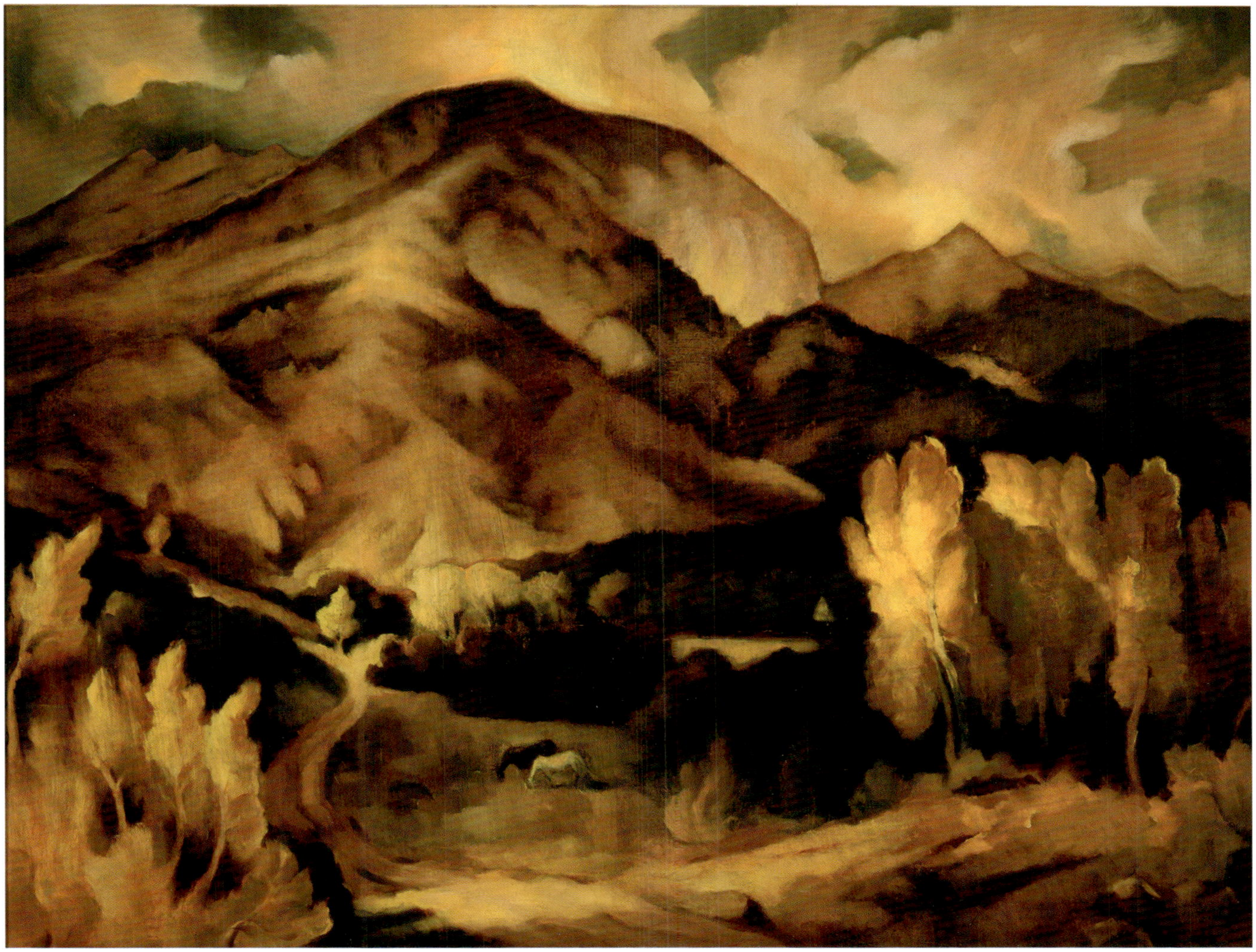

Alfred Morang

(1901–1958)

Harem of Colors, c. 1950

Oil on linen, 14 x 18 in.

1981.010.001

Museum Acquisition Fund

Alfred Morang's paintings are known for capturing the essence of Santa Fe in the 1940s and '50s. Morang was fascinated with the work of the French Impressionists. His paintings are colorful pieces that often have a sculptural quality, bestowed by the thickness of the paint and the richness of the color. He believed in art for people's sake and used art as a way to explore life to a depth that is unachievable by other means.

Morang's *Harem of Colors* conveys the spirit and liveliness of a landscape. Adobe houses and trees are nestled among the colorful, sunbaked curves of the mountain. The thick brushstrokes hide the true shape of the objects and instead suggest a dynamic and energetic emotional pull of the landscape

A native of Maine, Morang developed his skills as a painter under the direction of the American Impressionist Carroll S. Tyson and landscape artist Henry Bayley Snell. When Morang and his wife moved to Santa Fe in 1937 for his health, he quickly became an iconic figure in the Santa Fe art community as a teacher, writer and artist. Upon Morang's tragic death in a fire in 1958, one Santa Fe resident remarked that "he taught half of us how to paint; the other half how to see."

MR

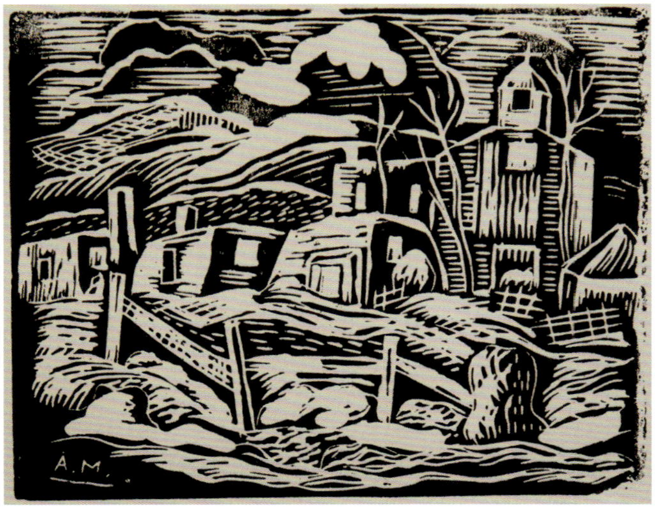

New Mexico Landscape with Church, mid-twentieth century. Linoleum block print, 6 x 8 in. 1982.034.001. Gift of Mr. and Mrs. Zeb B. Conley.

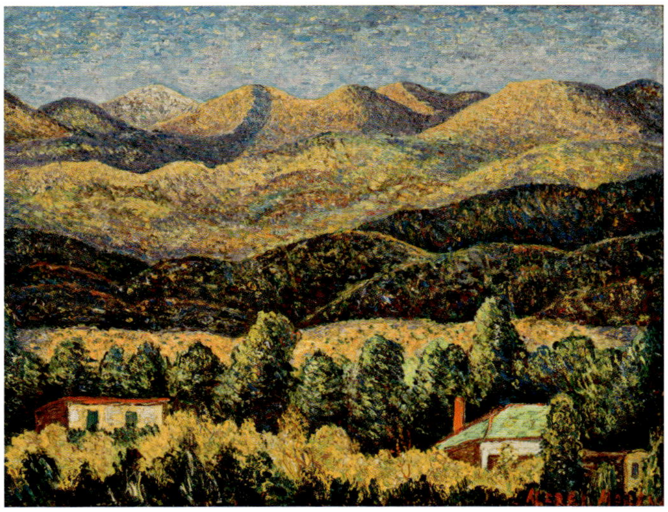

Golden Mountains, c. 1942. Oil on board, 17⅜ x 23¼ in. 1982.025.001. Museum Acquisition Fund.

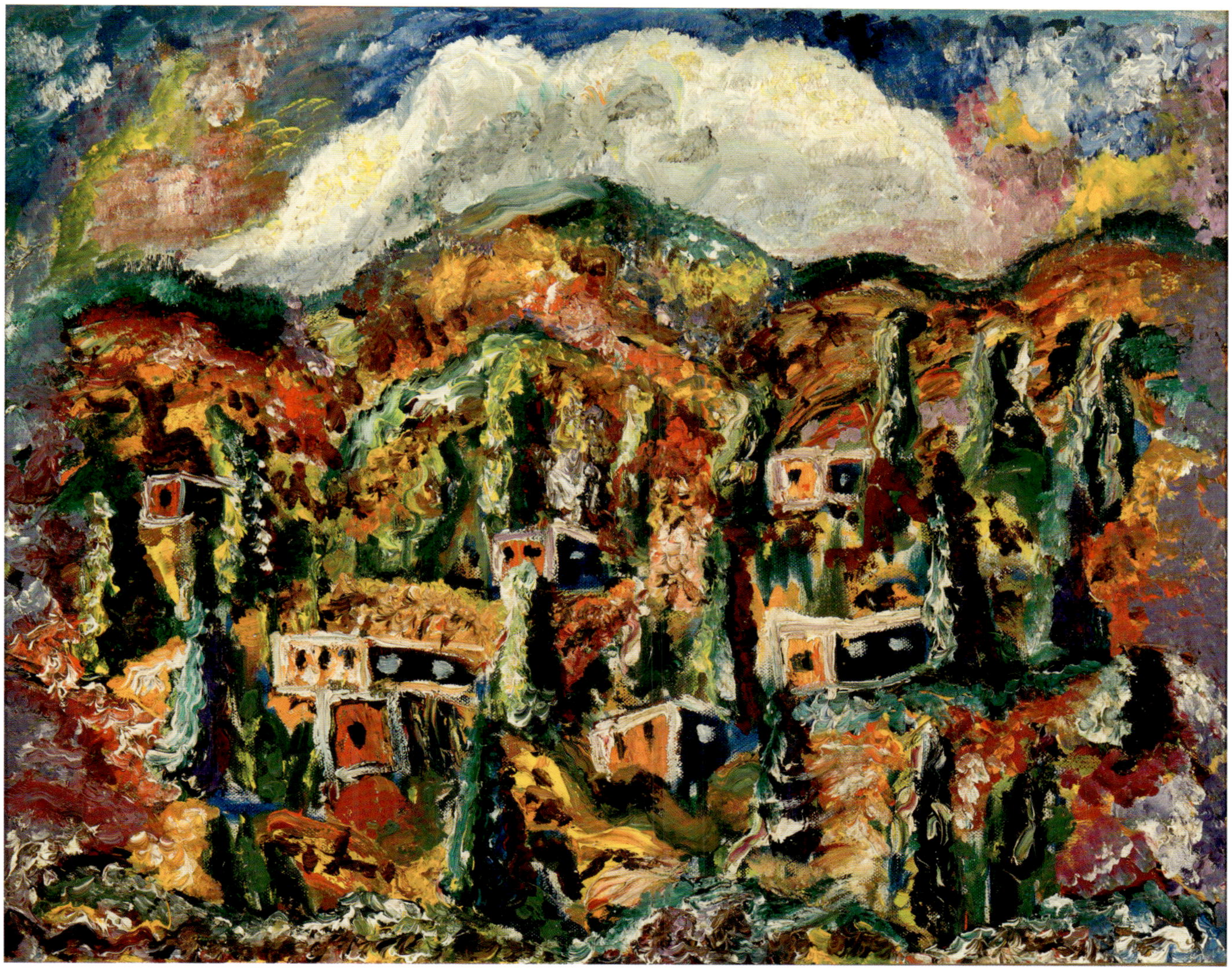

Mamie Woody

(dates unknown)

Navajo Pictorial Rug, c. 1981

Wool, 39½ x 26½ in.

1982.015.001

Museum Acquisition Fund

As a subgenre of Navajo (Diné) weaving, pictorial textiles are a more personal and time-specific glimpse into contemporary Navajo experiences. Pictorial textiles—as the name implies—utilize representational elements such as human figures, animals, buildings and landscapes in a decorative style. These works contrast with the traditional geometric abstract styles found in Navajo blankets and rugs.

This smaller rug, woven about 1981, is a fine representation of the style, with elements of the Western landscape combined with pickup trucks, mobile homes, horses and other details of reservation life in a flat, nonlinear perspective. One small woman in a white skirt, who may be the weaver Mamie Woody, is shown next to a house. At the top of the weaving geometric clouds lead downward to rock formations, with small figures in between that might be roadrunners. Triangular shapes create a black border, acting almost as a window frame onto the scene. Though pictorial designs differ in subject from the more widely known geometrics, the weaving technique is shared by all Navajo textiles, constructed on a loom in a tapestry style, meaning the designs are not embroidered onto the finished piece, but rather incorporated as the work is woven.

While some pictorial elements can be found throughout the history of Navajo weaving, the style became a growing segment of Navajo textile production in the latter half of the twentieth century, in large part due to its popularity with tourists. Because the charming rugs are often seen as tourist art, little critical analysis has been undertaken. However, these weavings can be read as a document recording the environment and concerns of an individual artist.

WE

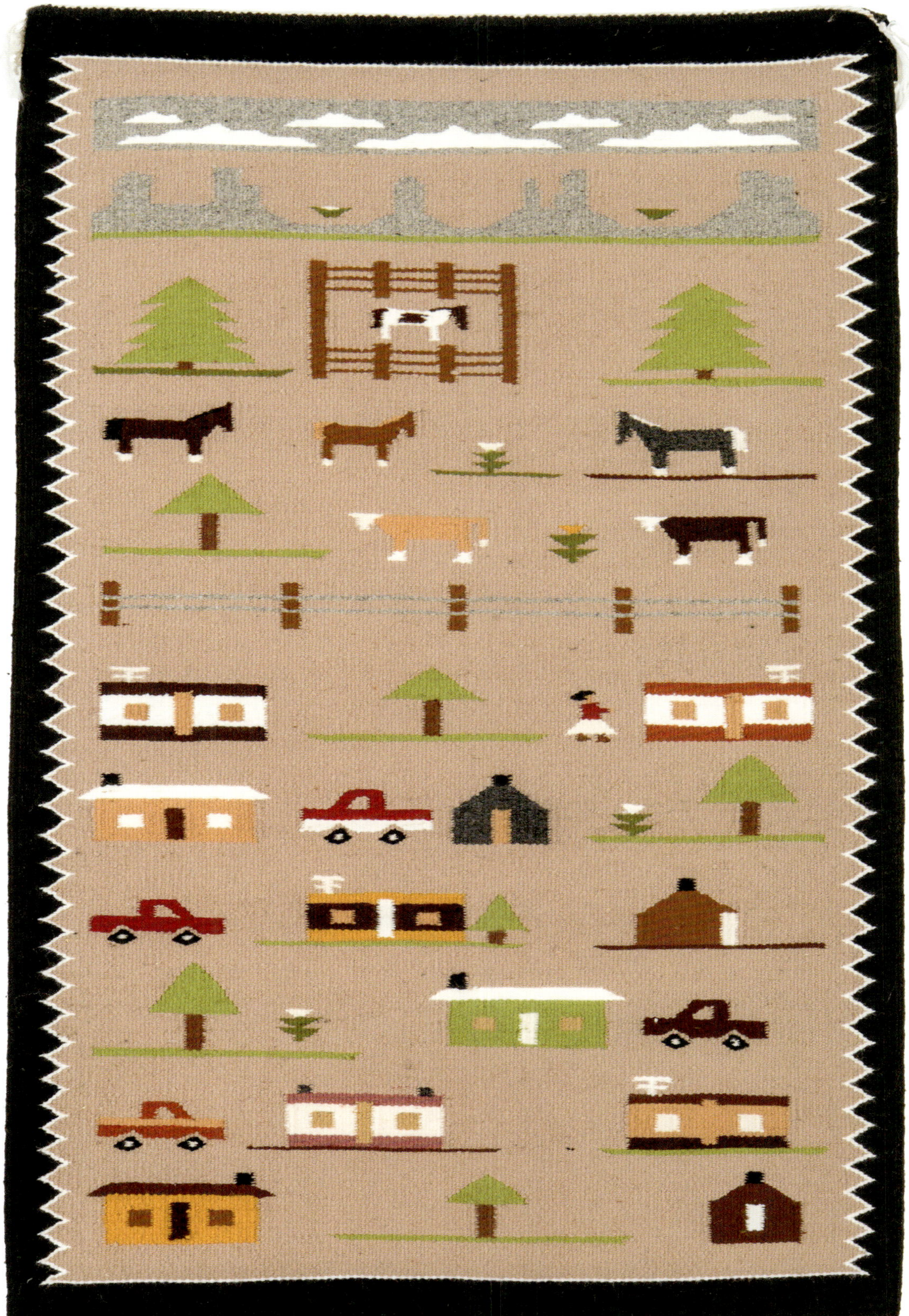

Grant Wood

(1891–1942)

February, 1937

Lithograph, 8¾ x 11½ in.

1982.017.001

Museum Acquisition Fund

The best-known artist of the Regionalists, Grant Wood was catapulted to fame when his first mature painting, *American Gothic*, was exhibited in 1930. For this and later works, Wood combined the formal training he received from the Minneapolis School of Design and Handicraft and the Art Institute of Chicago with his travels and observation in Europe, particularly of German and Flemish Renaissance painting. Using these influences and experiences, he produced images of rural America that are highly stylized but at the same time intensely detailed. Wood eventually returned to the Midwest, taking a teaching position at the University of Iowa. He completed several large mural programs at Iowa State University in Ames, and his sister Nan left his estate and papers to the Figge Art Museum in Davenport with her passing in 1990.

Wood's mature style was applied to portraits, large-scale murals, easel paintings and printmaking alike. Although only fifty when he died in 1942, the wide dissemination of his work and the international recognition of his American images ensured a lasting fame beyond his lifetime. The lithograph *February* includes several tropes utilized broadly across Wood's oeuvre, including the high vantage point from which are seen rolling midwestern hills, like those found in Iowa and eastern Kansas, covered in a blanket of snow. In the far distance at the edge of the picture plane is a barn or farmhouse shrouded in darkness, while a jagged line of barbed wire holds back three stylized horses silhouetted against the night sky. Despite the generalization of the horses, Wood still imbues them with a sense of curiosity as they approach the viewer on a cold and magical February night somewhere in Middle America. In this print, Wood used the soft-focus quality of lithographic printing to full advantage to complete an image on paper very close in style to his easel work.

BLW

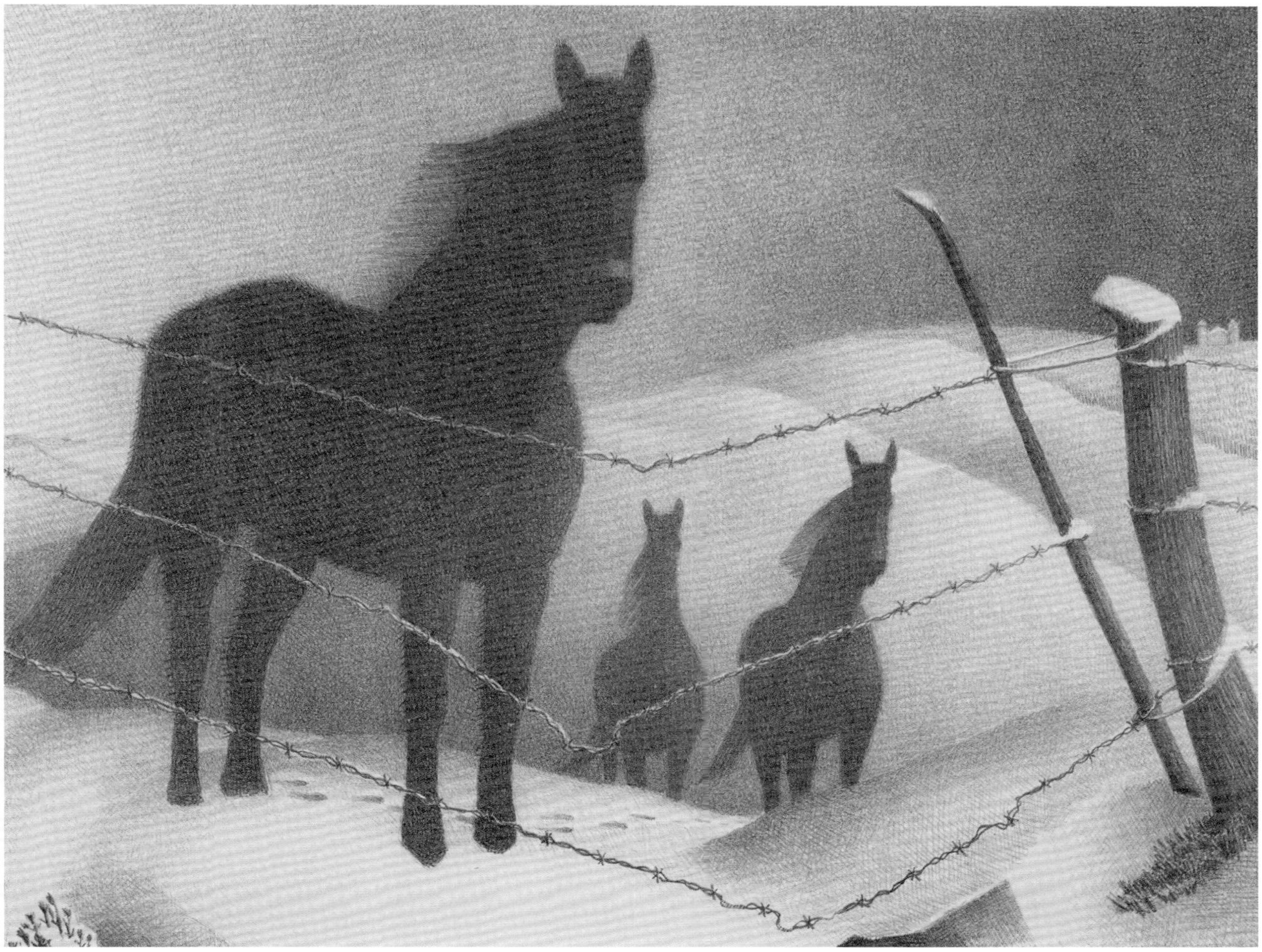

Doel Reed

(1895–1985)

Embudo Canyon, 1977

Aquatint engraving, 10¼ x 17¾ in.

1982.041.001

Museum Acquisition Fund

THE STRONG TONAL CONTRASTS are what draw viewers into the prints of Doel Reed. A lifelong printmaker and, as often characterized, a master of aquatint, he was born in Indiana and sought art education all his life, first at the John Herron Art Museum in Indianapolis and later at the Art Academy of Cincinnati, which included faculty member Joseph Henry Sharp. He served in France in World War I, then returned to his art education, influenced heavily by the aquatints of Francisco Goya. In 1924 he started a long teaching career at Oklahoma A & M College (now Oklahoma State University), building the art department he eventually would head. In 1952 he was elected to the National Academy of Design for his printmaking. Reed traveled extensively for artistic inspiration to places like France, Nova Scotia and Mexico, and made frequent summer trips to Taos, where, after retirement in 1959, he moved permanently, becoming a fixture in the art scene.

His works in New Mexico show a strong interest in the upland mountains and valleys of northern New Mexico. *Embudo Canyon* depicts the narrow valley along the Rio Embudo as it meets the Rio Grande southwest of Taos. The bright white trees punctuate the dark, mountainous topography and trace the riverbed narrowed by canyon walls. This aquatint etching by Reed may be one of the most evocative and expertly rendered Southwestern landscapes in the collection of the Museum of the Southwest. Other works by Reed include a serigraph of *The Cimarron*, the river that met the Santa Fe Trail and was one of his favorite areas to paint and sketch.

WE

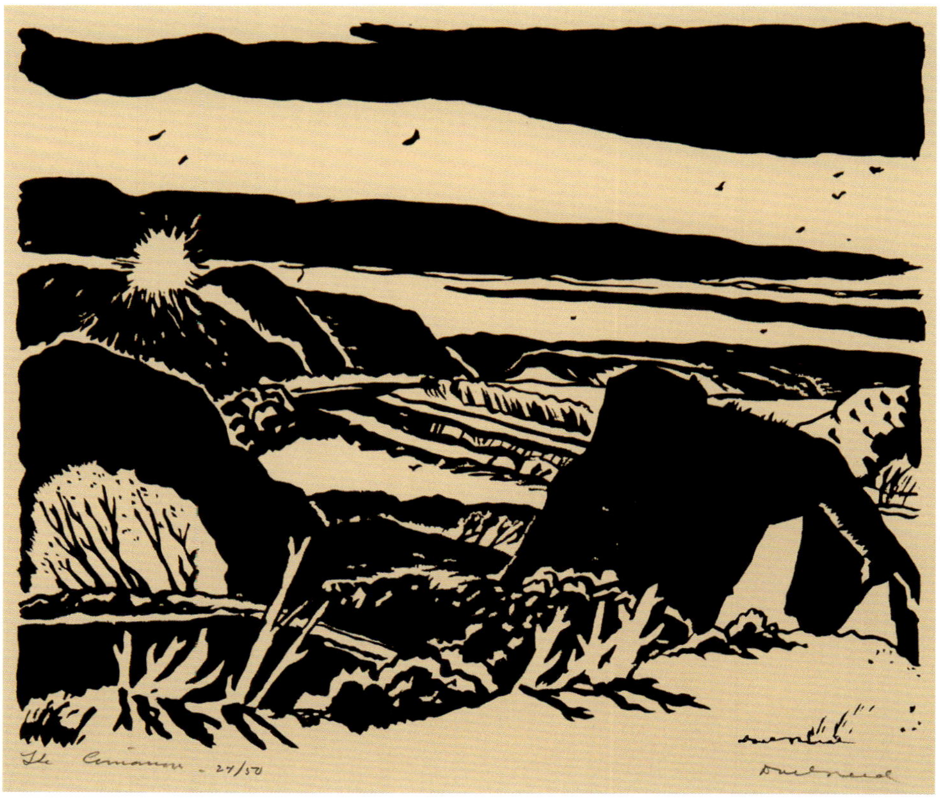

The Cimarron, 1941. Serigraph, 9½ x 9¼ in. 1983.006.011. Museum Acquisition Fund.

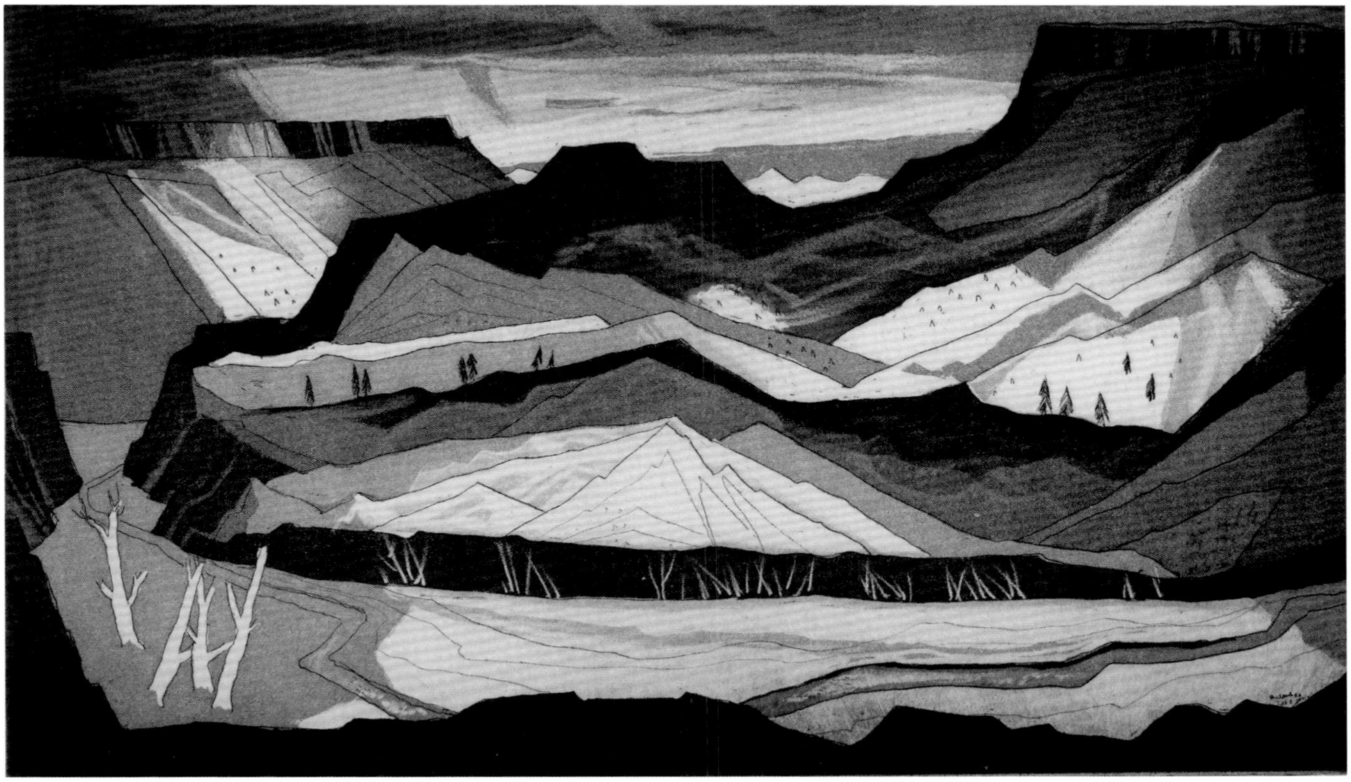

Fremont Ellis

(1897–1985)

Harvest Time at Taos Pueblo, 1928

Oil on canvas, 27½ x 35½ in.

1982.044.001

Gift of Mrs. Harvey H. Conger

Although Fremont Ellis was an important figure in the Santa Fe arts scene and lived in the city from 1921 until his death in 1985, his work has never earned significant scholarly attention. Ellis was born in a small mining town in Montana and received no formal education past the first grade. Living with an itinerant family, he moved to various places throughout Montana, the Carolinas, Georgia, Virginia, California and New York. Inspired by a trip to the Metropolitan Museum of Art when he was a teenager, he became enamored with art and began to paint with oils. He attended classes at the Art Students League for three months, the extent of his artistic education. As an adult he moved to El Paso and started exhibiting and selling his work. After a trip to Santa Fe at age twenty-one, he moved there permanently three years later.

Ellis was a founding member of the art-colony group Los Cinco Pintores in 1921, along with Willard Nash, Walter Mruk, Jozef Bakos and Will Shuster. The artists were exhibited that year at the New Mexico Museum of Art, itself a fledgling organization of newcomers. The five artists were loosely organized into this short-lived group largely for purposes of promoting their work, each displaying individual styles. Nash, Mruk and Bakos developed Modernist styles, while Ellis and Shuster were more traditional, although dabbling occasionally with Expressionist or abstract elements. Ellis' style has an Impressionist element in his brushwork and use of light, and he was fascinated with the Spanish influences in New Mexico. Although he lived in Santa Fe his work is more comfortably grouped with paintings from the Taos Society of Artists. *Harvest Time at Taos Pueblo* illustrates this connection beautifully. This 1928 painting is filled with strong light sources and big brushstrokes in a composition that fills most of the canvas with Taos Mountain and Taos Pueblo architecture.

WE

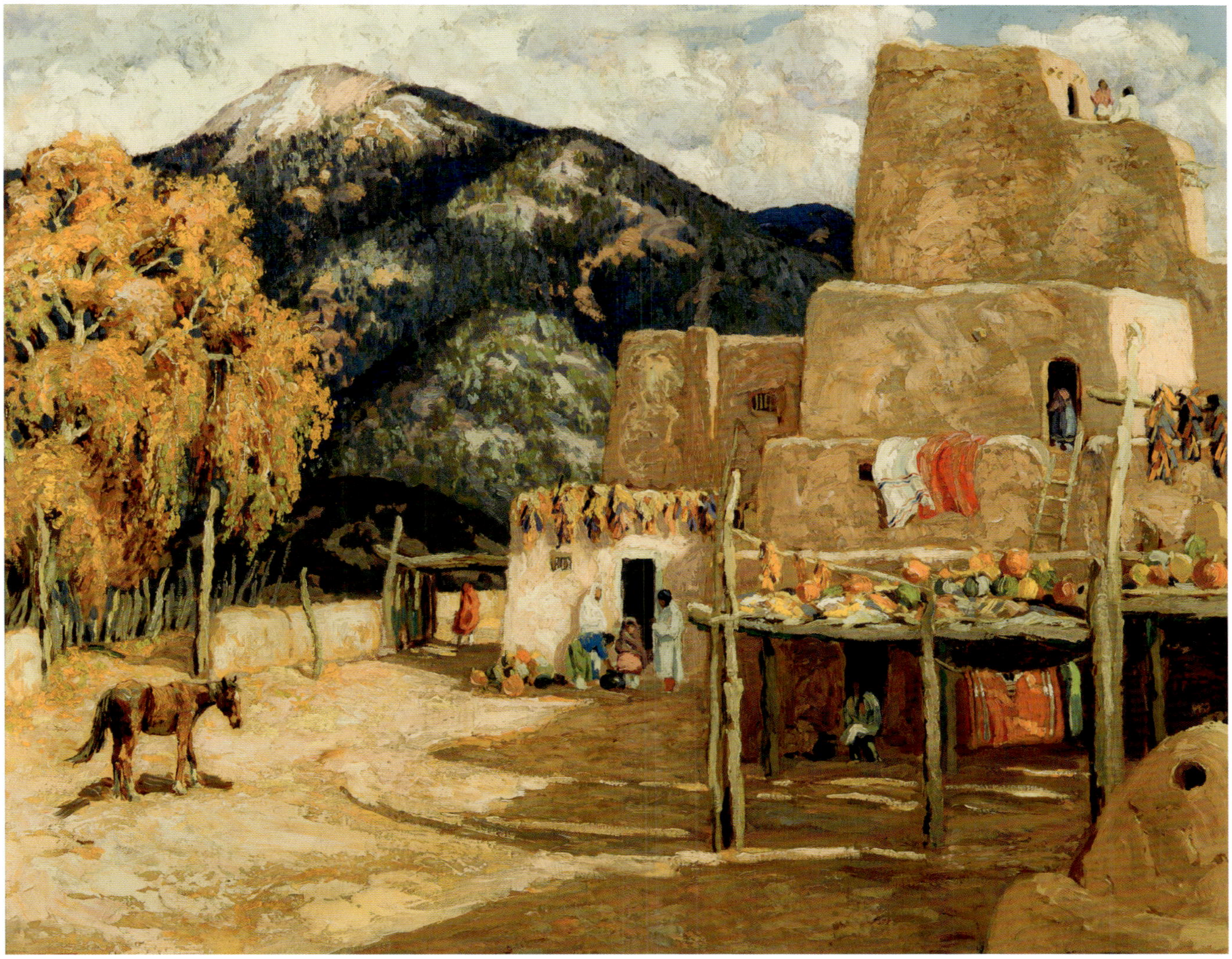

Thomas Moran

(1837–1926)

The South Dome—Yosemite Valley, 1887

Etching, 12 x 8½ in.

1983.002.001

Museum Acquisition Fund

One of the foremost American landscape painters of the nineteenth century, Thomas Moran is inextricably linked to the National Parks of the western United States, especially Yellowstone and Yosemite. Born in England, his family immigrated to the Philadelphia area in 1844. He became a successful and highly published artist, working as a painter and printmaker with a strong following from the general public due largely to his work as an expeditionary artist with the Hayden Geological Survey of 1871 of the Yellowstone area, allowing people in the eastern states to experience the area's splendors.

Moran was part of the Hudson River School, along with other artists in the Museum of the Southwest collection, including Albert Bierstadt and Thomas Hill. The Hudson River School was an art movement characterized by romantic and often large-scale landscape paintings. Although originally concentrating around the Hudson River Valley, artists associated with the movement journeyed afar to paint the magnificence of the western landscapes, earning the name the Rocky Mountain School.

Moran was one of the first American painters to also work in printmaking, focusing on etching and lithography. As a teenager he worked as a wood-engraving apprentice, then later in life worked as an illustrator, draftsman and watercolorist whose work was engraved by others. In *The South Dome—Yosemite Valley*, an etching based on a watercolor housed at the Cooper Hewitt Museum, Moran shows us a view of what would become Yosemite National Park. The dramatic scene rendered in black and white shows a large outcropping overlooking a mountain. Moran and his wife visited Yosemite for several months in 1872, and when Yosemite was declared a National Park in 1890 it was in part because of the artwork Moran created celebrating the area.

WE

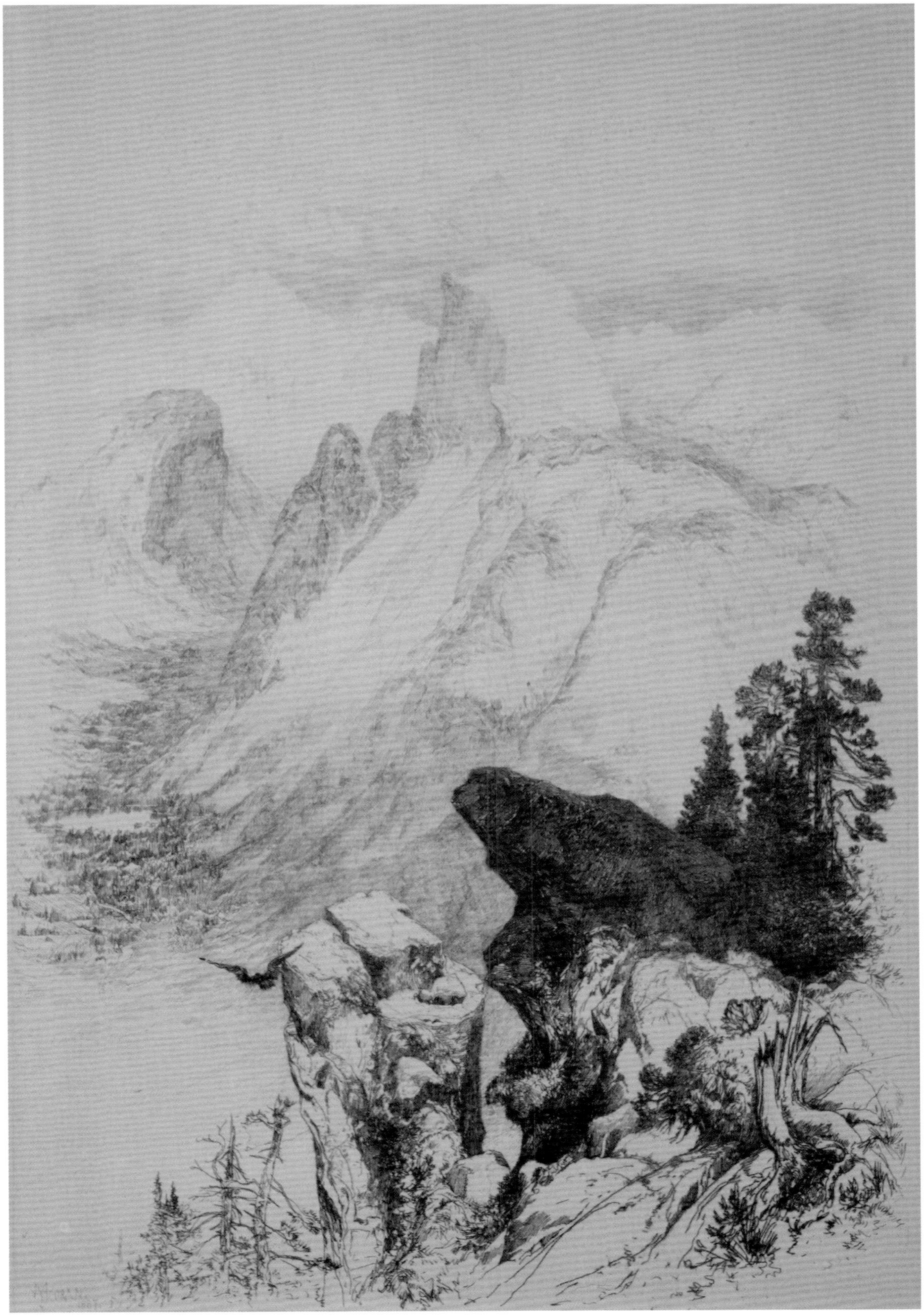

Willard Nash

(1898–1943)

Penitentes, c. 1930

Oil on canvas, 24 x 30 in.

1983.005.001

Museum Acquisition Fund

BOTH *Penitentes* and *Portrait of a Lady* reveal the painterly qualities that marked Willard Nash as the "American Cézanne." The angular outlines, bold and unblended shadows, dynamic contour lines and minimal backgrounds are characteristic of the artist's work. Born in Philadelphia, Nash spent his early years in Detroit and studied art at the Detroit School of Fine Arts. He had been a successful commercial artist from sixteen years old and first visited Santa Fe in his early twenties for a mural commission for a Detroit patron.

Nash moved to Santa Fe in 1920 and began studying with Andrew Dasburg, a Modernist artist heavily influenced by Paul Cézanne's techniques. He became one of the most influential artists of the Santa Fe Art Colony and was part of Los Cinco Pintores, the painting group. Nash lived in Santa Fe until moving to California in 1936, working in Hollywood briefly before returning to New Mexico in 1941 and shortly succumbing to tuberculosis.

Dabbling in Cubism, Fauvism and Expressionism, Nash painted portraits, landscapes and still lifes, as well as scenes of athletes, performers and the rituals of Los Hermanos Penitentes, the lay religious society active in New Mexico and Colorado since the early nineteenth century. The brotherhood's activities, at times open to the faithful public, center around the reenactment of The Passion of Jesus Christ. Artists, writers and many residents of Santa Fe have depicted these reenactments in various forms throughout the years. In Nash's *Penitentes*, the artist has shown the members of the society as flagellants, one on a life-sized cross and the others wearing hoods and white pants, with bloody bare backs, as was their custom. Nash is presenting a relatively unsensationalized account of the ritual that occurs every year during Holy Week.

WE

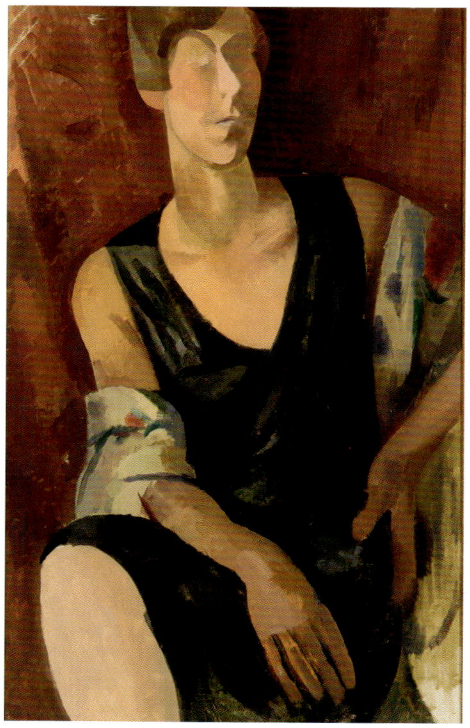

Portrait of a Lady, c. 1930. Oil on canvas, 29⅝ x 18¾ in. 1991.007.001. Gift of James W. McClary.

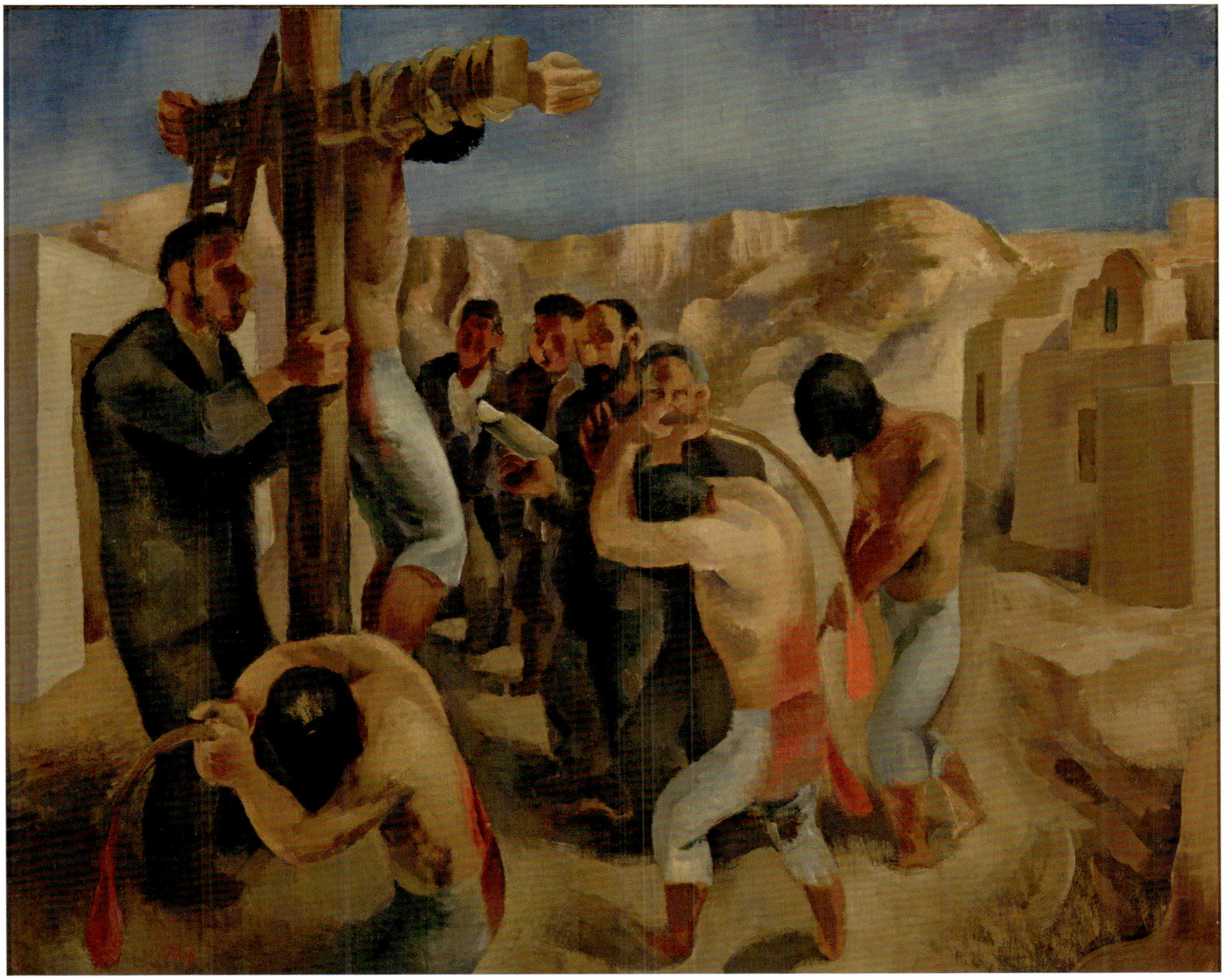

Unknown Navajo Weaver

Two Grey Hills Rug,
Mid- to late twentieth century

Wool, 74 x 102½ in.

1983.007.002

Museum Acquisition Fund

THOUGH SMALL IN NUMBER, the textiles in the collection of the Museum of the Southwest represent some of the best-known and visually appealing styles within the canon of Navajo rug weaving, including the Teec Nos Pos, Burntwater, Klagetoh, Chinle, Shiprock, Ganado Red, Two Grey Hills and Pictorial styles. Rug weaving in the twentieth century evolved from blanket weaving in the eighteenth and nineteenth centuries. Navajo weaving is a well-known textile tradition dating back to at least the arrival of the Spaniards in the Southwest, often featuring abstract and geometric patterns woven in a skilled and technically complex manner on a simple loom. Early Navajo weaving was for adornment and intertribal use, but with the arrival in the twentieth century of more tourists seeking the famed Navajo textiles, weaving evolved into a form mostly used by people outside of the tribe for decorative and educational purposes. Regional styles became a mark of pride, with trading posts, usually run by non-Navajos, encouraging weavers to develop distinctive and more complex patterns more desirable to tourists.

Two Grey Hills is one of the best-known and easiest-to-identify styles within modern Navajo weaving, and emerged from one of the most remote trading posts in the Navajo Nation, near the Chuska Mountains in northwest New Mexico. Two Grey Hills weavers have been known for the last century for using only undyed wool from a variety of sheep that yield black, brown, tan, gray and white wool. Typical rugs have several layers of borders around the central symmetrical geometric designs. The large *Two Grey Hills Rug* from an unknown weaver has two large borders with geometric I-shaped motifs inside them, surrounding a complex central pattern with stepped motifs. The rug below, from Mary Silentman, features rows of zigzags in the different sheep wools of tan, brown and black, stunning when viewed closely.

WE

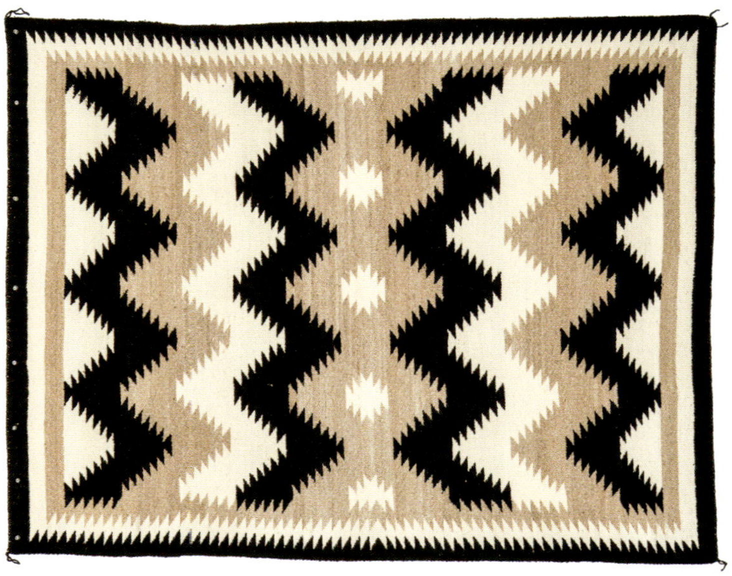

Mary Silentman. *Two Grey Hills Navajo Blanket*, 1969. Wool, 47 x 62 in. 2002.001.001. Gift of Mr. and Mrs. Charles N. Wade.

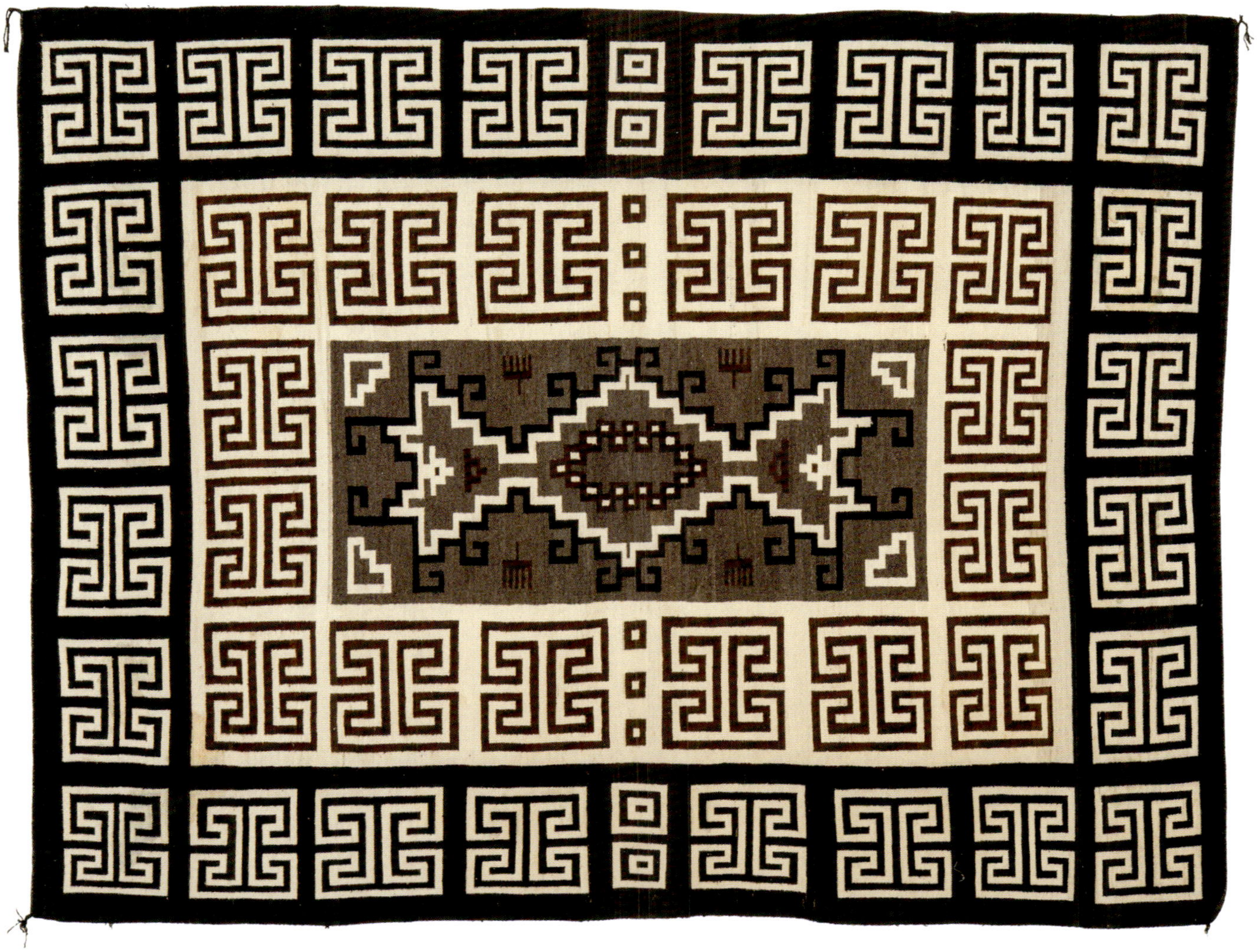

Doug Hyde

(b. 1946)

The Naming, 1981

Limestone, 60 x 44 in. diam.

1983.010.001

Gift of Fred T. and Novadean Hogan

A student of the Institute of American Indian Arts and the San Francisco Art Institute, Doug Hyde, Nez Perce, Assiniboine and Chippewa, was a trained artist who studied under Allan Houser. Hyde's sculptures are unique in their mystical quality, Native mythological allusions and the artistic method in which he works.

Hyde enlisted in the army in 1967, served two tours of duty in Vietnam and was honorably discharged after being severely injured in a grenade explosion. Upon his return to the United States he served as a monument maker, using his skill as an artist but also becoming trained in the use of large power tools. He began to see how this new skill could influence his own artwork.

Hyde's sculptural creations, typically made from limestone, alabaster and marble, are subtracted down using power tools to reveal animals or people that tell the stories Hyde grew up hearing. The use of these tools allows Hyde to work quickly, forming the stone freely and fluidly as his mind forms the image of the final product. Hyde does not work from models or drawings; he allows the stone to speak to him and inform what he creates. Natural lines, imperfections and textures help to dictate what form the sculpture will take.

In the case of *The Naming*, Hyde tells the story of a Hopi christening ceremony. Four women hold on to a young child; one of the women holds an ear of corn over the group. The work is simple but filled with symbolism and detail. These women, three aunts and the mother, are communing with Mother Earth, symbolized in the ear of corn, to find a name for the child. Each of the women is similar in form but unique in detail, which can be seen in the etched waves of hair, the implied textiles each is wearing and the use of the stone's natural texture.

KW

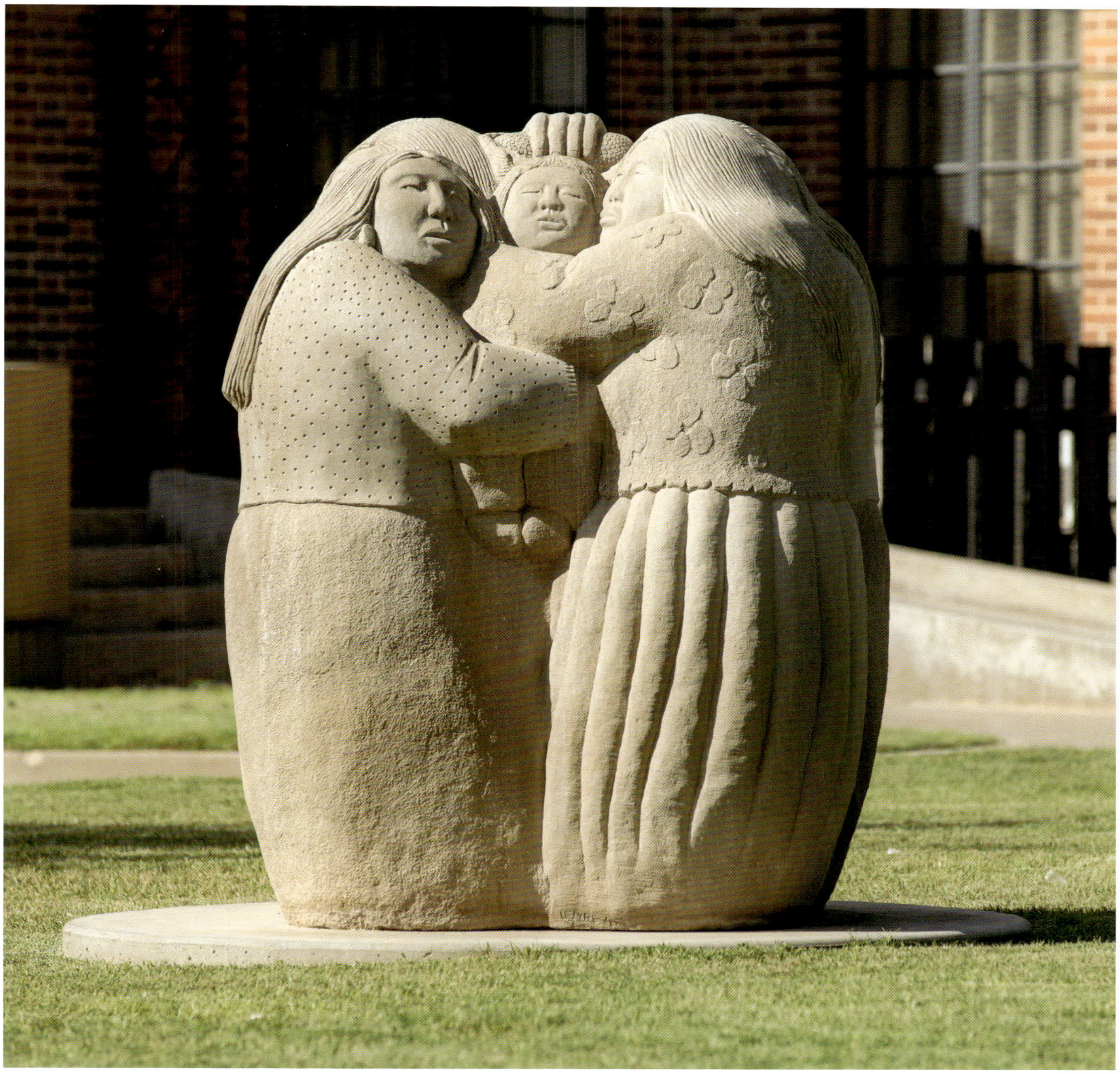

William Penhallow Henderson

(1877–1943)

Portrait of Tesuque Indian Woman, c. 1920

Oil on board, 23½ x 17¼ in.

1983.013.001

Museum Acquisition Fund

Portrait of Tesuque Indian Woman presents us with an almost stark portrayal of an anonymous woman, with thick lines outlining large blocks of color and minimal shading and texture. The accompanying study in oil pastel gives us an insight into the artist's process, showing a much greater concern with color and pose than with presenting an accurate rendering of subject.

William Penhallow Henderson traveled all over Europe, and the influence of Post-Impressionists like Cézanne and Gauguin is evident in his portrait depictions of Pueblo Indian women in the villages near Santa Fe. Tesuque was one of the many pueblos he visited, and the woman in the painting is shown in period hairstyle and jewelry, with a blackware vessel of the kind produced at Santa Clara and San Ildefonso Pueblos to the north. Henderson's work differs from other Anglo New Mexican artists, offering less detail and romanticization and instead conveying a more universal feeling.

Born in Massachusetts, Henderson studied at the Massachusetts Normal Art School and the School of the Boston Museum of Fine Arts. As a young artist he traveled extensively, then moved to Chicago, where he made a living by painting portrait commissions and teaching at the Academy of Fine Arts in Chicago. While there he met and married his wife, the poet Alice Corbin. Her poor health and battle with tuberculosis necessitated a move in 1916 to Santa Fe, a burgeoning art colony where many tuberculosis sufferers found respite. In addition to painting on canvas, during his many years in New Mexico Henderson worked as a muralist and furniture designer. Henderson was also an architect and accomplished building designer; the Wheelwright Museum of the American Indian in Santa Fe is a Henderson design in the style of a Navajo hogan.

WE

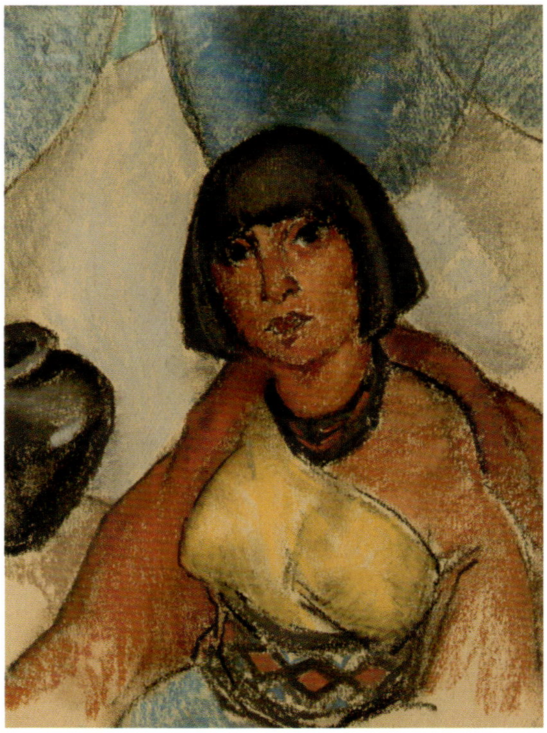

Study for *Portrait of Tesuque Indian Woman*, c. 1919. Pastel on paper, 10 x 7⅞ in. 1984.006.001. Museum Acquisition Fund.

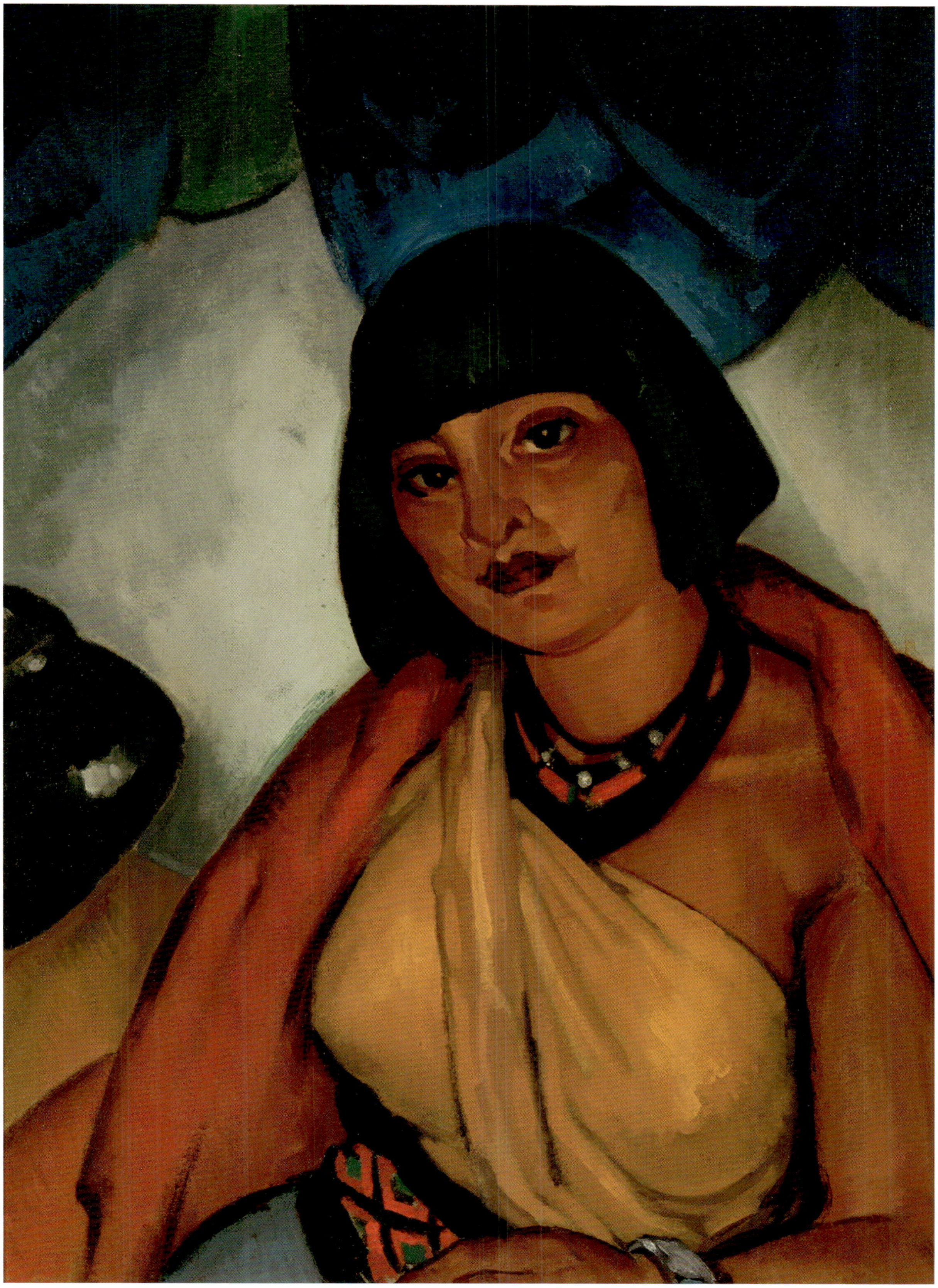

Woodrow Wilson (Woody) Crumbo

(1912–1989)

Crow Dancer, c. 1970

Silk screen, 12 x 9 in.

1983.015.006

Gift of Mr. and Mrs. Ed A. Vogler

As a prolific painter and printmaker concerned with Indian subjects and documentation, Potawatomi artist Woody Crumbo's work is highly invested with information and meaning. The Museum of the Southwest's forty-six prints by Crumbo illustrate the depth of his chosen subject matter and the creativity he imbued into each composition. He held various positions within the art world, as a professional dancer, flautist, painter and printmaker, as well as director of art at Bacone College, consultant and curator to the Thomas Gilcrease Museum and director of the El Paso Art Museum.

Primarily a painter, he turned to printmaking in the 1950s as a way to disseminate his artwork—and that of other Indian artists—to a wider audience nationally and internationally. *Crow Dancer* and *Rainbow Horse* illustrate important facets of his style. Crumbo painted in the traditional Indian style of his day, utilizing few backgrounds and flat areas of color, but what makes his work stand the test of time is his dynamic figures, always graceful, rhythmic and full of energy. With *Crow Dancer,* the figure has his back turned to the viewer and is covered with rich, detailed costume elements. Crumbo was a dancer himself, and learned about dance and music traditions from several tribes, including the Creek, Sioux and Kiowa. He wrote a pamphlet about the importance of many of his dance and ceremonial depictions, providing layers of research about elements of the costumes, performance and movements. The Crow Dance takes its name from the "crow" or "bustle," the feather ornament with streamers that hung down the back. The crow was worn in various dances, including the War Dance, Grass Dance and Victory Dance, and often served as a warning to the dancer that death was always at his heels. These feather ornaments could also be symbolic of the thunderbird and had connections with the early Sun Dance.

WE

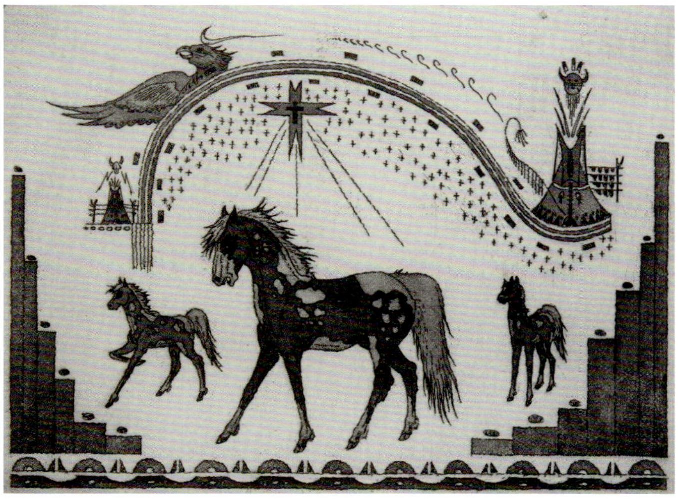

Rainbow Horse, c. 1945–1950. Etching, 4 x 5½ in. 1983.015.030. Gift of Mr. and Mrs. Ed A. Vogler.

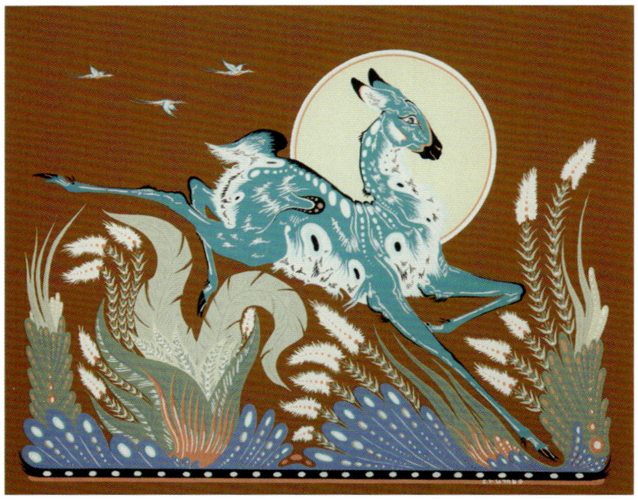

Untitled (Deer with Moon and Plants), c. 1945–1950. Silkscreen, 15 x 19¾ in. 1999.003.001. Gift of Mary Griffith.

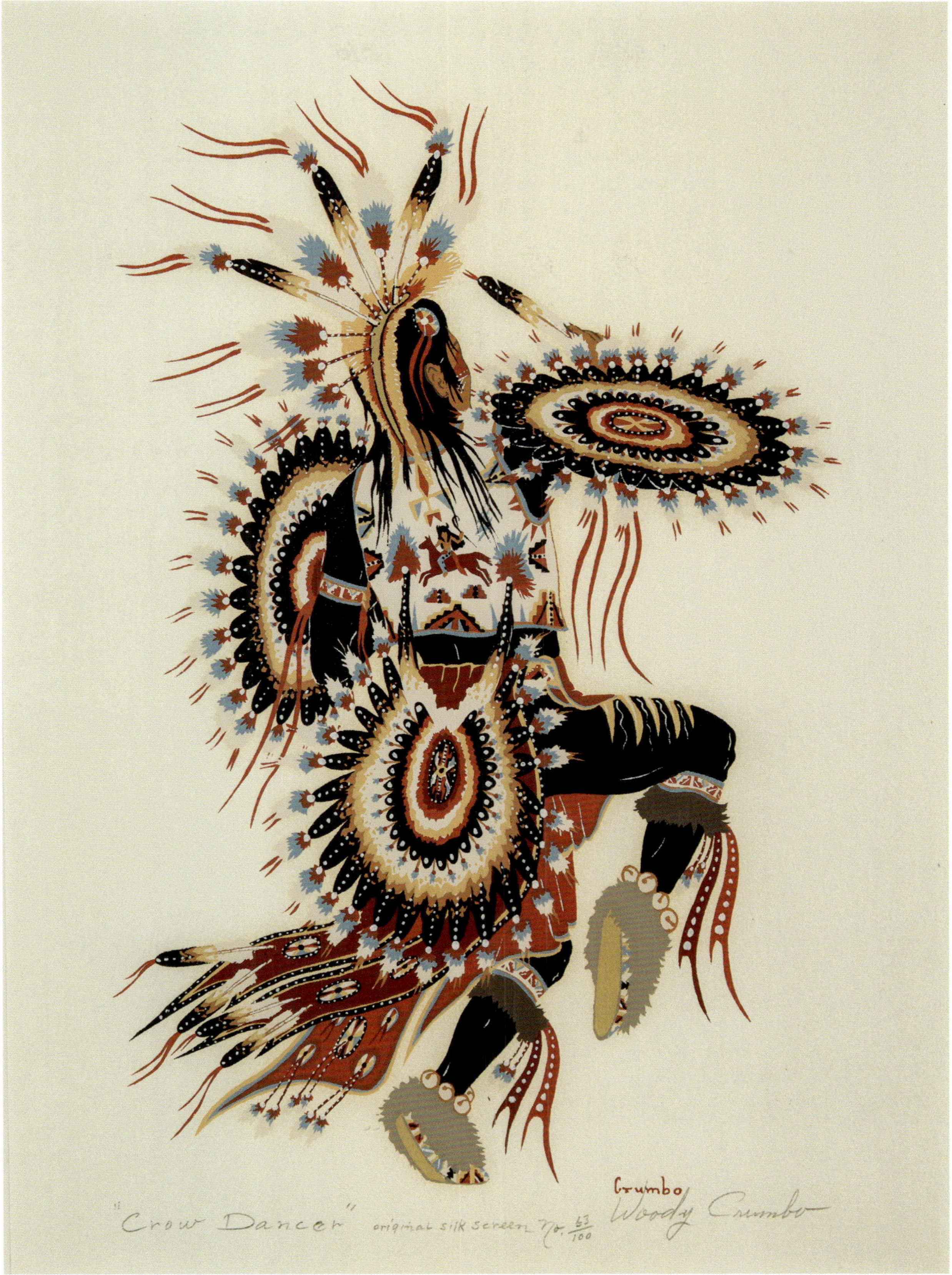
"Crow Dancer" original silk screen No. 63/100
Crumbo
Woody Crumbo

Karl Bodmer

(1809–1893)

Facsimile of an Indian Painting, 1833

Hand-colored aquatint engraving, 11¾ x 17 in.

1984.008.055

Bodmer Acquisition Fund

THIS ENGRAVING WEAVES TOGETHER a narrative of two artists from very different worlds. It all started with an 1833 painting created by Mató-Tópe (also known as Four Bears), a chief of the Mandan tribe in North Dakota. Mató-Tópe was a fierce warrior who created works of art depicting his prowess in battles. For his painting *Battle with a Cheyenne Chief*, which is in the collection of the Joslyn Museum of Art, he was given pencils, paint and paper by the Swiss and French artist Karl Bodmer. Bodmer traveled with the expedition of the German Prince Maximilian of Wied from 1832-1834, documenting cities, landscapes and Indian tribes found throughout the United States. The text and artwork produced during this expedition were published in Maximilian's *Travels in the Interior of North America*.

Bodmer worked in watercolor painting and produced several portraits of Mató-Tópe and other members of the Mandan tribe during his several months in North Dakota. He also produced a faithful rendition of Mató-Tópe's painting entitled *Facsimile of an Indian Painting*. The aquatint was created by a French engraver, then published by a London firm that created an entire series of hand-colored aquatint prints based on Bodmer's watercolor paintings. The Museum of the Southwest owns one of the few complete suites known to exist. The series shows a wonderful progression of reinterpretations of a very early Indian painting by a non-Indian artist. Several other explorers and artists had visited the Mandan villages and created portraits of Mató-Tópe, including George Catlin. Mató-Tópe died in a smallpox outbreak in 1837; thus, Bodmer's works are some of the last records of him.

WE

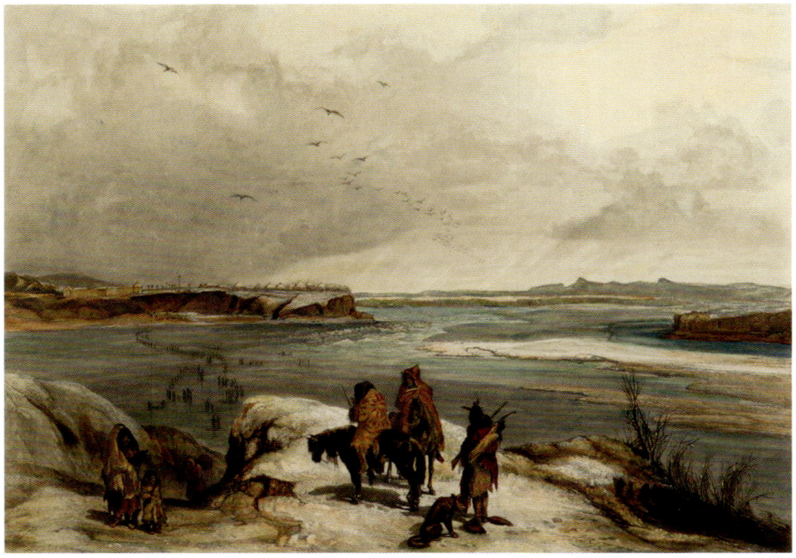

On the Missouri, 1833. Hand-colored aquatint engraving, 11¾ x 17 in. 1984.008.048. Bodmer Acquisition Fund.

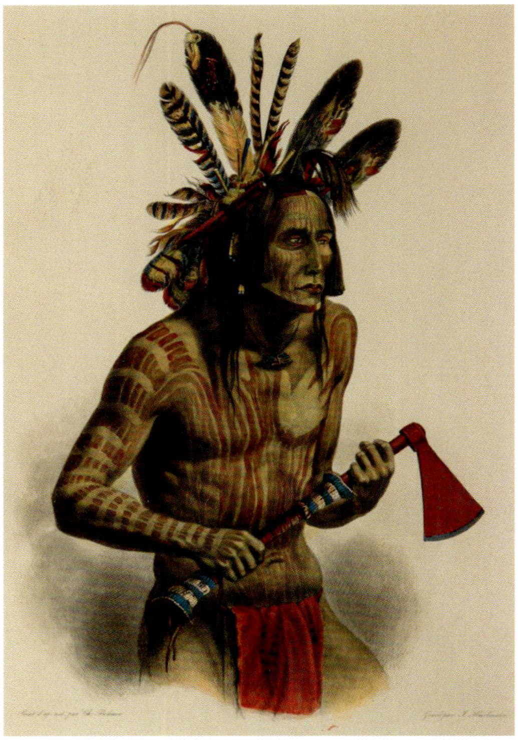

Mató-Tópe, A Mandan Chief, 1833. Hand-colored aquatint engraving, 16½ x 12¾ in. 1984.008.046. Bodmer Acquisition Fund.

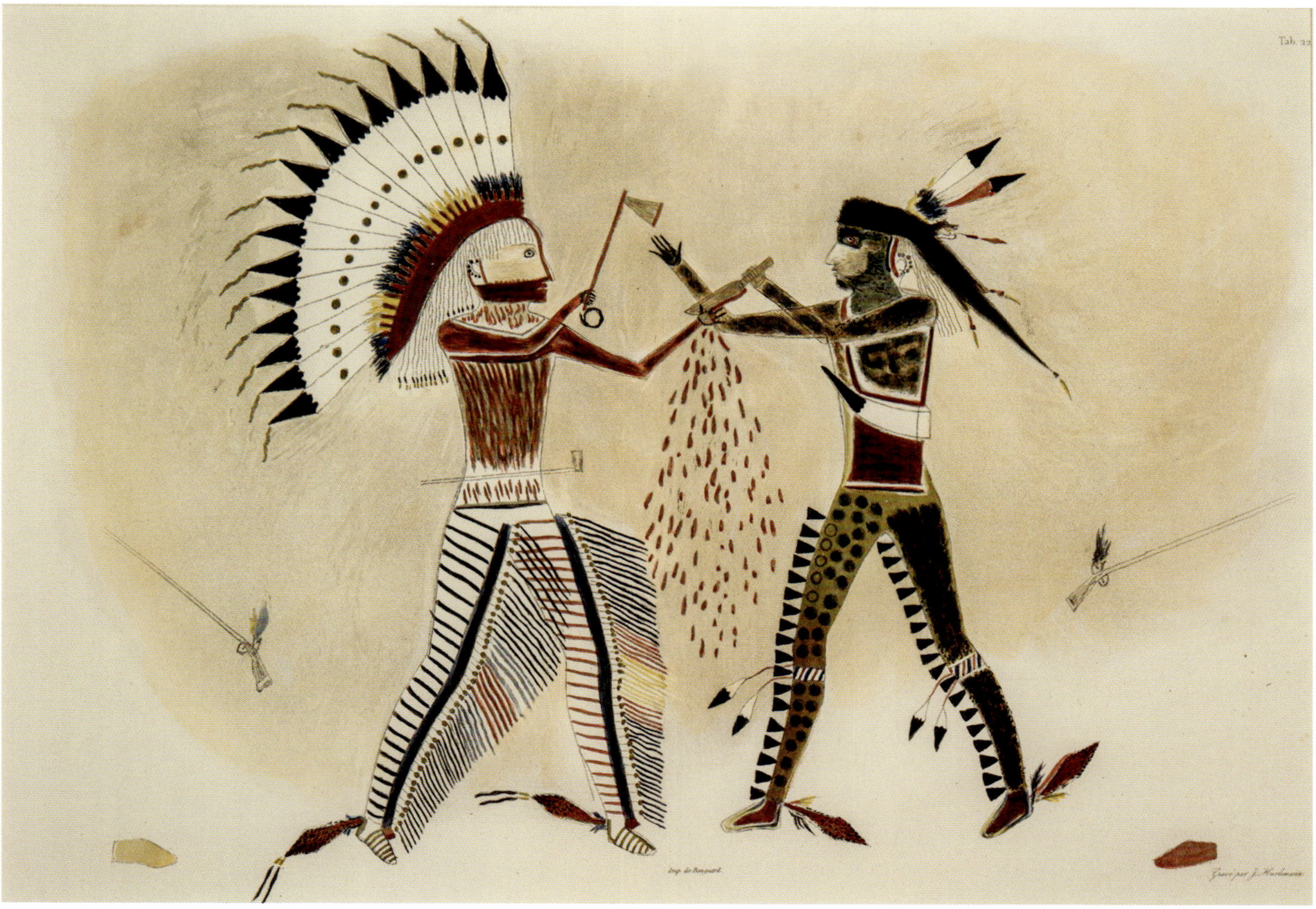

Nicolai Fechin

(1881–1955)

Portrait of
Mrs. Ralph van Vechten,
c. 1926–1928

Oil on canvas, 23½ x 19½ in.

1985.004.001

Museum Acquisition Fund

A NATIVE OF KAZAN, RUSSIA, Nicolai Fechin immigrated to the United States in 1923 after the fallout from the Russian Revolution had caused devastation to his parents, who died of typhoid fever. Fechin was rescued by the American Relief Association. Shortly thereafter he, his wife, Alexandra Belkovitch (daughter of the director of the Kazan School of Art), and their daughter, Eya, settled in New York where his major collector, the architect John Burnham, arranged housing for the family. Fechin's work was already known to audiences in the United States, as in 1910 he had exhibited paintings at the prestigious Carnegie International Exhibition in Pittsburgh.

Fechin's early work in Russia, where he had studied at the prestigious Imperial Academy of Arts and won the Prix de Rome (enabling him to travel around Europe), is said to favor imagery related to violence and death. In America Fechin turned to portraiture and, upon settling in Taos, where he moved for health reasons, took up painting the landscape and the native population. A few of his more renowned subjects include Vladimir Lenin, Karl Marx, Frieda Lawrence, Lillian Gish and Mrs. Ralph (Fannie) van Vechten, the wife of the prominent Chicago banker and stockholder of the Chrysler Corporation.

Ralph van Vechten died in 1927 and Fannie the following year; thus, this portrait was painted about 1926. Fannie appears sullen and introspective in the artist's characteristic loose brushstroke technique that curator Jo-Anne Birnie Danzker has described as "Fechin's early preference for thick layers of color and pigment with very little oil, and a penchant for conflating the real and the abstract."

MBW

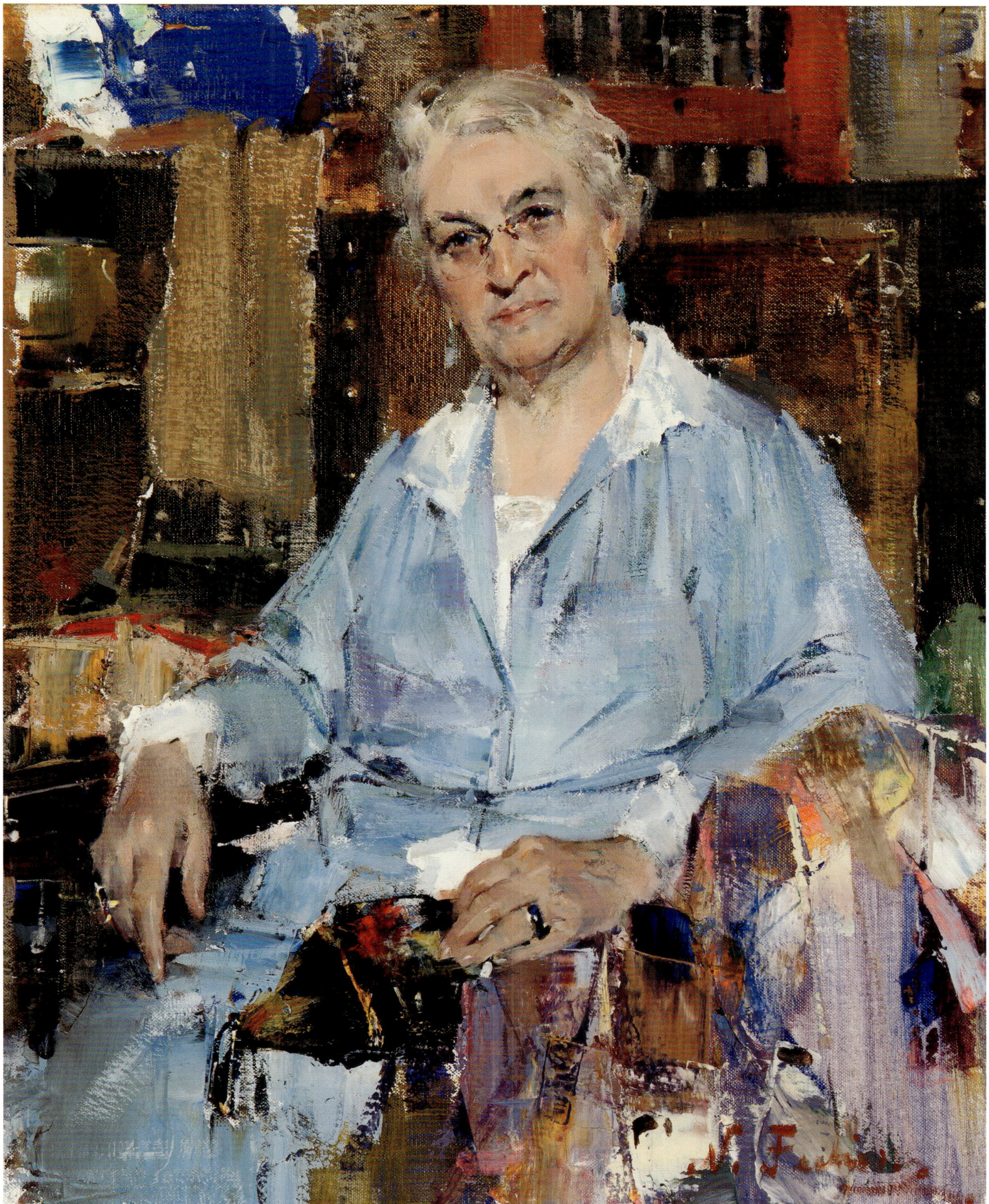

Norman Rockwell

(1894–1978)

Spring Song, 1925

Oil on canvas, 31 x 24 in.

1986.003.001

Gift of Fred T. and Novadean Hogan

In more than 300 paintings that Norman Rockwell created for the covers of the *Saturday Evening Post,* no two are alike. With scenes of American life spanning five decades, his work captures the essence of representational art in the twentieth century. Rockwell was an artist from an early age, studying at the Chase Art School starting at age fourteen, with additional training at the National Academy of Design and the Art Students League. He found success early in his career, illustrating books and becoming a staff artist and later art editor for *Boy's Life* magazine while still in his late teens. He submitted his first cover to the *Saturday Evening Post* in 1916 when he was twenty-two.

Most of the paintings that served as *Saturday Evening Post* covers, along with his hundreds of other paintings, are now in public collections. In his lifetime he was famous in popular culture but often derided by art critics, who preferred to call him an illustrator instead of an artist and often used the terms "kitschy" or "sentimental." *Spring Song*, in the collection of the Museum of the Southwest, while not a Southwestern painting, does tie Rockwell together with the work of illustrators like Andrew Loomis and with the Regionalist painters depicting other facets of American life, including Jerry Bywaters, Thomas Hart Benton and Merritt Mauzey. *Spring Song*, sometimes referred to as *Flutist*, was a *Post* cover in May 1925, a time when the Roaring Twenties were in full swing with a national focus on youth and beauty. This painting—like so many of Rockwell's works—responds to the artistic impulses of the day in Rockwell's signature style, depicting an old man playing the flute to a composition entitled *Spring Song*, likely the piece composed by Mendelssohn. The man is seated at an old-fashioned desk but still striving to create and capture the youthfulness that is the essence of spring.

WE

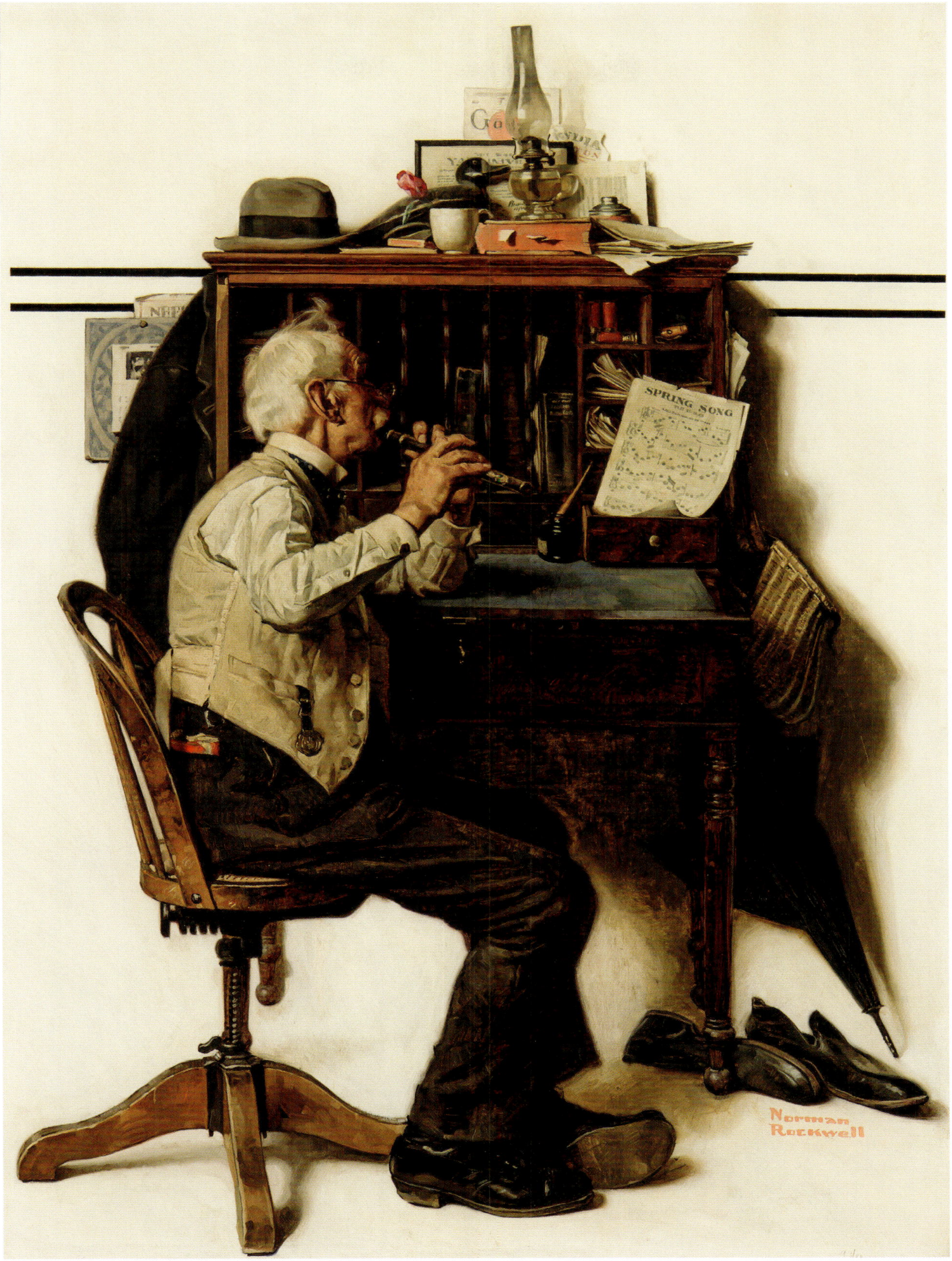
SPRING SONG
Norman
Rockwell

Eanger Irving Couse

(1866–1936)

Flower of the Prison, 1888

Oil on canvas, 45½ x 37½ in.

1986.007.001

Gift of Fred T. and Novadean Hogan

Born in Michigan, educated in Paris, and a summer resident of Taos, E. Irving Couse became a leading artist of American Indian genre scenes in the early twentieth century. His intimate and harmonious depictions of Native life lent humanitarian insight into a culture that was seen as a mystery to much of the nation. Working among a close group of artists and friends, Couse was a founder and first president of the Taos Society of Artists in 1915 and used his ties with the New York art world to shed light on northern New Mexico and the Taos Indians.

Known predominantly for his rustic and impressionistic glimpses into Native life, Couse's *Flower of the Prison* serves as a visual precursor to his later work with Native American models and subject matter. Created as his first entry for the Paris Salon in 1888, this painting is a rich portrayal of Couse's formal training in art and the influence of his artistic mentor at Académie Julian, William Bouguereau. Couse's studies as a young man in Paris focused heavily on technique, the human form and draftsmanship. Bouguereau praised his student and pressed him in the direction of classical and academic art and an intimate understanding of European art history. This training he would take back to America, where his style as an artist fully formed as his subject matter changed.

The use of symbolism and allegory in this work lends itself to a deeper understanding of Couse's later depictions of Native American life. The young girl's yellow flower may symbolize religious redemption, especially in conjunction with the illuminated book in the background, presumably a Bible. However, Couse's true interest was in the human form and the humanity found behind that form. Using light and shadow to create contemplative and peaceful environments, his numerous subjects are romanticized and humanized, as seen in *The Image Maker* and *The Purple Shawl*.

KW

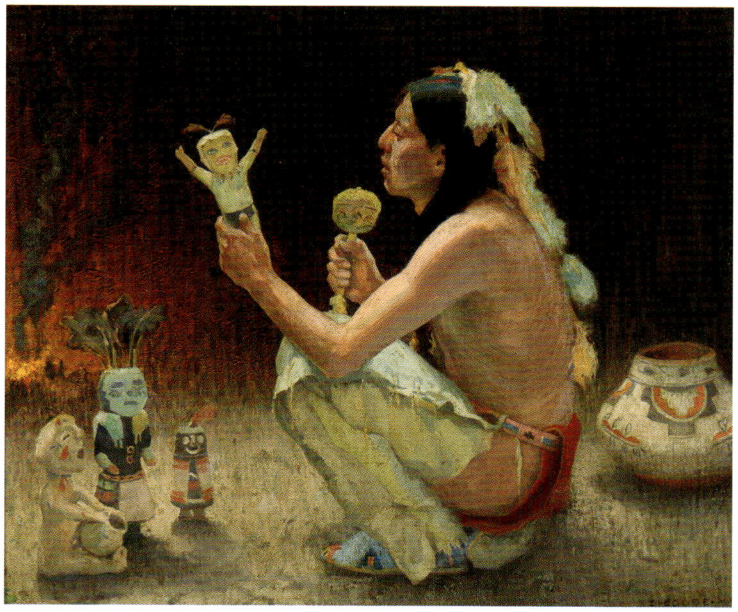

The Image Maker, c. 1910–1930. Oil on canvas, 24¼ x 29 in. 1972.003.001. Gift of Mr. and Mrs. Lynn Durham.

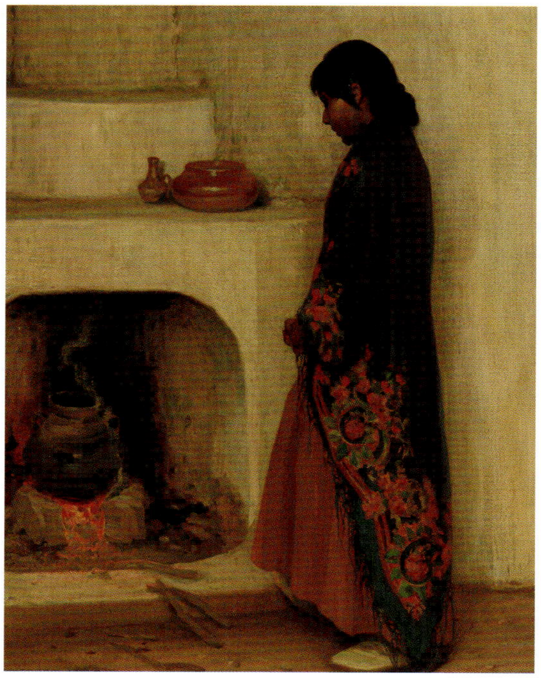

The Purple Shawl, 1911. Oil on canvas, 1980.009.005. 29¼ x 24 in. Gift of Fred T. and Novadean Hogan.

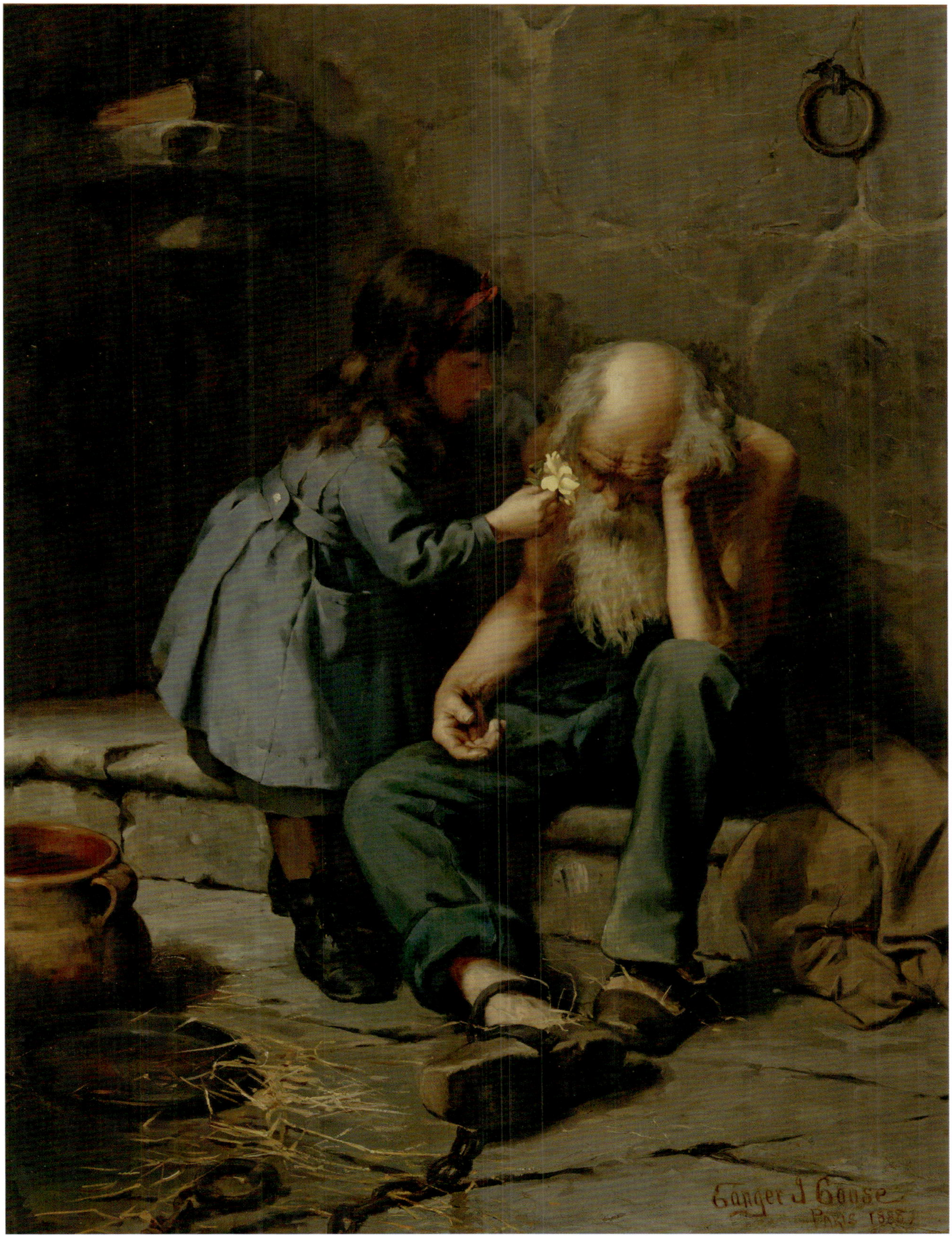

Nora Henio

(dates unknown)

Rainbow Chant of Mother Earth and Father Sky, Late twentieth century

Sandpainting, 24 x 36 in.

1986.011.001

Gift of Mr. and Mrs. Stan Lamphere

Sandpaintings—also called dry paintings—were originally sacred Navajo iconography used in healing ceremonies. The designs were not made to last; the act of placing the sand upon the floor and then dismantling the composition after the ceremony are what made it effective for healing. Sacred sandpaintings were a performance rather than an object. Beginning in the 1940s, some enterprising Navajos started to make commercial sandpaintings that were secular and permanent, which could be sold to non-Navajos. The technique used to create the permanent work involves trickling sand through the hand onto a glue-covered board, working from the center outward to create the design. The designs normally used in ceremonies are changed—either through an inversion of the colors or a deliberate removal of certain elements—in order to ensure that the power of the original act is not compromised.

Reproducing sandpainting designs outside of ceremonial settings can be done to create permanent secular works of art, as demonstrations in places like trading posts or museums, or even as designs for textiles. Commercial sandpainting artists place a greater emphasis on aesthetic qualities, transforming the designs into true works of art. These pieces come in a variety of sizes and utilize many themes, including sacred figures, plants and animals. The figures are elongated and striking, adorned with many details and set against stark backgrounds.

According to a note from the maker Nora Henio, *Rainbow Chant of Mother Earth and Father Sky* contains a chant for the sick for nine days and nights. The artist states, "The medicine man put sand on the ground floor to heal and bring luck. The sands are natural, and their different colors are achieved by boil dying with weeds and flowers or stone grind and sandstone." Sometimes sandpaintings can be contextualized, with notes like the one that accompanied *Rainbow Chant*, but often the maker and specific ritual associations are lost, as with the piece below.

WE

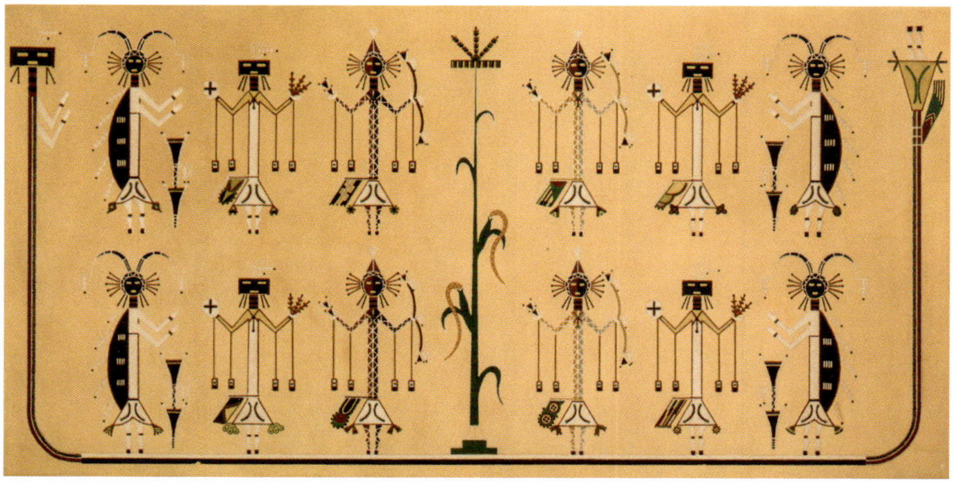

Unknown artist. *Corn Dance*, c. 1945–1955. Sand on board, 66 x 126 in. 1982.033.001. Gift of Mr. and Mrs. Lynn Durham.

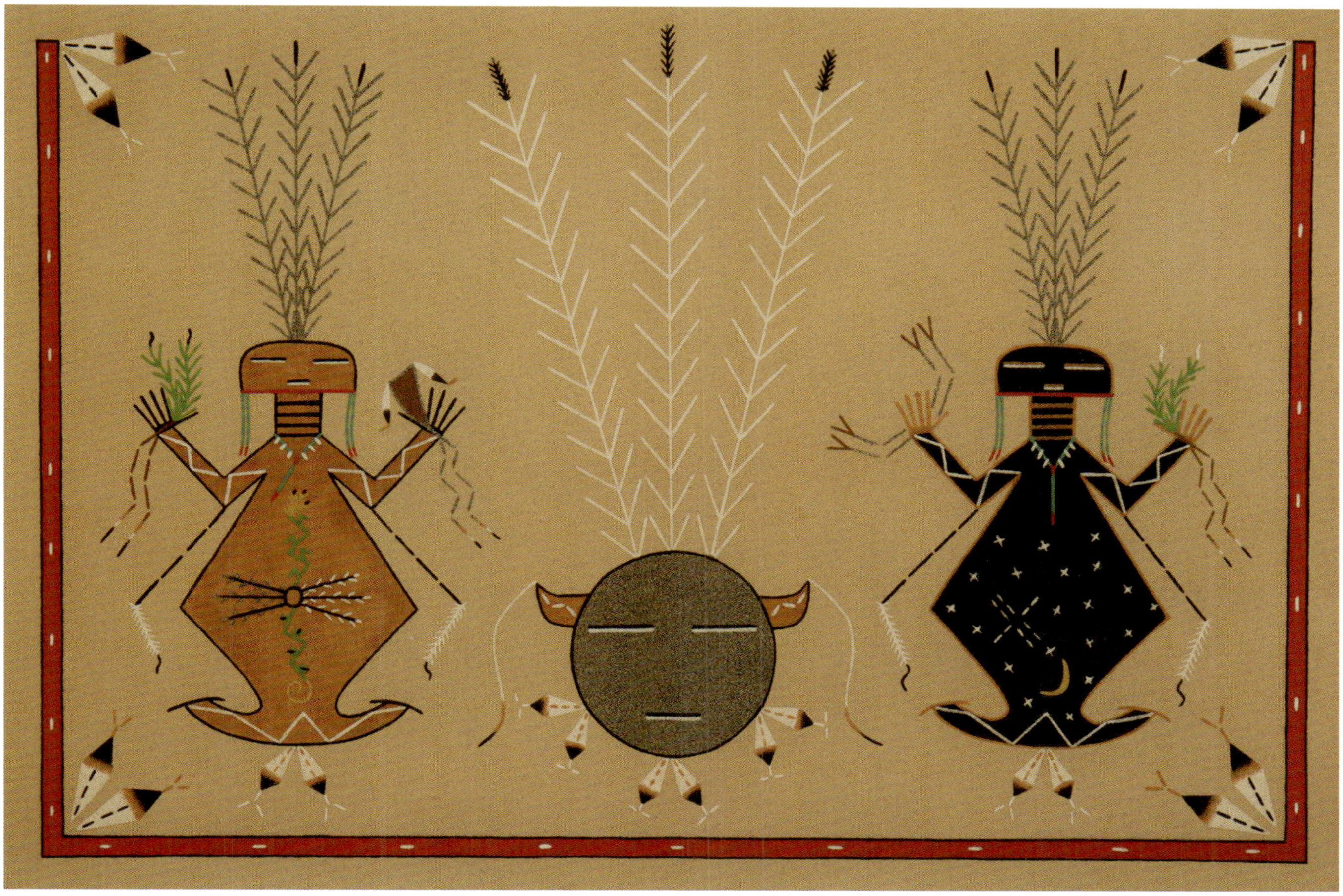

Casas Grandes Culture

Polychrome Bowl, 1200–1450

Ceramic, 7 7⁄16 x 5 3⁄8 in. diam.

1987.004.005

Gift of Dr. Kirby B. Tarry

Casas Grandes, located in the Chihuahuan Desert of northern Mexico, was part of the Greater Southwest sphere of Pueblo cultures. From 1200–1450 the site of Casas Grandes, also known as Paquimé, was a trade center heavily involved in the import and export of tropical birds, shells, pottery and other goods within the Southwest. Throughout the fourteenth and fifteenth centuries, Casas Grandes was the key link between the Southwest and Mesoamerica with its geographic position giving it much of its political power.

Most Casas Grandes art that has survived is painted ceramics, with designs tracing a clear stylistic lineage to older pottery of the Anasazi, Mimbres and Mogollon traditions. The most common type of ceramic is the Ramos polychrome (in black, white and red), as seen in the collection of the Museum of the Southwest. At first glance these pots seem to be painted with abstract patterns that don't immediately convey any meaning. Knowing more about the culture, especially the crucial importance of macaws and other tropical birds, gives viewers an insight into the designs and meanings of the artwork. Macaws were imported from the tropical forests of southeastern Mexico and Guatemala into the southwest regions of Texas and New Mexico because the brightly colored feathers were highly valued for rituals and costumes.

Macaw motifs are found throughout Casas Grandes art, especially the birds' hooked beaks and beady eyes, which artists rendered naturalistically in some vessels but in other vessels abstracted by depicting wavelike forms and bull's-eyes. Other artistic motifs included intricate and complex geometric patterns, plumed serpents, and innovative new forms and designs that combine figures and concepts from Mesoamerica into the style of the Southwestern ceramic tradition. These ceramics are archaeological objects but also works of art connecting the past and different cultural traditions.

WE

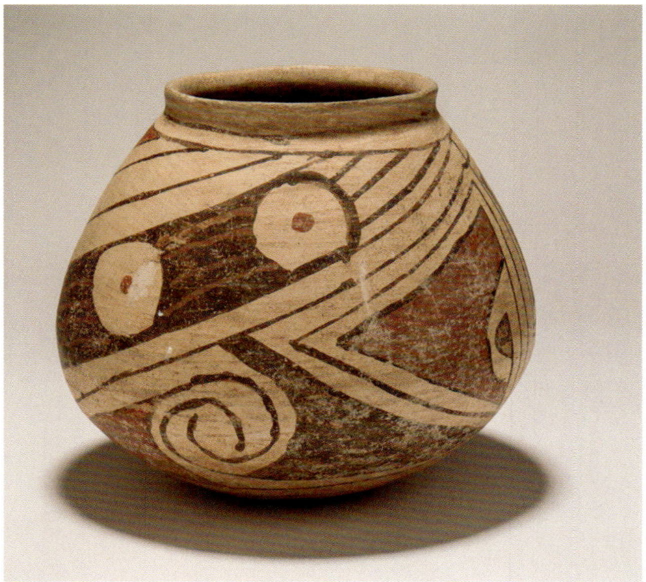

Polychrome Jar, 1200–1450. Ceramic, 8¼ x 8 in. diam. 1986.012.008. Gift of Dr. Kirby B. Tarry.

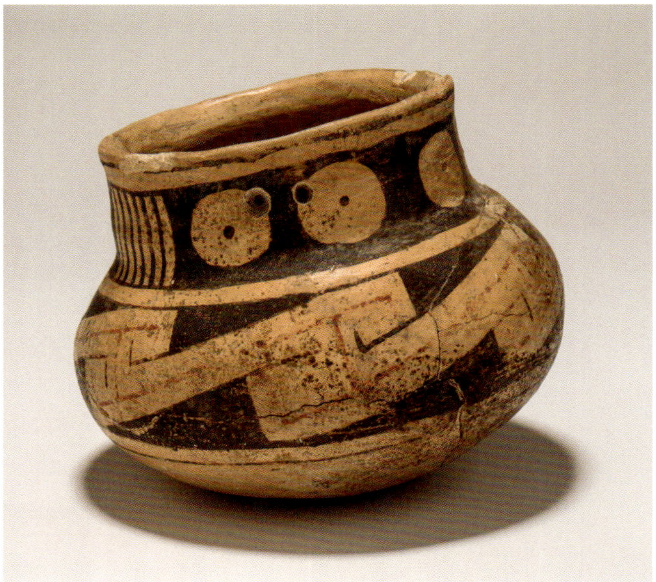

Polychrome Bowl, 1200–1450. Ceramic, 5¼ x 6 in. diam. 1986.012.005. Gift of Dr. Kirby B. Tarry.

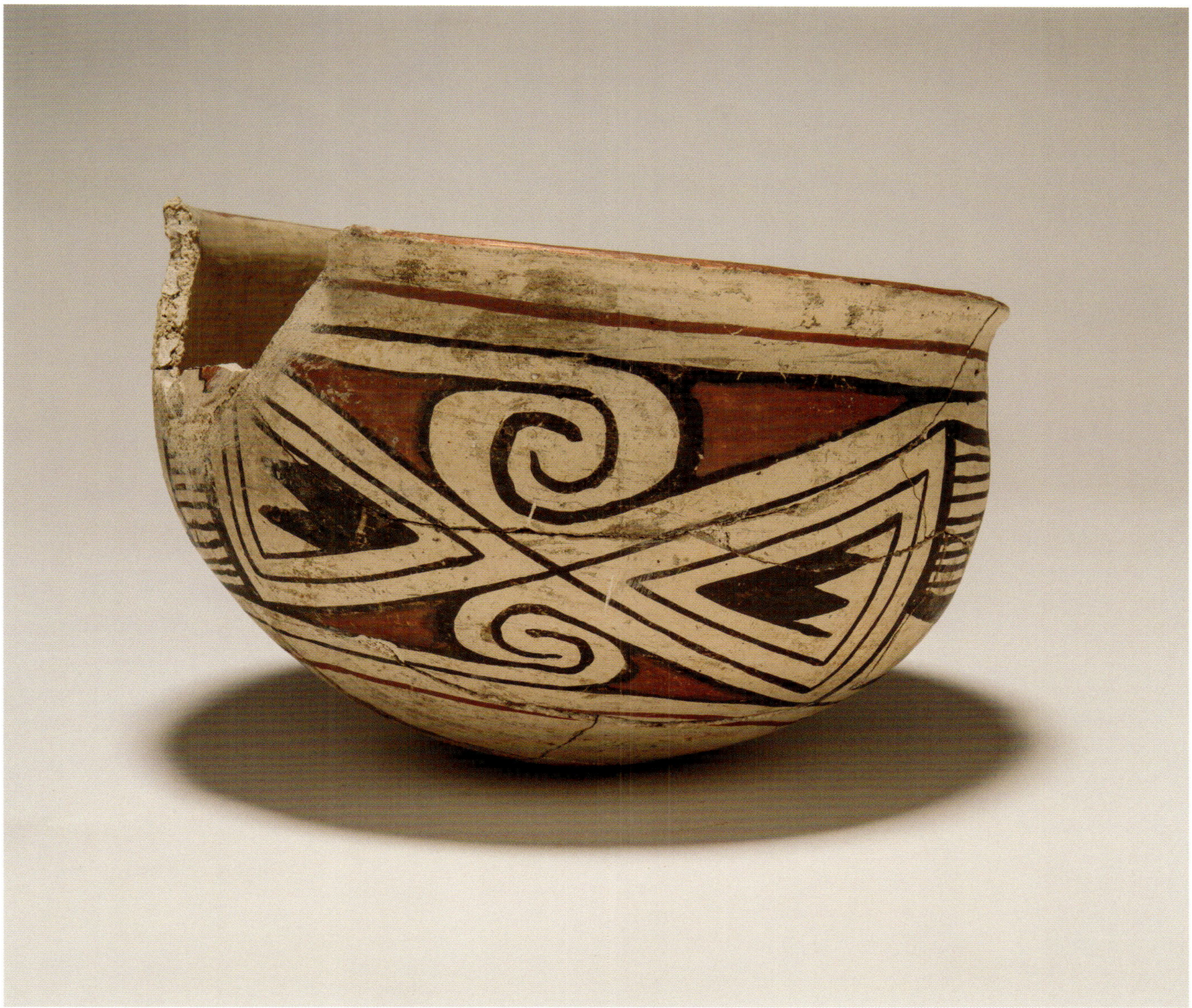

Julius Rolshoven

(1858–1930)

Portrait of a Young Male Indian, c. 1916–1930

Oil on canvas, 23¾ x 19¾ in.

1989.001.001

Gift of BLee Dorn

JULIUS ROLSHOVEN'S *Portrait of a Young Male Indian* presents the viewer with one of the most visually inviting works in the Museum of the Southwest collection. The young man is in the process of turning towards the viewer, bare chested and with an enigmatic expression that would not be out of place on a young person today. The background is stark, and though he wears a red hair wrap and a blanket or some sort of clothing loosely draped around him, all of the attention is drawn towards his bare chest and face. The path that led the artist to paint this portrait of an Indian from New Mexico is a circuitous one.

Rolshoven was born in Detroit in 1858, one of the earliest born members of the Taos Society of Artists. There are some conflicting details within his biographies, but he was a highly skilled painter in the academic tradition. He began his education at the Cooper Union in New York before moving to Europe. There he studied at the Düsseldorf Academy, the Royal Academy of Munich and finally the Académie Julian in Paris, where he stayed to teach. Among his many teachers was William Bouguereau, who also taught E. Irving Couse. During his time in Europe he also lived in London, Venice and Florence and ventured to North Africa in 1910, finding inspiration from Tunisian subjects. Around 1916 he moved to Santa Fe and set up a studio at the Palace of the Governors and, although he did not live in Taos, was quickly elected into the Taos Society of Artists. He preferred his studio in Santa Fe, where he was often able to paint local Pueblo Indians who visited the main plaza. For the remainder of his life he divided his time between New Mexico and Florence, constantly refining his artistic skills.

WE

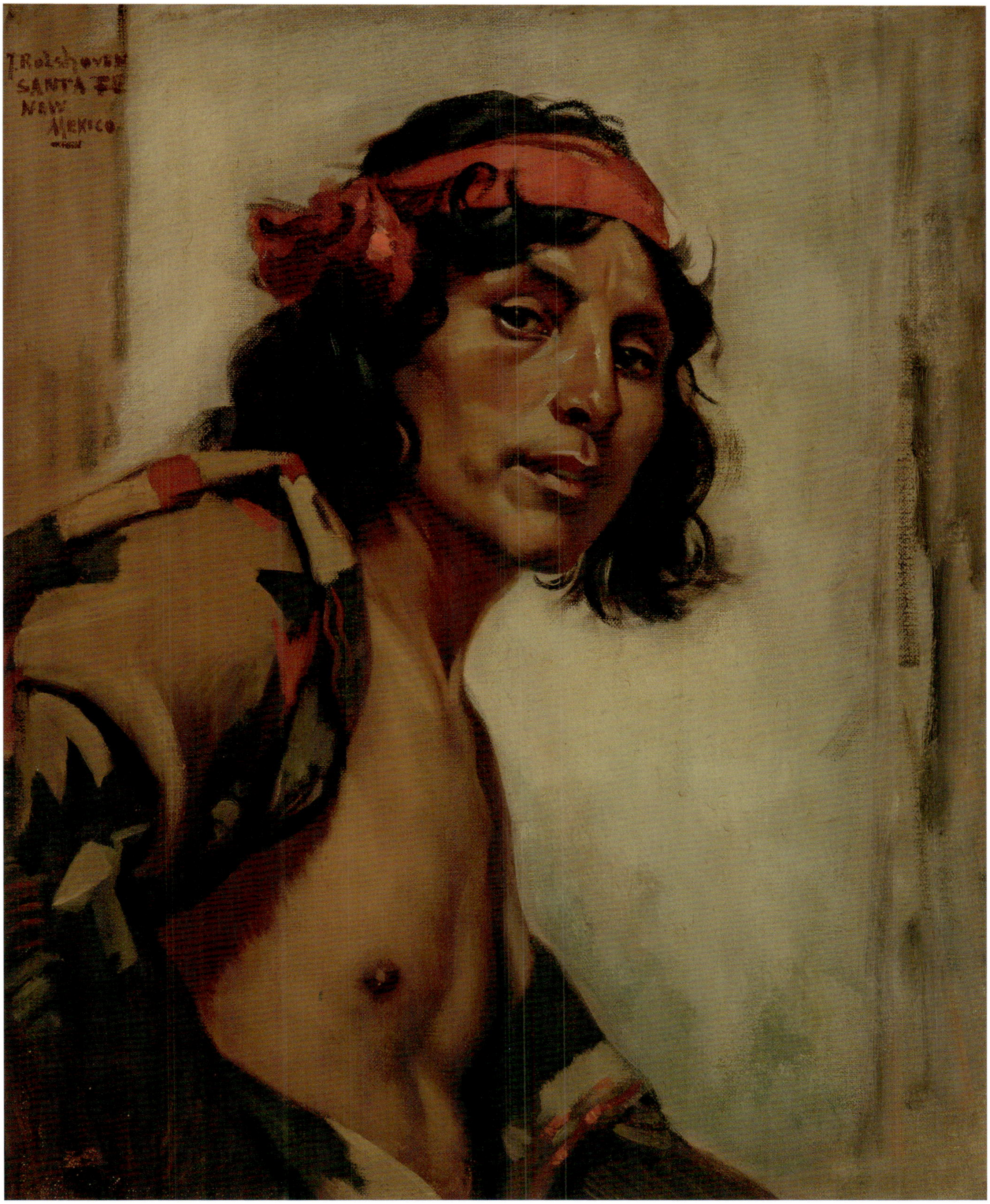
J. Rolshoven
SANTA FE
NEW
MEXICO

Dorothy Brett

(1883–1977)

Untitled, 1962

Acrylic on board, 27 x 31 in.

1989.002.001

Gift of Joanie and Bobby Holt

Twelve years after New Mexico became a state, artist Dorothy Brett made her way from the sophistication of London's Bloomsbury Group to the relative wilds of New Mexico. Brett did so in the company of author D. H. Lawrence and his wife, Frieda, arriving in Taos in 1924. Lawrence had invited several of his friends to join in the venture he envisioned would terminate in the creation of a utopian society he would call Rananim, but only Brett accepted. Although the Lawrences provided a great deal of influence in Brett's decision to visit and, ultimately, to resettle in Taos, it may also have been the sideshows of Buffalo Bill Cody that fueled the young Englishwoman's interest in the Wild West.

In Taos she turned her attention to depicting the Taos Indians with the sense of dignity and monumentality in *War Widows,* painted in 1916. It may be that Brett's deafness made her more sensitive to the customs and rituals of the Pueblo Indians. She referred to these paintings as "Ceremonials." Some critics, however, argue that Brett's paintings were commercial—created for the tourist trade.

Although *Untitled* is acrylic on board, it gives the appearance of having been done in pastels and is reminiscent of a short-lived movement known as Tonalism. Painted in 1962, the work depicts the three aspects of San Geronimo (St. Jerome) Feast Day at Taos Pueblo, an annual celebration on or about September 29 in honor of the patron saint of the pueblo. In the upper half of the composition the sun god or goddess is depicted above San Geronimo in a mandorla, likely signifying the equality of each in contributing to the success of the harvest. A diagonal separates the two figures from dancers in the lower half of the picture. The men dressed with headdresses of antlers are dancing the deer dance. In 1925 artist and writer Blanche Grant wrote in *Taos Today*, "Below in front of the ladder which leads to the shrine, drums sound again and aspen branches rustle gently while runners form a semi-circle…." Perhaps Brett had read Grant's passage or had seen this ceremony take place firsthand.

MBW

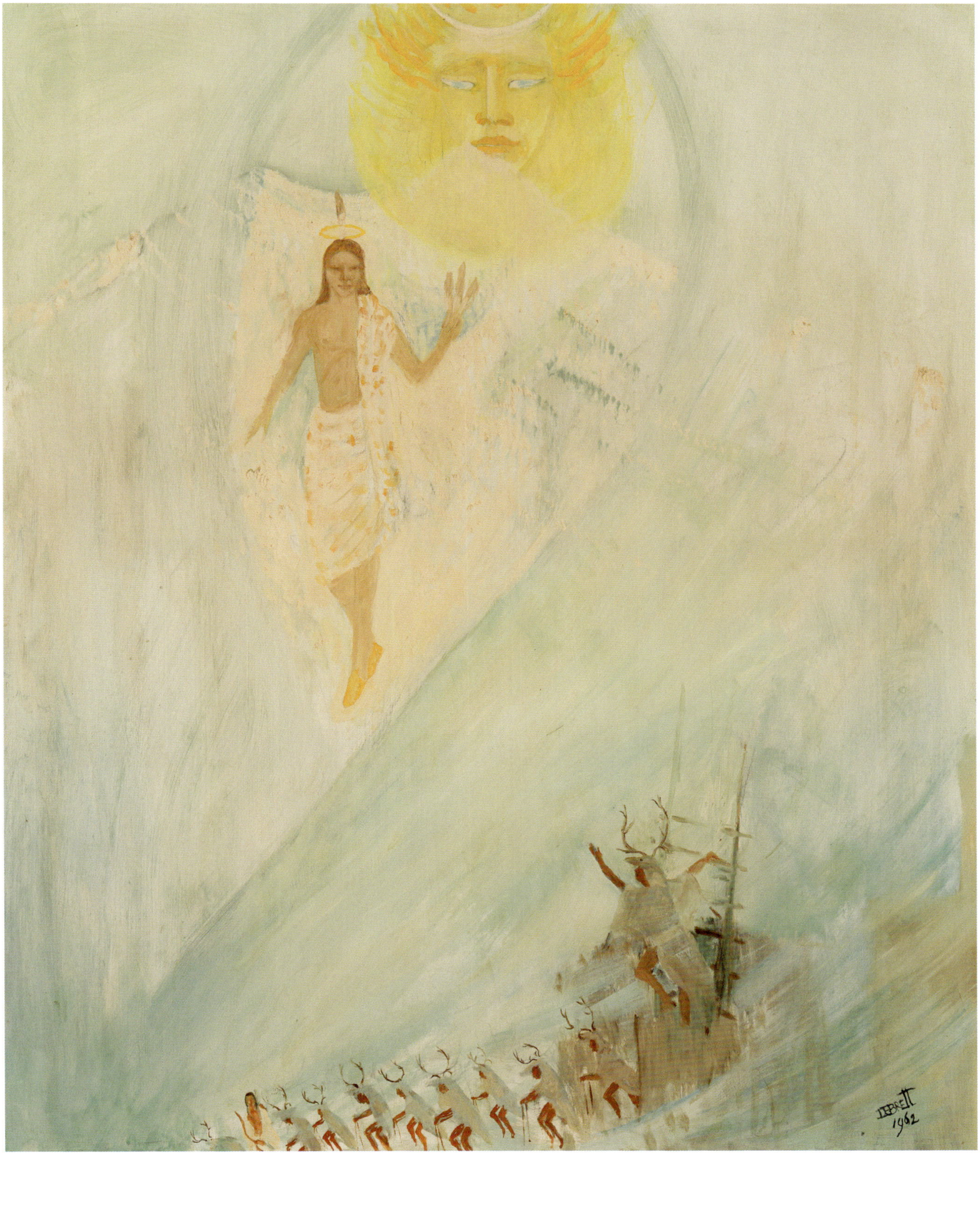
1962

Woody Gwyn

(b. 1944)

Arroyo Wall, 1975

Acrylic on canvas, 72 x 107½ in.

1993.001.001

Gift of Dwayne and Carol Fitting Chesnut in Loving Memory of Carol Lowe Fitting and James Lowell Fitting

Born in San Antonio in 1944 and raised in Midland, Woody Gwyn knew he wanted to be an artist from a very early age. Encouraged by his art teachers, Gwyn apprenticed himself to Peter Hurd, one of the best-known artists in the Southwest at that time. Hurd emphasized a respect for light and attention to precise detail that became entwined with Gwyn's aesthetic. At his mentor's suggestion Gwyn studied painting at the Pennsylvania Academy, Hurd's alma mater, but Gwyn soon decided to follow his own path and moved to Santa Fe, where he felt he could connect with the many independent artists who lived and worked there.

Like many of his other paintings from this period, *Arroyo Wall* focuses the attention of the viewer on the details of the landscape from a viewpoint very different from what might be experienced in reality. *Arroyo Wall* is an incredibly large canvas with the details of the landscape rendered in an extremely precise manner. Gwyn's interpretation of his subject is never beholden to reality, as he utilizes artistic license to develop finished compositions in the studio from drawings and sketches produced on site. *Interstate/Overpasses* is a similarly large-scale painting also showing immense detail seen by the viewer from an unusual place within the picture plane. Gwyn, however, is not limited by scale or media, as a smaller lithograph titled *Interstate* of a similar subject shows how easily his point of view is translated. In the end, Gwyn's paintings are less about the subject matter of landscape and more about light, movement and the transience of human experience.

BLW

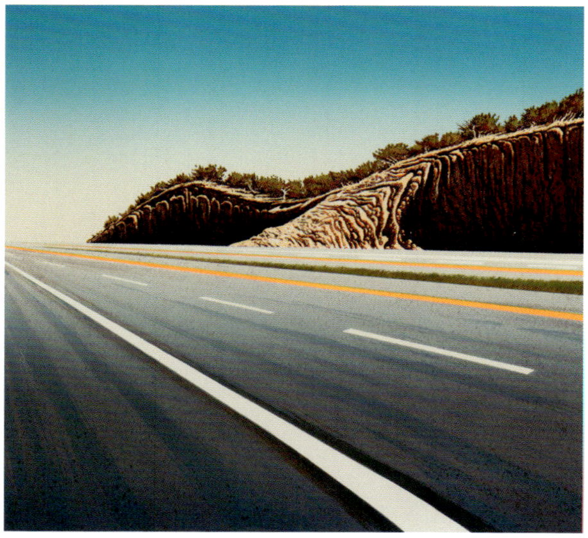

Interstate, 1981. Lithograph, 18 x 20 in. 1986.002.001. Gift of the Artist.

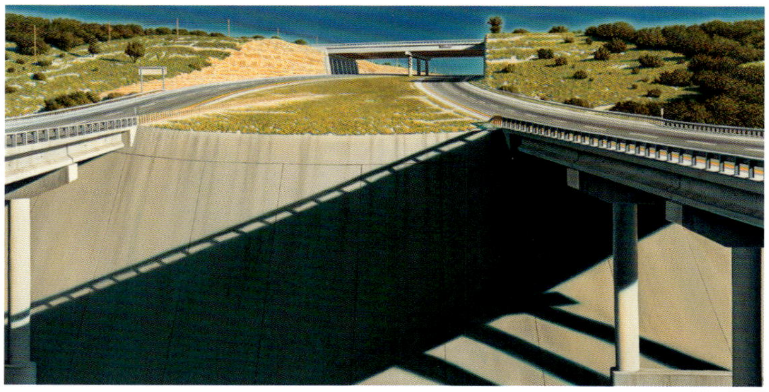

Interstate/Overpasses, 1985. Oil on canvas, 49½ x 96½ in. 1986.002.002. Museum Acquisition Fund.

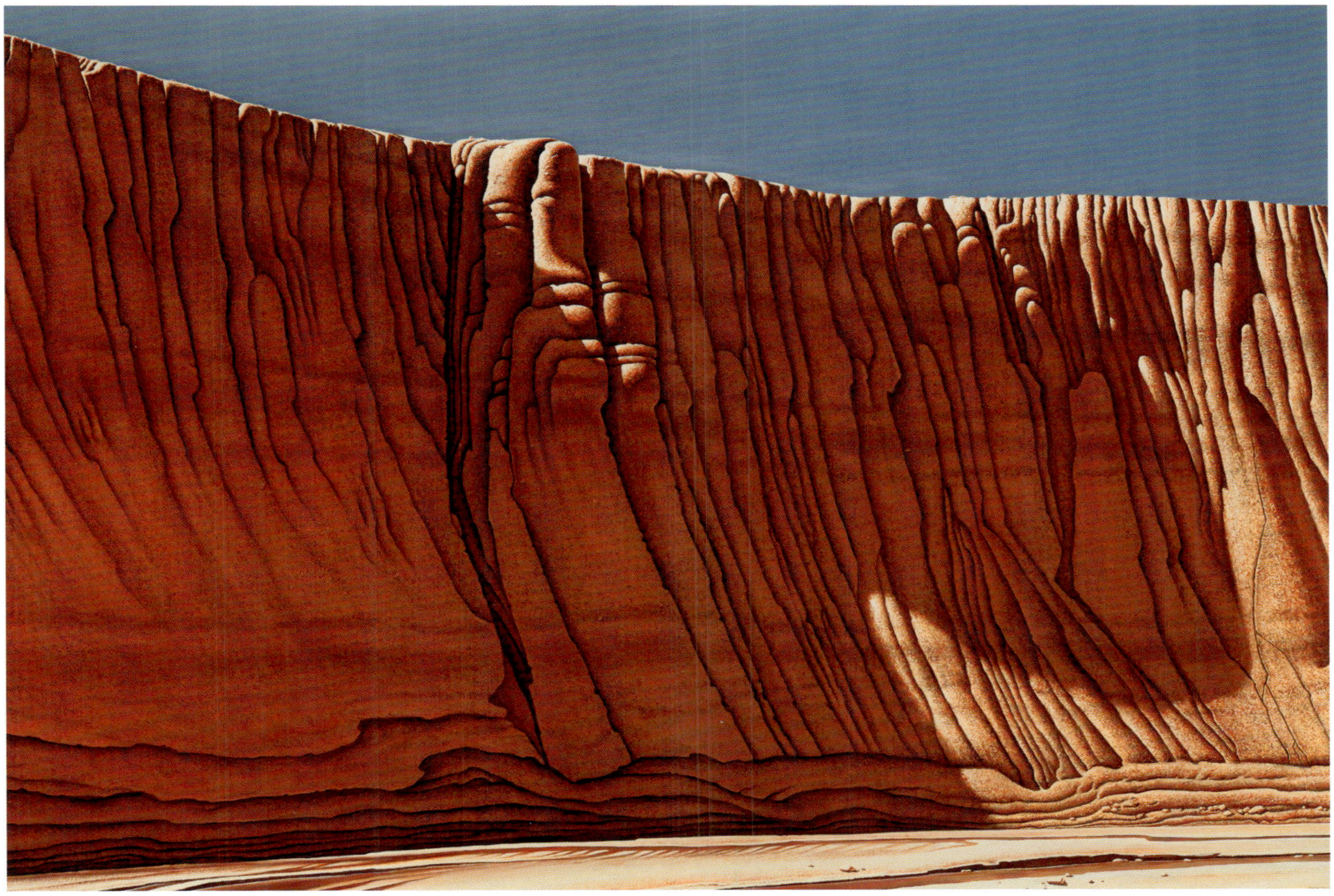

Julian Onderdonk

(1882–1922)

Early Spring, Southwest Texas, 1912

Oil on canvas, 15¾ x 23½ in.

1995.001.001

Museum Acquisition Fund

THE BEST-KNOWN ARTIST OF THE TEXAS IMPRESSIONISM MOVEMENT, Julian Onderdonk was a *plein air* landscape painter who captured a moment in time during the early twentieth century. He was born in San Antonio in 1882, when the population of Texas was rapidly growing and the Impressionist style was making its way into America. He was encouraged to be an artist at a very young age by his father, painter Robert Jenkins Onderdonk. At eighteen he moved to New York to study at the Art Students League with the renowned artist William Merritt Chase. *Misty Twilight* was painted eight years later in 1908 during Onderdonk's last year in New York, where by then he was working professionally as an artist.

The artist returned to Texas, moving to Dallas and sketching and painting the Texas landscape from Dallas, the San Antonio Hill Country and the southwestern portions of the state. Works from this period include the landscape *Early Spring, Southwest Texas* in 1912. This oil painting documents trees just starting to bloom, a herd of sheep and an expanse of cacti in the foreground, giving viewers a sense of the diversity of the Texas landscape. Onderdonk constantly refined his *plein air* techniques, growing from the influence of such artists as Robert Henri and George Inness. In his short career his misty and illusory paintings found popularity with art collectors in Texas, New York, Chicago and Los Angeles.

Onderdonk first created a bluebonnet painting around 1911, with subsequent wildflower landscapes inspiring exhibitions and the rise of the Bluebonnet School, still going strong in Texas today. Onderdonk's career parallels the Texas Impressionism movement, which lasted from around 1885 to 1935 and found later champions in artists such as Porfirio Salinas. In the 1920s and 1930s Texas Regionalist artist Jerry Bywaters and others rejected the hazy lines and softer pastel color palettes in favor of bolder colors and decisive line work.

WE

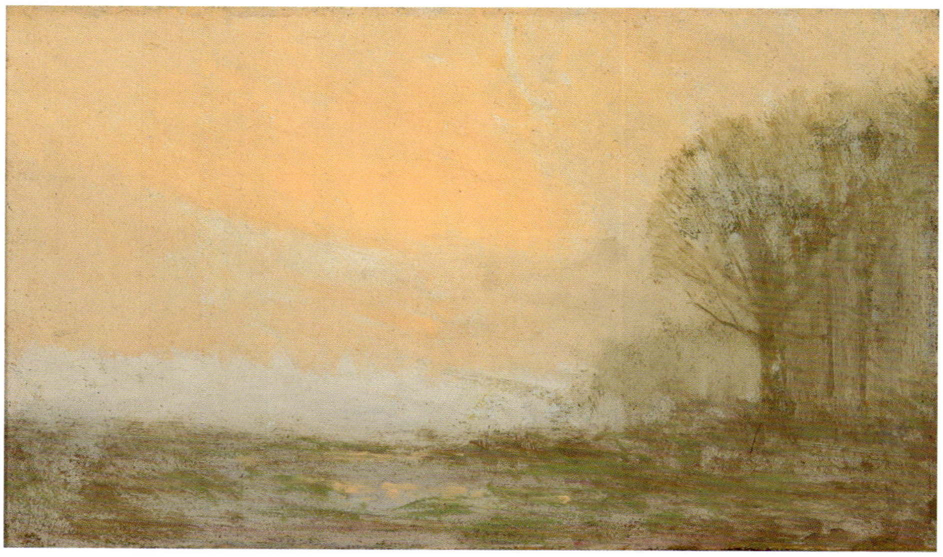

Misty Twilight, 1908. Oil on panel, 4¼ x 7 in. 1995.004.001. Museum Acquisition Fund.

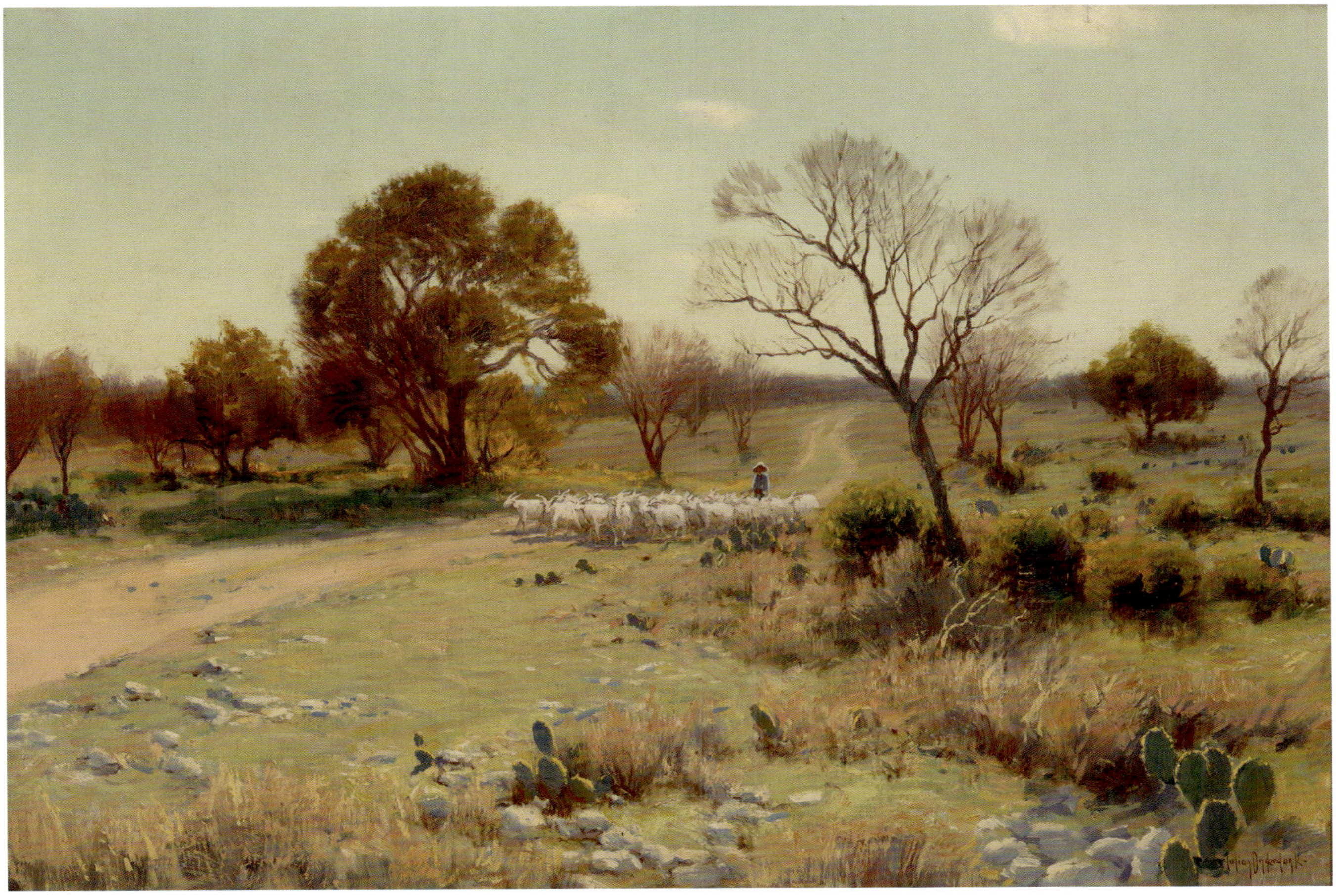

Porfirio Salinas

(1910–1973)

Autumn, Edwards Plateau, 1966

Oil on canvas, 15½ x 19¼ in.

1995.005.001

Gift of Edgar S. Keefe in Memory of Maurine Igou Keefe

Porfirio Salinas is an artist almost entirely defined by his location in the Texas Hill Country. Born in Bastrop, Texas, to a family of tenant farmers, he spent most of his life in San Antonio and the Hill Country. Salinas started taking *plein air* sketching trips with the noted Texas Impressionist artists and teachers Robert Wood and José Arpa beginning in 1925. Salinas quickly became an important part of the Texas Impressionism movement and part of the unofficial Bluebonnet School.

Wildflower and especially bluebonnet painting was popularized by Julian Onderdonk and became a standard subject for Texas artists. In 1927 an oilman named Edgar B. Davis, along with the San Antonio Art League, created the Texas Wildflower Competitive Exhibition, later called the San Antonio Competitive Exhibition. The short-lived event awarded some of the biggest prizes available at the time, and artists who won included Salinas, Oscar Berninghaus, Joseph Fleck and E. Martin Hennings. Lyndon Johnson hung Salinas' works in the White House, bringing national attention to bluebonnet painting and making it one of the highest exemplars of traditional Texas art.

Autumn, Edwards Plateau does not depict the bluebonnets most closely associated with Salinas, but it does show his color sense and finesse for Hill Country scenes. One of the first nationally recognized Mexican-American artists, during his lifetime he was considered one of the state's most accomplished landscape artists. His vast body of paintings was repetitious but always true to the realities of the natural world, neither adding nor subtracting from what he saw. His favorite subjects were wildflowers, oak trees, mesquite, buffalo grass and the Texas skies.

WE

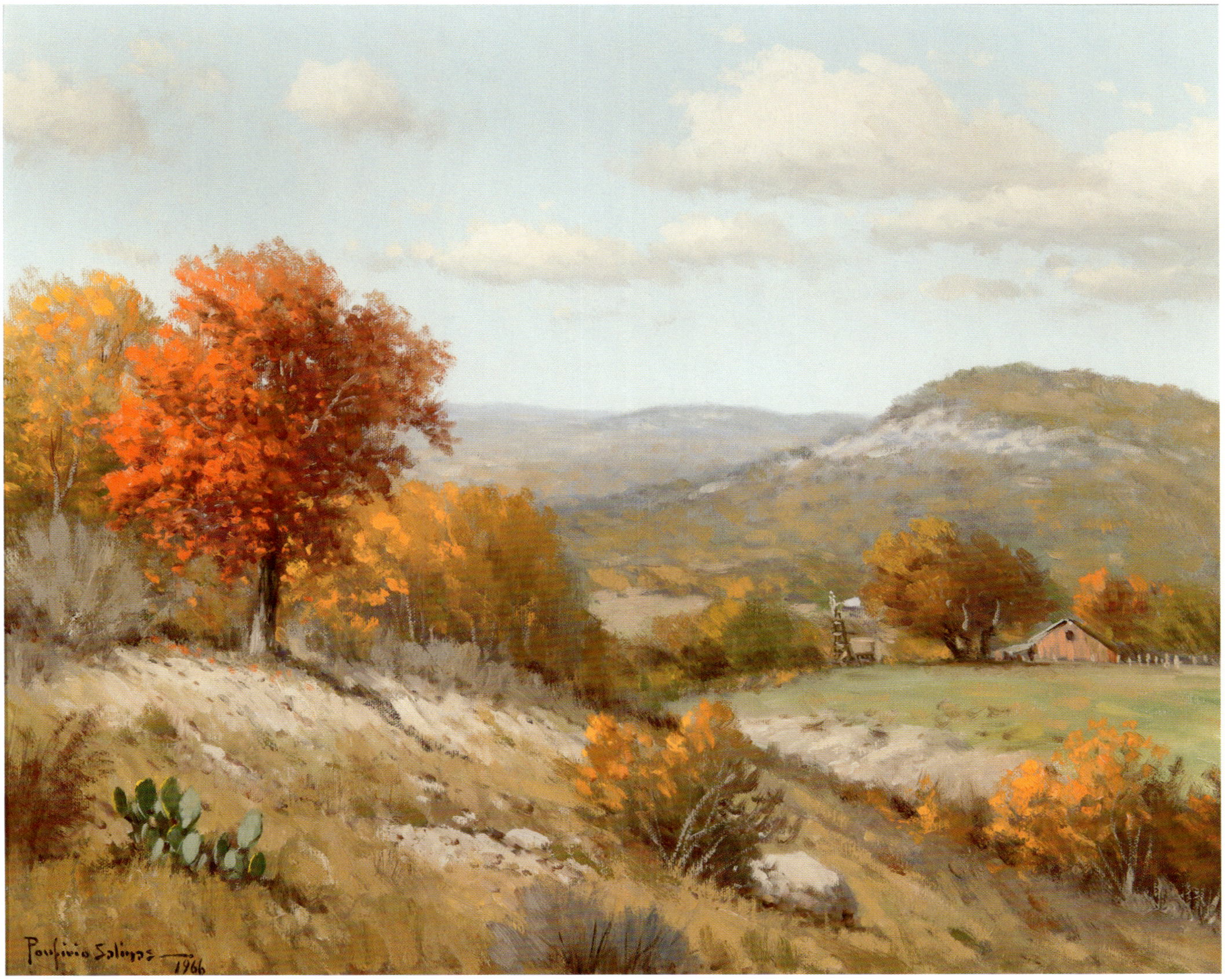
Porfirio Salinas
1966

Thomas Hill

(1829–1908)

Bridal Veil Meadow, Yosemite, 1882

Oil on canvas, 17¾ x 23¼ in.

1996.002.004

Gift of Fred T. and Novadean Hogan

Thomas Hill's *Bridal Veil Meadow, Yosemite* presents a characteristic nineteenth-century landscape, with the sweeping view of Yosemite towering over the small figures in the forefront. This technique of painting man on a small scale compared to the vastness of nature was typical of the Hudson River School with which Hill was associated.

Hill was born in England and moved to the United States in 1844, settling in Massachusetts. He trained at the Pennsylvania Academy of Fine Arts and was an active landscape painter in Boston in his early years. Seeking a warmer climate due to his poor health, Hill moved his family to San Francisco in 1856. He opened a studio in 1861 and made his first trip to Yosemite Valley in 1862, one of the first East Coast painters to venture there. Hill created both smaller and monumental landscapes of Yosemite, which were exhibited around the country—including at the National Academy of Design. Although he enjoyed a long and successful career in California, he never reached the popularity of other Hudson River School artists such as Albert Bierstadt.

The Western landscapes of Hill and his contemporaries are sometimes viewed as documentary works, views into a part of the United States that few people on the East Coast got to experience firsthand. These paintings show the diversity and scale of their subjects and stimulated more travel and tourism. Yet the isolation of human figures in these works, especially the small figures on horseback in Bridal Veil Meadow, Yosemite, could also be seen as warning of the dangers of overdevelopment caused by tourists and the displacement of indigenous groups living in these areas.

WE

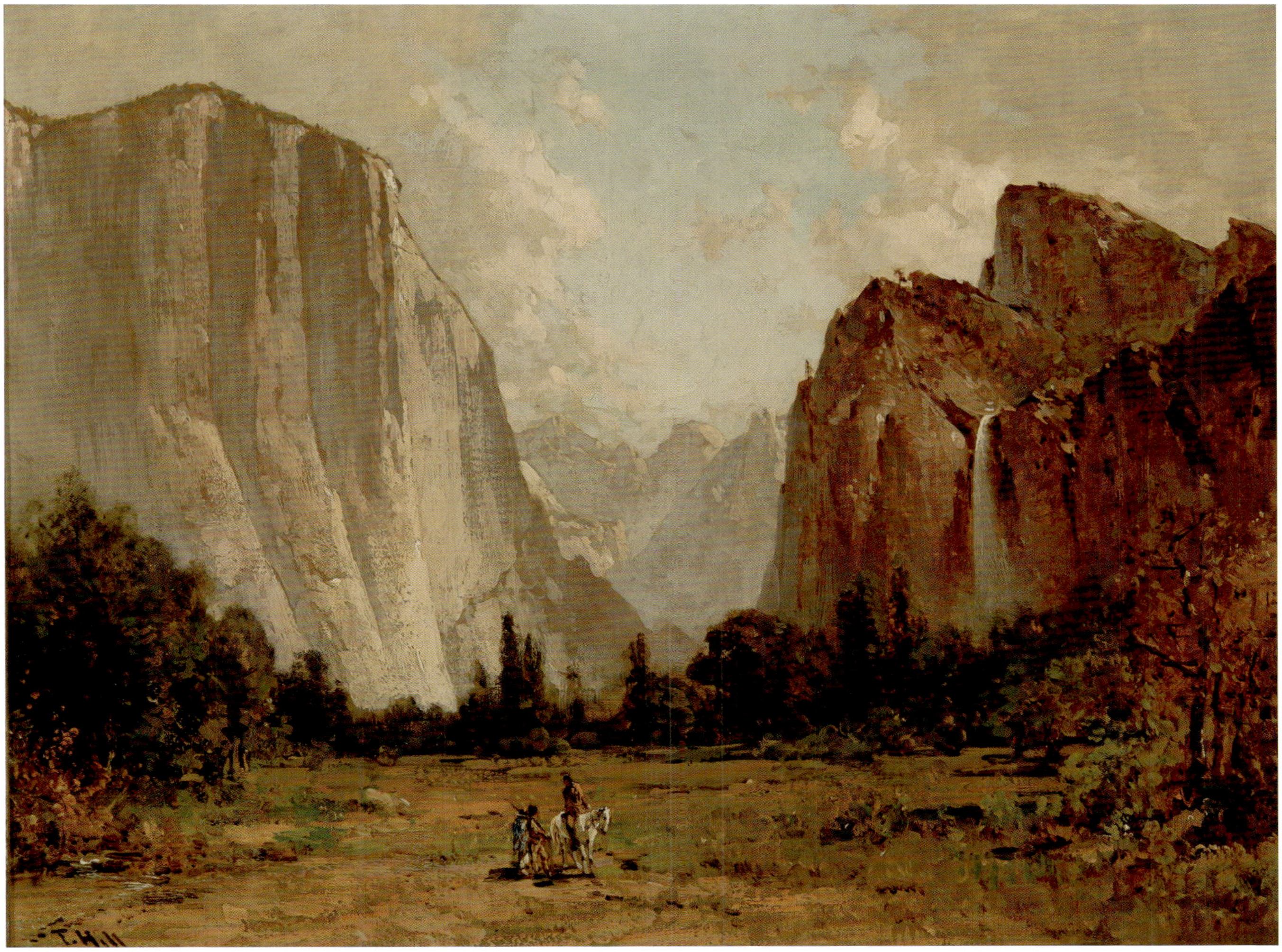

Marie-Rosalie (Rosa) Bonheur

(1822–1899)

Deer in the Forest, c. 1882

Oil on panel, 11¼ x 15¼ in.

1996.002.005

Gift of Fred T. and Novadean Hogan

MANY PEOPLE CONSIDER ROSA BONHEUR the best-known and most-celebrated female painter of the nineteenth century. Bonheur was the first woman to be awarded France's most coveted prize, the Cross of the Legion of Honor. Bonheur's talent was encouraged by her father, Oscar-Raymond Bonheur, who was also her teacher. He was a member of the Saint-Simonian sect, a religious order that stressed gender equality. He frequently related stories about the French artist Elisabeth Vigée-Lebrun as someone Rosa could emulate and surpass, as she did in achieving the medal of the Legion of Honor. The artist's work is among the collections of major museums throughout the world. As art historians have noted, Bonheur was very cognizant of shaping her reputation for posterity and entrusted her American friend, the artist Anna Klumke, with the task of recording her words and preserving her letters and sketches.

Although she never visited the United States, Bonheur was fascinated with the American West when Buffalo Bill Cody took his Wild West Show to Paris for the Exposition Universelle in 1889. This is where Bonheur sketched the "American" animals in the troupe, as well as the Native Americans who were part of his show. These sketches provided the basis for her painting *The Buffalo Hunt,* 1889, and the image became the trademark of Cody's publicity campaign.

It seems appropriate that Bonheur's small painting *Deer in the Forest* is among the collections of the Museum of the Southwest, given the artist's interest in the western United States. Painted about 1882 at the height of her career, the work exhibits Bonheur's realistic treatment of a pair of does drinking under the watchful protection of a young male. Bonheur's extreme fondness for animals caused her to be dubbed the "Queen of Beasts." She visited stockyards and animal fairs, frequently in trousers, and was known as an independent woman and a model for younger women.

MBW

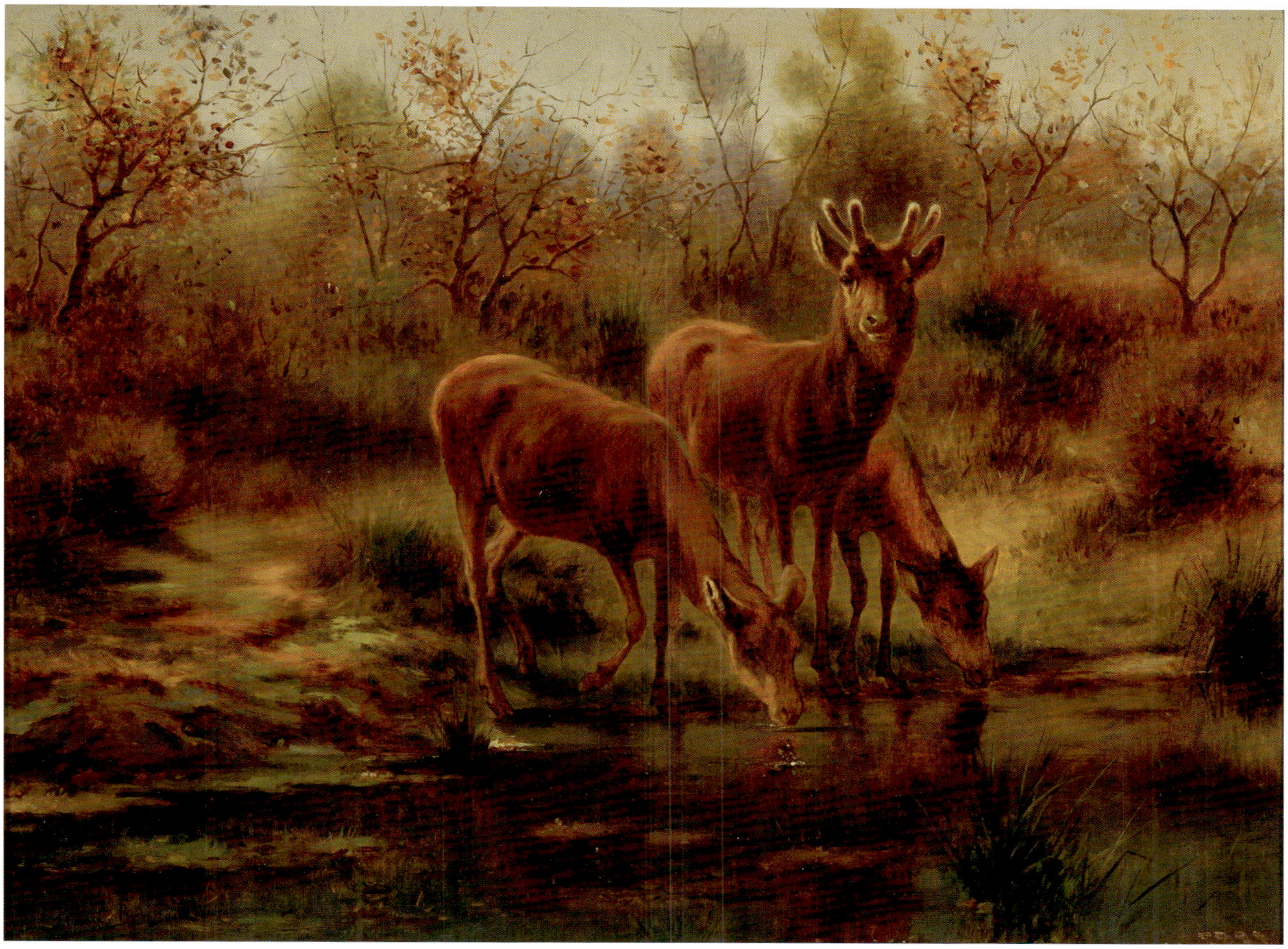

Albert Bierstadt

(1830–1902)

Buffalo Trail to Waterhole, 1867–1869

Oil on canvas, 17¾ x 23¼ in.

1996.002.010

Gift of Fred T. and Novadean Hogan

An immigrant from Germany at the age of two, Albert Bierstadt grew up in New England surrounded by the landscape that inspired the first generation of Hudson River School painters. He returned to Europe to study painting at the Düsseldorf Academy, a favored destination for American art students in the late nineteenth century that was of great influence on the development of landscape painting in the United States.

In 1858, Bierstadt made his first trip into the West, followed by another trip into Yosemite Valley five years later. These were the first of numerous expeditions where he sketched and painted quick studies, and on later visits used a camera, to capture what was then new and unfamiliar landscape to most people in the world. Bierstadt took the lessons of the Hudson River School and applied them to these dramatic landscapes of the American West. He combined attention to detail with a luminescent light that relayed a perspective many later considered highly romanticized. These canvases, some of them ten feet across, provided some of the first images of a landscape that captured easterners and international audiences alike and garnered numerous prestigious awards and wide recognition for the artist.

At the height of his production, Bierstadt was probably the most financially successful of his peers. He combined his talent for painting with a shrewd business sense and an ability to move through the social spheres of art collectors and aristocracy with great ease. Likewise, he profited from the reproduction of his large canvases by newspapers around the world and also painted many smaller canvases, such as *Buffalo Trail to Waterhole,* for patrons without the means to acquire his monumental works. Even though small, this canvas contains many of the elements that made Bierstadt's work instantly recognizable. The sun rising over distant hills infuses the entire landscape with a magical quality that illuminates the scene with a quiet, almost internal, light, while a herd of bison moves silently across the picture plane, pausing at the mirrorlike watering hole for refreshment.

BLW

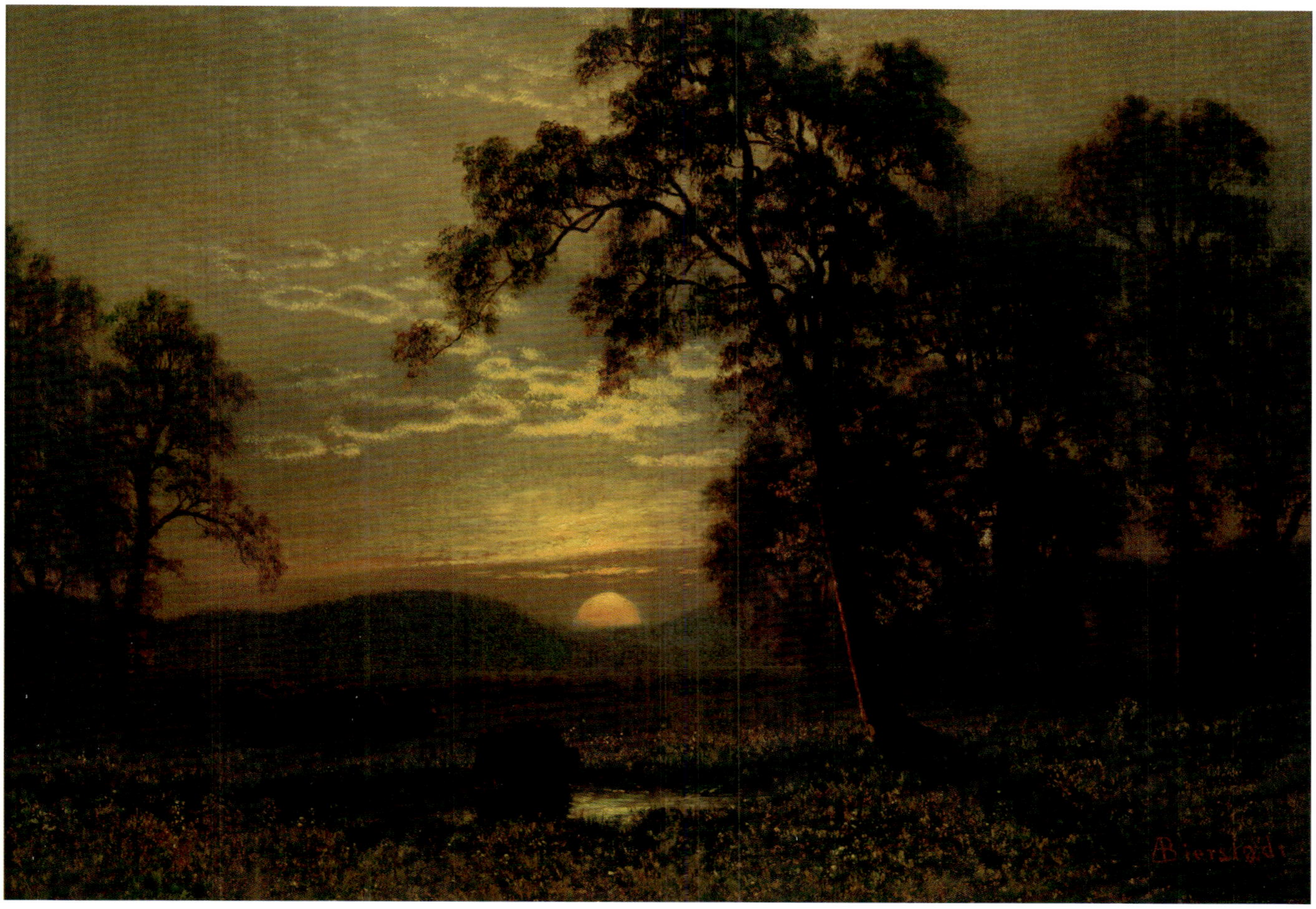

John Phillip

(1817–1867)

El Cortejo, 1857

Oil on canvas, 24½ x 18½ in.

1996.002.011

Gift of Fred T. and Novadean Hogan

The Royal Academy of Arts in London developed from a petition signed by thirty-four artists and presented to King George III in 1768. The petition requested a lyceum for artists to exhibit and receive education through sharing and trading techniques. Among the Royal Academy's myriad traditions is the Summer Exhibition, which has occurred with great fanfare every year since the Academy's inception. It accepts work from visual artists around the globe and showcases the art world's ever-changing trends.

El Cortejo, by John Phillip, was accepted into the Royal Academy's annual exhibition in 1858. It was the second work of Phillip's to be chosen, the first having been selected and exhibited in 1838. A native of Aberdeen, Scotland, Phillip traveled to Spain, where he earned the name "Spanish Phillip" and developed his formal artistic style strongly represented here in an intimate portrait of a Spanish couple. Soft lines and muted colors romanticize the couple who bask in their courtship.

Phillip then moved to London under the patronage of British politician Lord Panmure. A student of the Royal Academy beginning in 1837, Phillip was recognized for his work as a portraitist and landscape painter and was selected as a Royal Academician in 1859. Royal Academicians are chosen by their peers for their dedication to the visual arts and their potential to flourish during their time at the Academy; selection is considered a high honor. Compositions such as *El Cortejo* illustrate the rigorous training Phillip had to complete as an academician in order to effectively translate his life experiences onto canvas.

KW

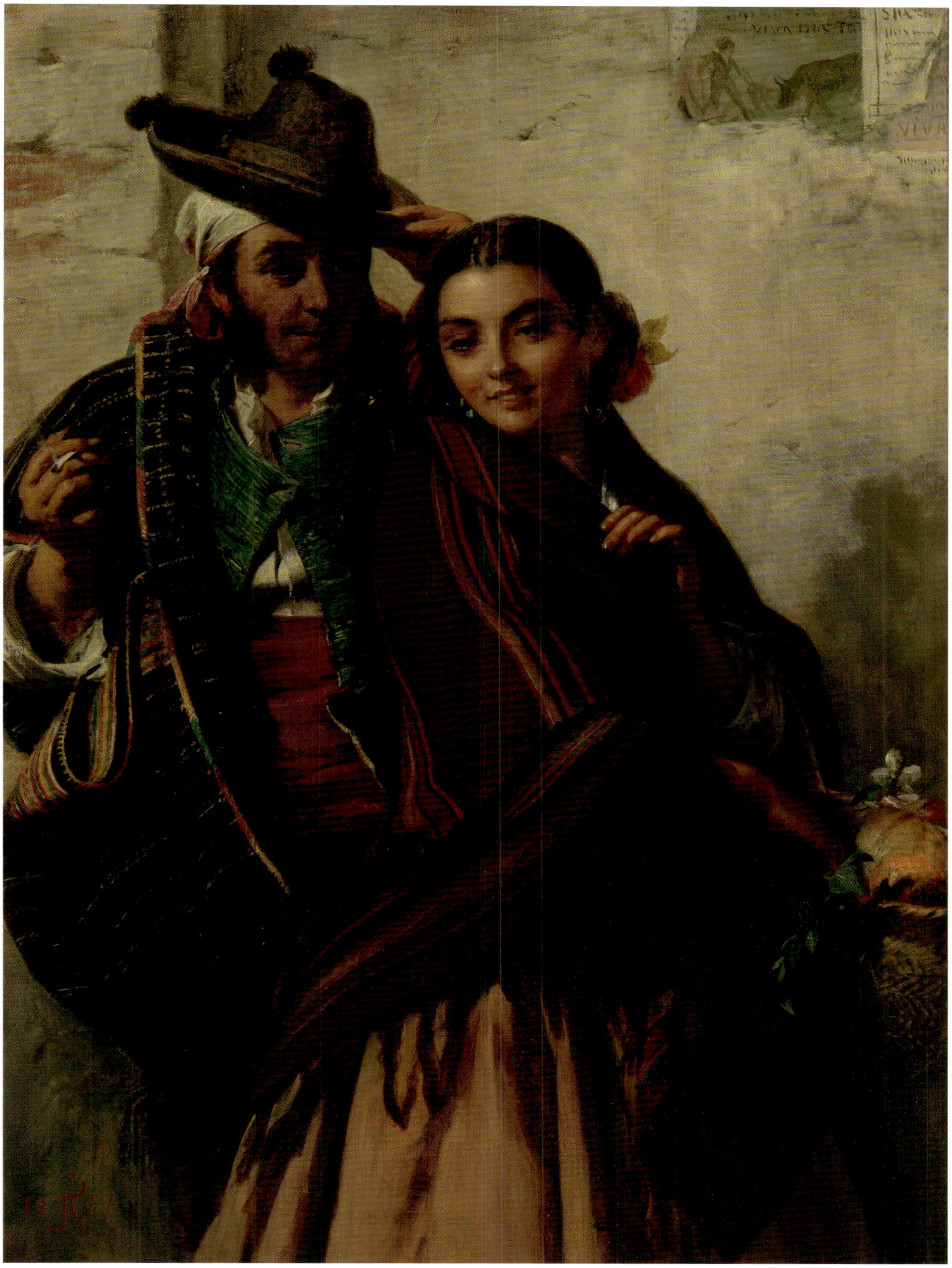

Clark Hulings

(1922–2011)

Man from Spain, 1967

Oil on canvas, 19¼ x 15½ in.

1996.002.012

Gift of Fred T. and Novadean Hogan

THE OEUVRE OF CLARK HULINGS sits neatly within the classification of art historical genre painting. Rural scenes of the working class, peaceful slow-moving life and the occasional landscape or portrait reveal the artist's classical talent. Hulings received a degree in physics from Haverford College but began his adult career as a portraitist in Louisiana. His artistic interests led him to scenes of daily life inspired by his travels throughout America and Europe. One word that succinctly describes the tone of Hulings' work is nostalgia. The two examples found in the collection of the Museum of the Southwest, *Man from Spain*, 1967, and *Impressions of Old Santa Fe*, 1978, are representative of two very distinct periods in the artist's career.

Man from Spain serves as a reminder of the time Hulings spent in Spain. The people he passed every day on the streets are still alive in this work, a man seen in close-up as if an enlargement of a detail from one of Hulings' more typical distant street scenes. His face is wrinkled from a lifetime of working in the sun, and he wears his age proudly.

Impressions of Old Santa Fe is a testament to Hulings' fascination with the quickly fading American West. Burros, dogs, men and women go about daily routines while Hulings captures the moment like a photograph. As Hulings reflected, "For an artist who likes to study and paint what he can see rather than what he can imagine, modernism presents a problem." Scenes of everyday life in rural villages are not the subject of modern art nor the focus of the artist's contemporaries. Hulings' work does more than preserve the past; it evokes a memory or sparks a feeling of remembrance. As modern-day advances fade the great American West, the last frontier, Hulings grasps at imagery that may one day be long forgotten.

KW

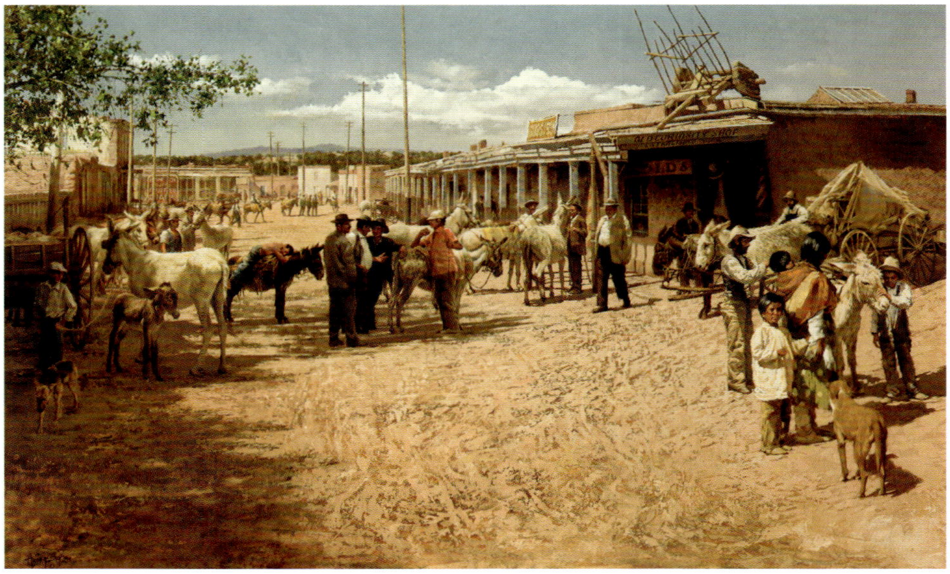

Impressions of Old Santa Fe, 1978. Oil on board, 29¼ x 49 in. 1978.008.001. Museum Acquisition Fund.

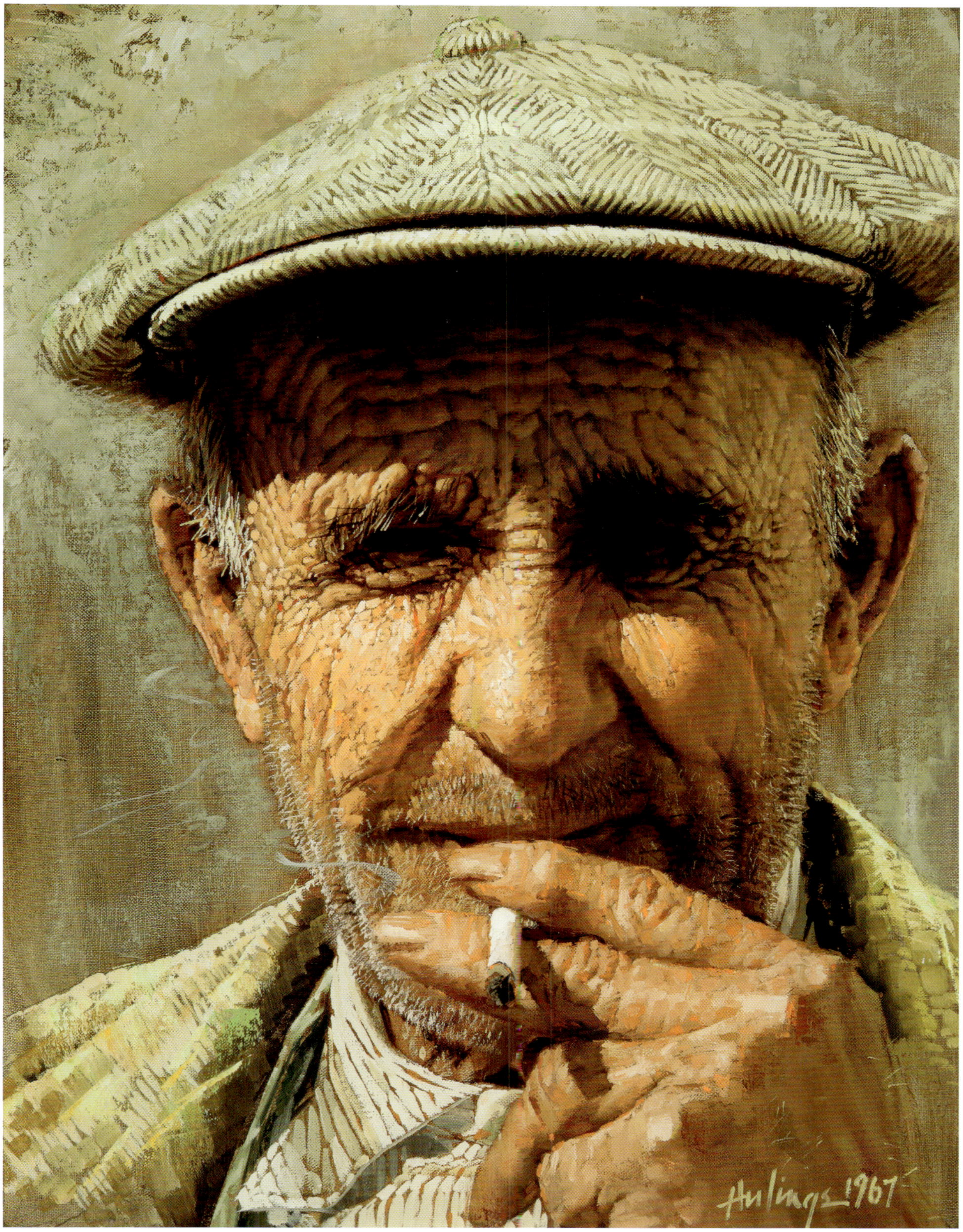
Hulings 1967

John George Brown

(1831–1913)

The Old Bobsled, c. 1870s

Oil on canvas, 14¾ x 23 in.

1996.002.015

Gift of Fred T. and Novadean Hogan

A PROLIFIC ARTIST who produced between twenty and thirty paintings a year, John George Brown was one of best-known American artists of the nineteenth century. Widely successful in his lifetime, he was known as a genre painter, depicting scenes of everyday life, often with sentimental depictions of children. After his death, his work was largely dismissed by twentieth-century critics and scholars.

Brown was born in 1831 in Durham, England, and apprenticed with a glass cutter before immigrating to New York City at the age of twenty-two. Working in a glass factory by day, at night he studied at the National Academy of Design. He studied life drawing and taught himself to paint, soon becoming successful enough to devote himself to art full-time. He was heavily involved in the National Academy of Design, becoming its vice president.

The Old Bobsled is most likely part of Brown's earlier work, depicting children in the countryside in the 1860s and 1870s. This period in the United States is marked by great changes, partly as a result of the Civil War and partly due to societal changes resulting from greater urbanization and industrialization. As a result, art patrons during this time looked to idyllic country scenes as a distraction, often out of a sense of nostalgia. In *The Old Bobsled*, five children are shown on a bobsled in a well-lit and generically rural environment. Somewhat off-putting by modern standards, the piercing stare of a bonneted girl confronts the viewer, while the other figures are focusing their attention somewhere outside the canvas. Starting in the 1880s Brown shifted from his rural subjects to depict now-iconic scenes of young children in the city. He was one of the first artists to capture the subject of the urban poor, often depicting subjects such as newsboys, shoeshine boys and street urchins.

WE

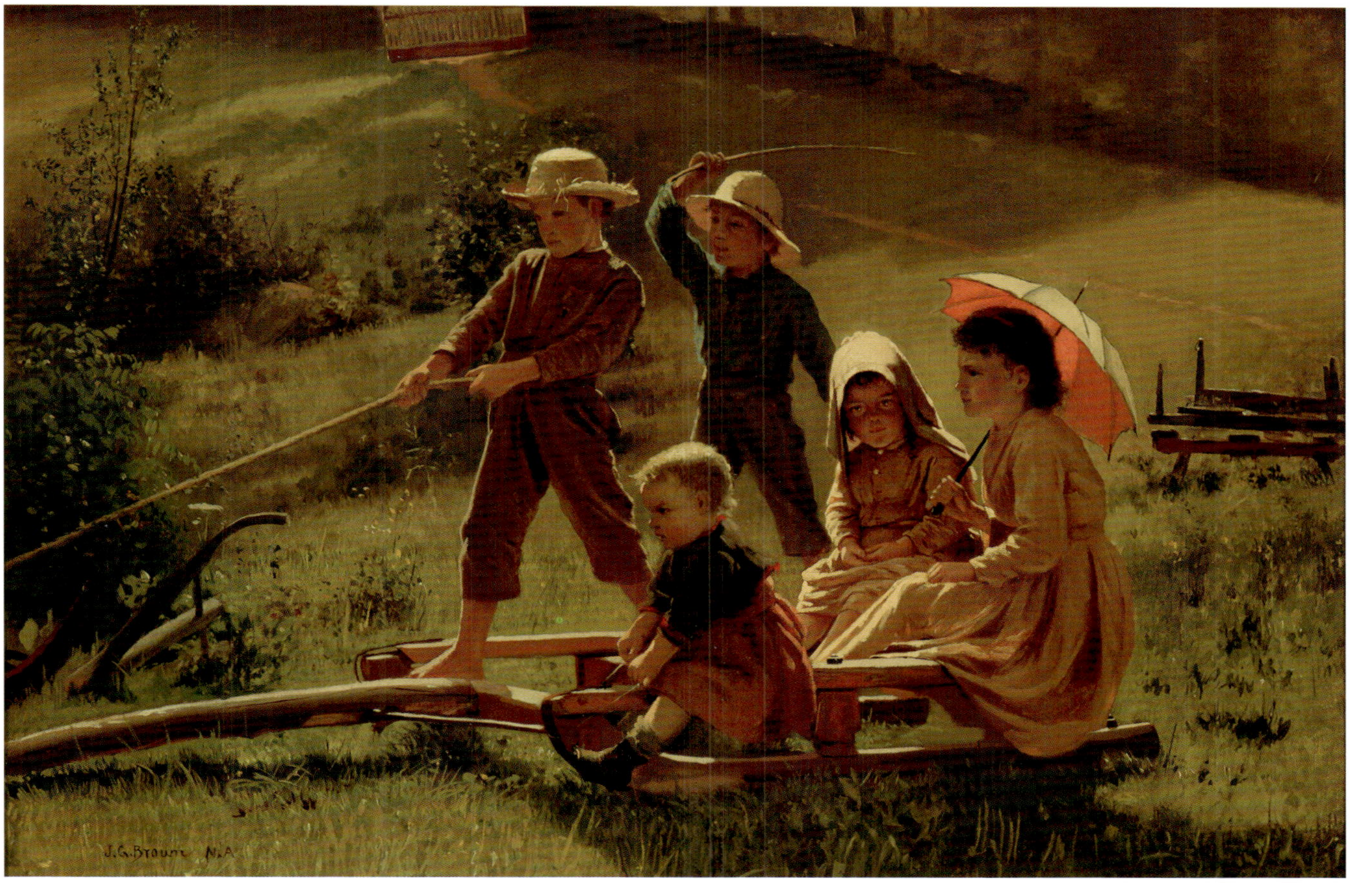
J.G.Brown N.A.

(William) Andrew Loomis

(1892–1959)

The Little Bather, c. 1950

Oil on board, 19½ x 23½ in.

1996.002.017

Gift of Fred T. and Novadean Hogan

Through his widely printed books and active career, Andrew Loomis was considered one of the most important illustrators of the early twentieth century. Loomis was born in Syracuse, New York, but raised in Zanesville, Ohio, and spent most of his career in Chicago. He received his art education at the Art Students League and the Art Institute of Chicago and later taught at the American Academy of Art. After military service in World War I, Loomis opened his own studio in Chicago, working as a commercial illustrator and painter.

Loomis' highly realistic style of illustrating is well regarded, and his teaching style was widely disseminated through several published books. His six art instruction books include *Fun with a Pencil* and *Figure Drawing for All It's Worth* and focus on figure drawing, with many of the outlined techniques invented by Loomis and described in a casual, humorous style.

Loomis had one of his paintings printed as a cover of the *Saturday Evening Post*, but unlike fellow *Post* artist Norman Rockwell, Loomis never achieved fame in the realm of fine art. Though best known for his commercial works, his paintings like *The Little Bather* convey his expertise in figure drawing and composition. The thickly applied brushstrokes allow the viewer to see the artist's hand. The anonymous figure is bathing, seated on a rock near a rushing river and surrounded by foliage. Although nude, the female has her back turned to the viewer, allowing for some modesty, but the shadow of the trees somewhat resembles a hand intruding upon her privacy. The scene might be an homage to works like Pierre-August Renoir's *The Large Bathers*, which features three women bathing in a similar environment.

WE

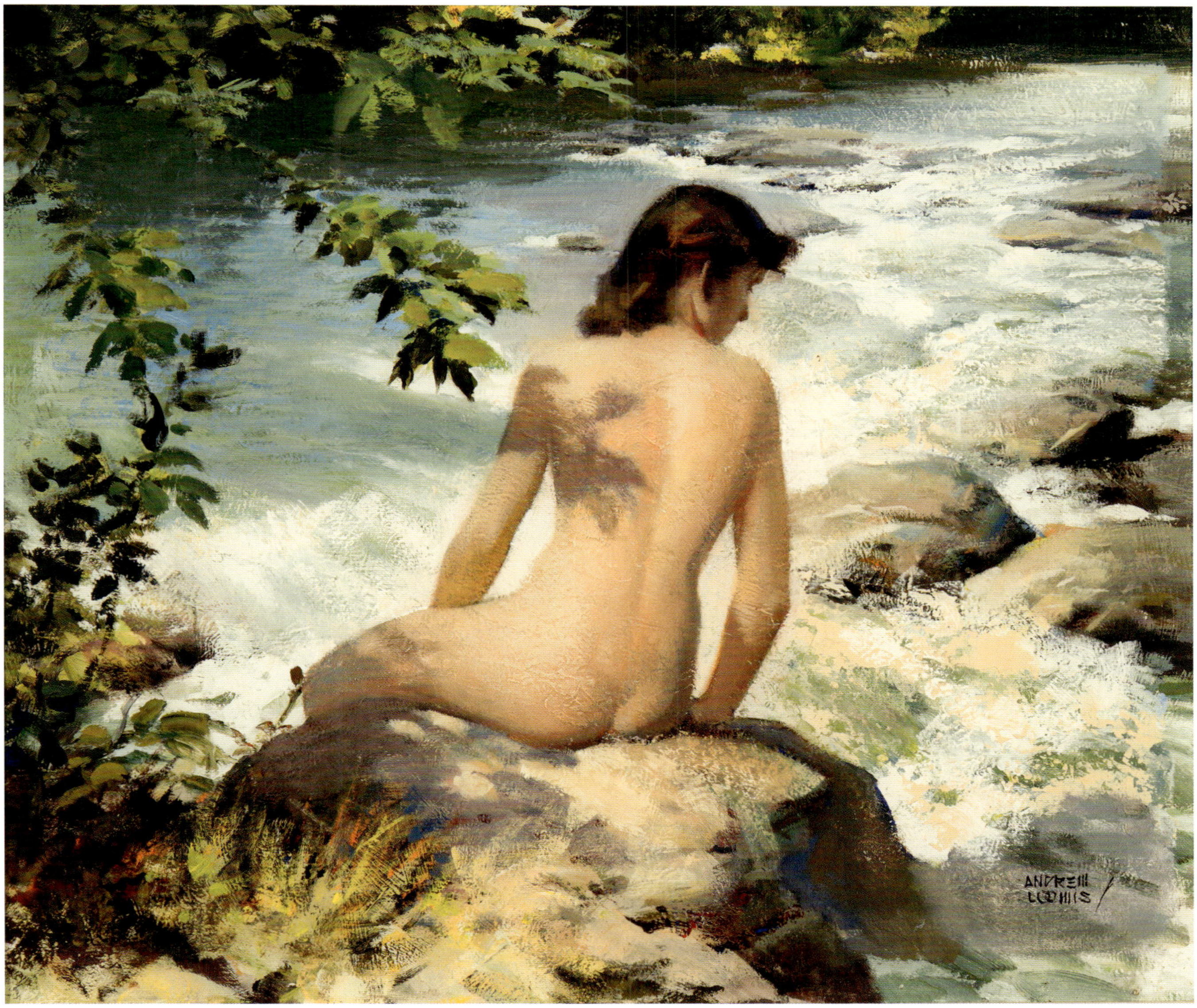
ANDREW
LOOMIS

John James Audubon

(1785–1851)

Red Texan Wolf, 1845

Lithograph, 13¼ x 25½ in.

1997.005.003

Museum Acquisition Fund

The Museum of the Southwest is home to a nearly complete collection of prints from John James Audubon's *The Viviparous Quadrupeds of North America.* This series is the second and last collective work of the noted naturalist and artist. Born in 1785 in present-day Haiti and raised in France, Audubon began traveling and exploring from a very young age. Immigrating to the United States at the age of eighteen, his family settled on a farm, Mill Grove, in Pennsylvania. His interests in the natural world developed considerably, and in 1820 Audubon left to begin his monumental project in documentation. His collection of bird illustrations eventually became his most famous tome, *The Birds of America*, published in a large-format series between 1827 and 1838.

Audubon traveled across the United States, arriving in the new Republic of Texas in April 1837. During his visit Audubon documented a variety of regional birds, as well as an assortment of mammals, including the red Texas wolf, the black-tailed hare and the collared peccary (also known as the javelina). These records, along with specimens sent to him by colleagues and a second trip to Texas in 1845, would soon take shape as the *Quadruped* series. The series became a collaborative work, as Audubon fell ill and his son John Woodhouse Audubon continued work on many of the 150 illustrations for *The Viviparous Quadrupeds of North America.*

The birds Audubon drew required the sacrifice of their lives to be posed and positioned in natural form while being sketched. While Audubon's oeuvre has benefited the work of cataloguers, naturalists and conservationists alike, his methods are no longer used.

KW

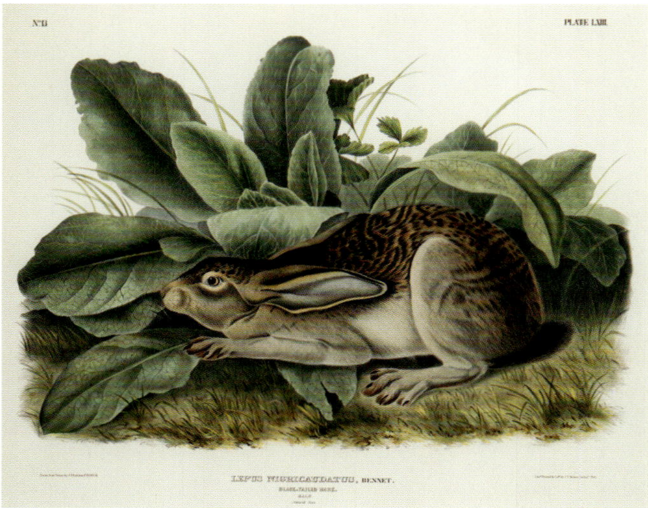

Black-tailed Hare, 1845. Lithograph, 15½ x 23½ in. 1995.002.001. Gift of Mary W. de Compiegne in memory of Margaret How Wallace.

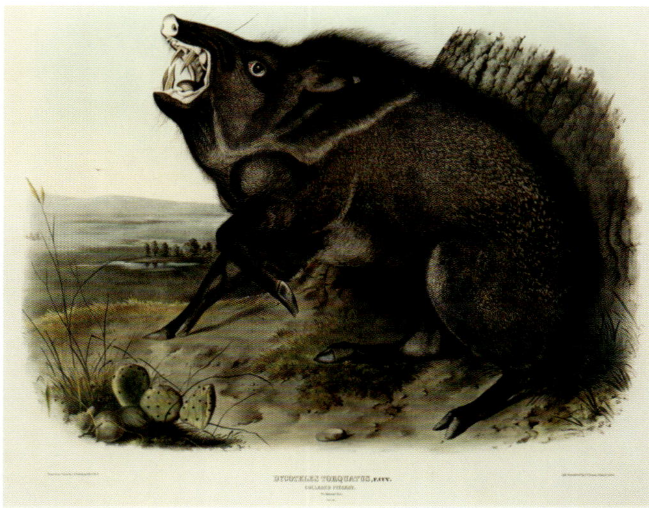

Collared Peccary, 1844. Lithograph, 16½ x 23¼ in. 1996.001.001. Audubon Acquisition Fund. Gift of Charles A. Bird, Earle M. Craig, Jr., L. Decker Dawson, BLee Stringer Dorn, Richard Gibson, J. H. Herd and Jack B. Wilkinson, Jr.

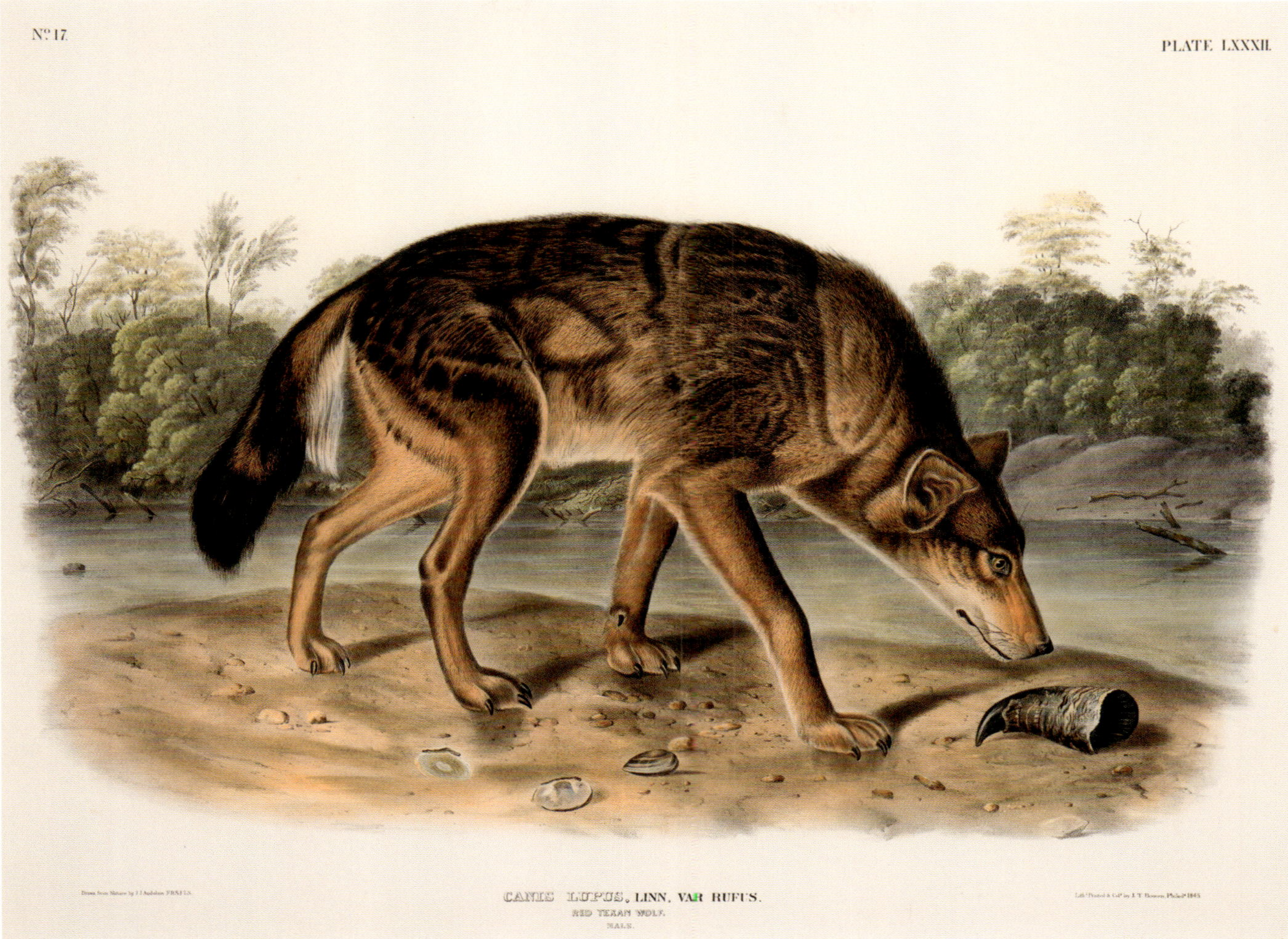

No. 17.
PLATE LXXXII.
Drawn from Nature by J. J. Audubon, F.R.S. F.L.S.
CANIS LUPUS, LINN. VAR RUFUS.
RED TEXAN WOLF.
MALE.
Lith. Printed & Col. by J. T. Bowen, Philada. 1845.

Otis Dozier

(1904–1987)

West Texas, 1978

Oil on canvas, 24 x 48 in.

2000.003.001

Museum Acquisition Fund

Otis Dozier was born in Forney, Texas, and raised on a farm in Mesquite before moving to Dallas in the 1920s. He was a charter member of the Dallas Arts League and created several murals for the Public Works of Art Project and Treasury Relief Art Project as part of the New Deal. On the tenacity of artists, he once said in a 1965 interview with the Archives of American Art at the Smithsonian that "There's quite a number of us here that art means so much to us it was sort of like a priesthood, we wanted to do it and we sacrificed a great deal to be able to paint and in later years it paid off."

In general, the Texas Regionalist artists are known for being strong draftsmen, with solid lines and clear contrasts, features which translate well to printmaking. Among the artists associated with the Texas Regionalists, Otis Dozier had one of the most painterly styles, as shown in the oil painting *West Texas* and the lithograph *Mountain Town*. While some artists, such as Jerry Bywaters, rejected the "weak" lines of Impressionism, others, including Dozier, found inspiration in the Avant-garde movements of the time, incorporating style elements from Surrealism and Cubism into their regional subject matter.

West Texas is a fine example of the color palette most often utilized by the Dallas-based artists of this era, with the muted, earthy tones of pinks and grays conveying a mountain scene, most likely the Davis or Guadalupe Mountains found in this part of Texas. *Mountain Town* is a great exemplar of why lithography worked better than many other modes of printmaking for the Lone Star Printmakers, an art circuit comprised of members associated with the Texas Regionalists. In lithography the artist is able to paint directly onto a stone, rewarding the skill of the draftsman.

WE

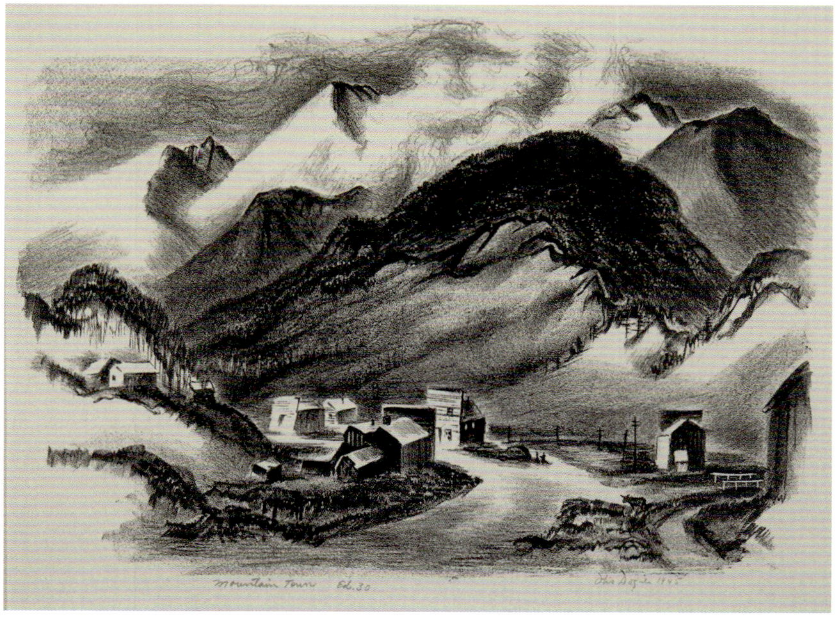

Mountain Town, 1945. Lithograph, 9 x 12¾ in. 1970.015.004.
Gift of Merritt Mauzey.

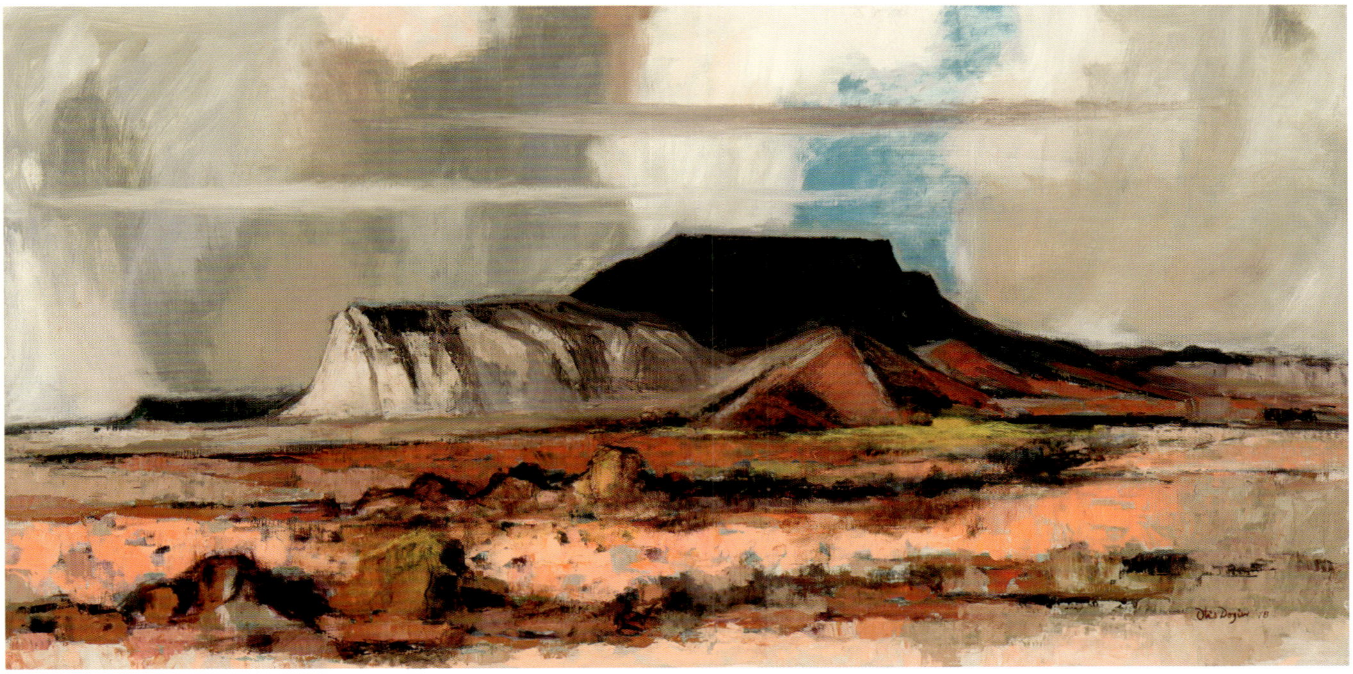

Florence Elliot White McClung

(1894–1992)

Taos, N. Mexico, c. 1930

Woodblock print, 14¾ x 17½ in.

2000.003.002

Museum Acquisition Fund

Florence McClung was not a native Texan but moved to the Lone Star State as a child and remained in Dallas the duration of her long life. A skilled printmaker and painter, her work shares a definite kinship with that of American Regionalists Grant Wood and Alexandre Hogue, the latter with whom she studied. By the late 1920s McClung was also pursuing an academic career and became head of the Art Department at Trinity University in Waxahachie (now located in San Antonio).

McClung's painting *Lancaster Valley* is said to be the first work by a Texan to enter the collections of the Metropolitan Museum of Art, but unfortunately it has been deaccessioned. She likely painted it for the Dallas Centennial Exposition, as the year was 1936. In 1939 it was exhibited again at the *Exhibition of Contemporary American Art* at New York's World's Fair, and was subsequently presented to the MET. According to the *Bulletin of the Metropolitan Museum of Art*, it was among thirty-one works that the fair purchased to allocate to museums across the country.

The artist began traveling to Taos around 1928, where she joined the circle that included Alexandre Hogue, hosted by Mabel Dodge Luhan and Tony Luhan. She painted the local landscape and made prints, including *Taos, N. Mexico,* a woodblock print that illustrates a town scene of two women, one carrying a baby, strolling along a street of adobe houses with mountains in the background. This print entered the Museum of the Southwest's collections in 2000 and is indicative of McClung's propensity for illustrating local people in their natural environment.

In addition to her painting and academic careers, McClung was a member of several Texas art associations and organizations. She was loosely affiliated with the Dallas Nine but her name does not appear on the list of "official" male members. McClung was also a member of the "women only" Dallas Printmakers Guild.

MBW

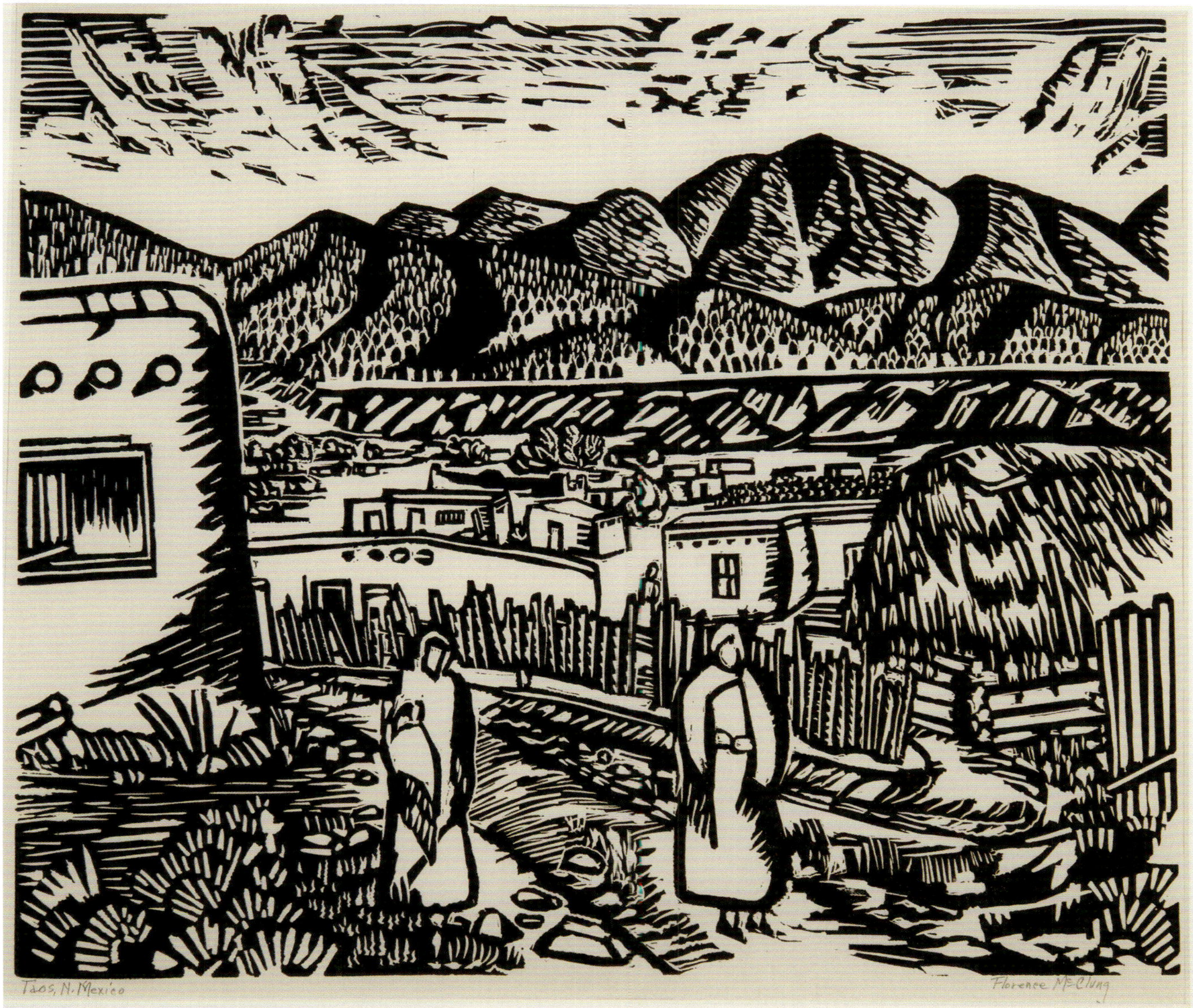
Taos, N. Mexico
Florence McClung

Gustave Baumann

(1881–1971)

Lost in the Desert, 1920

Color woodblock print, 7 x 7 in.

2002.003.001

Museum Acquisition Fund

GUSTAVE BAUMANN'S COLOR WOODCUT PRINTS reveal a consummate craftsmanship and mastery of the medium with an emphasis on the Southwestern landscapes of Santa Fe. Baumann focused on woodcuts, but he also worked in oil painting, sculpture and marionette making. Born in Germany, he moved with his family to the United States when he was ten. As a teen he attended night classes at the Art Institute of Chicago while working at an engraving house by day. He later studied wood carving and the techniques of woodblock printing in Munich, then returned to the United States and around 1908 started making his living as a graphic artist. In 1918 he traveled to New Mexico, first visiting Taos, which he found too crowded. He ultimately settled in Santa Fe, where he lived for more than fifty years. He primarily worked as an artist, but also served as area coordinator of the Public Works of Art Project of the Works Progress Administration in the 1930s.

Baumann's *Lost in the Desert* is a woodblock print of a lone burro, rendered in green, pink, blue and brown. Like many of Baumann's prints, the outline is minimal, inviting the viewer to spend some time studying the work to get a clearer sense of it. The colors are expertly blended; the woodblock created for the pink inking is also owned by the Museum of the Southwest, giving a particular insight into how the artist created this piece. The isolation of the scene reflects the necessity for solitude for woodcut printers. Color woodcuts involve a labor-intensive process, typically requiring the carving of at least four blocks to achieve the desired picture. A steady hand and quiet studio is of utmost importance. *Lost in the Desert* was created in 1920, just two years into Baumann's long life in Santa Fe, and reflects the techniques and interests that the artist would carry with him throughout his career.

WE

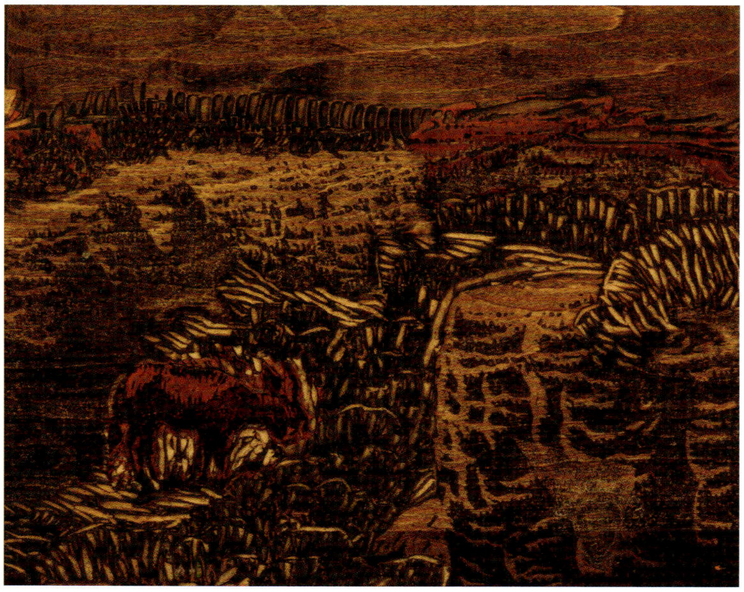

Lost in the Desert, c. 1920. Basswood printing block, 6½ x 7⅞ in. 1996.002.001. Gift of Fred T. and Novadean Hogan.

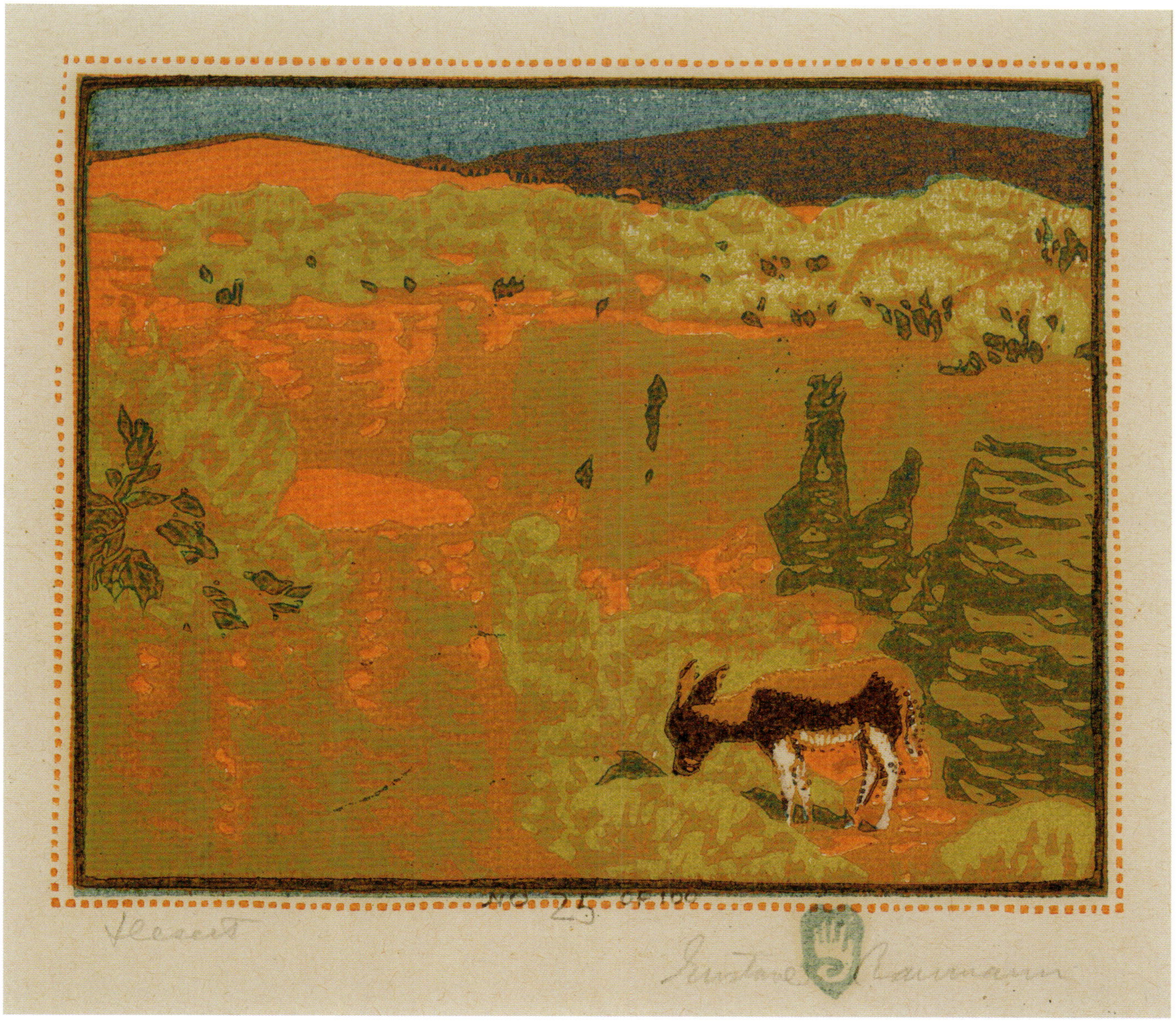

Maria Martinez

(1887–1980)

Red Wedding Jar, 1963

Ceramic, 11 x 7½ in. diam.

2002.004.001

Gift of Adrian Randle

No Southwestern art collection is complete without at least one black ceramic piece by the prolific Pueblo potter Maria Martinez. The pots she created with her husband, Julian, and later her daughter-in-law Santana and son Popovi Da have been known worldwide since at least 1918. Maria's hand-thrown pottery is always exceptionally symmetrical, thin-walled and unglazed, with the decoration achieved through hand burnishing and drawn motifs outlined with matte black. The undecorated redware wedding vase features two identical spouts, connected by a single handle, thought to symbolize two individual lives united. The symbols and designs were usually drawn by Julian, then later Santana, and include the stylized feathers seen in the plate below, as well as other Pueblo designs including serpents, birds, rain, clouds and mountains. Many of these were adapted from ancient vessels, especially those of the Mimbres culture.

In the San Ildefonso Pueblo, the typical ceramics are polychrome on white, jet black, gunmetal silver or terra-cotta red, and they come in a variety of shapes, with plates and jars as a common form. The famous blackware—matte black on polished black—is achieved through a longer polishing process followed by firing at a lower temperature, smothering the fire with dung.

Another well-known San Ildefonso Pueblo potter, Rose Gonzales (originally from San Juan Pueblo), whose work is shown below, represents another great tradition of carved black or red ceramics. Gonzales started this carving tradition in 1930. This redware vessel features a deeply carved avanyu design of a water serpent or plumed serpent found on prehistoric pottery and used by potters at several pueblos.

WE

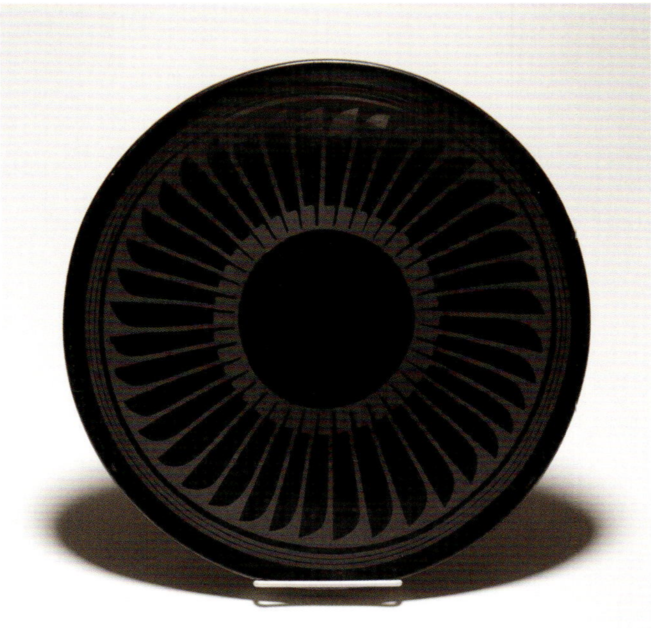

Maria and Santana Martinez. *Ornamental Plate*, c. 1943–1956. Ceramic, 12½ in. diam. 1994.004.001. Gift of Jean O. Smith.

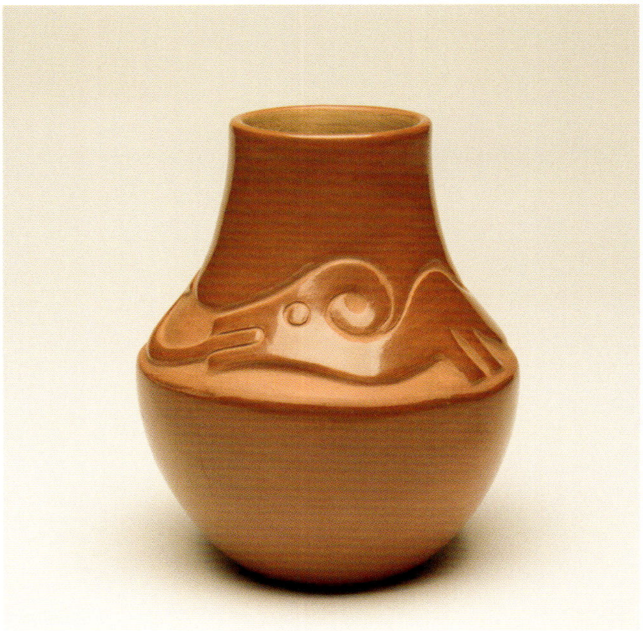

Rose Gonzales. *Incised Vase*, 1973. Ceramic, 7¾ x 6¾ in. diam. 1973.003.001. Museum Acquisition Fund.

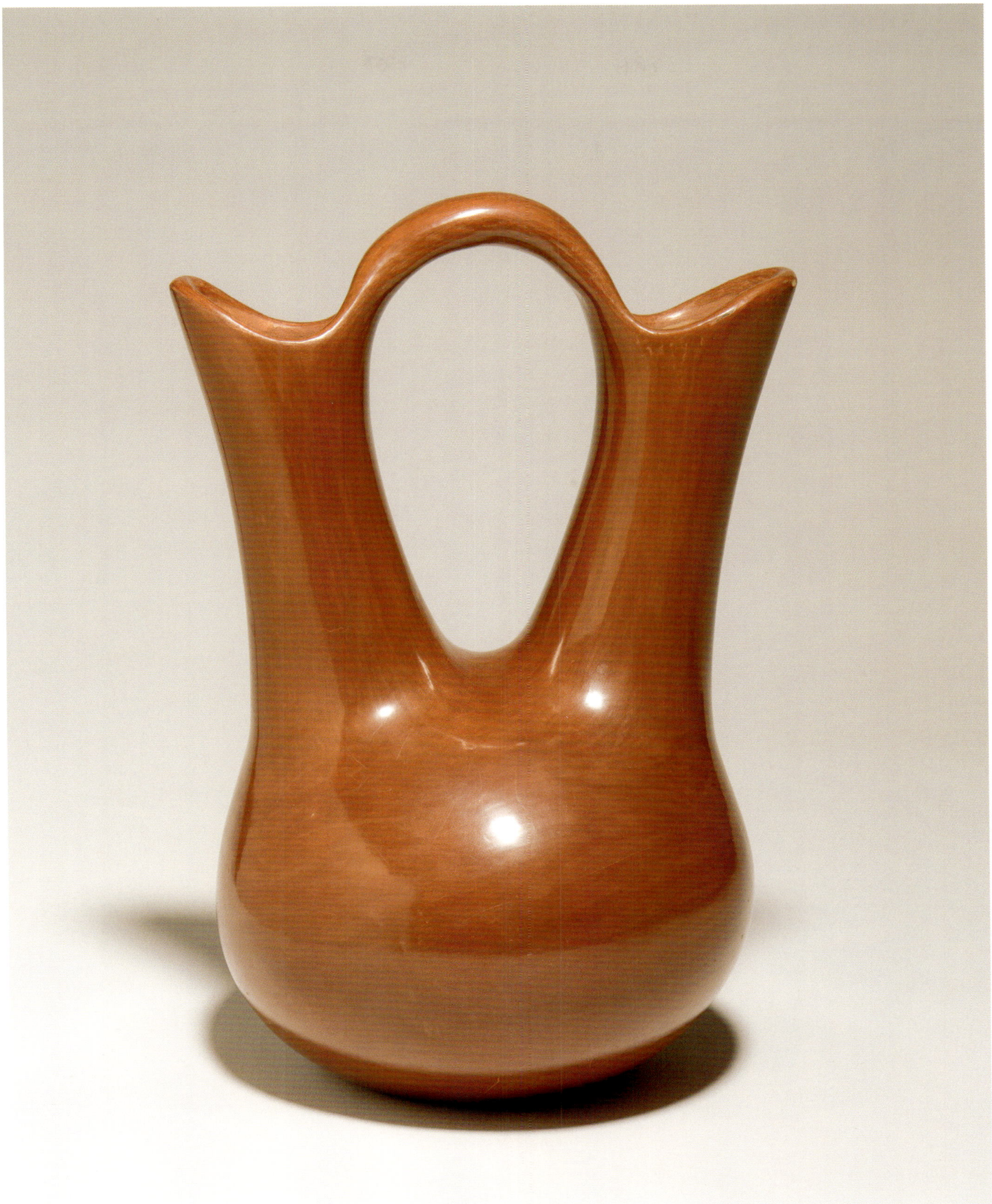

Unknown Hopi Basketmaker

Coiled Hopi Tray, Mid- to late twentieth century

Galleta grass or rabbit brush with yucca strip stitching, 13¼ in. diam.

2003.003.001

Gift of Ron Price in Memory of Miriam Price

Among American Indian tribes of the Southwest, basket weaving is one of the oldest crafts, dating back to at least 6000 BC. Basketry declined in the late nineteenth century with the introduction of railroads that brought cheap, factory-made goods from the East. However, several tribes, such as the Hopi represented here, have engaged a continuous tradition of basket weaving, both for personal use—mainly for ceremonial and intertribal obligation—and for sale to outsiders. As a result, so-called tourist baskets such as this coiled plaque present an interesting intersection of the continuation of millennia of weaving and construction techniques and new innovations in forms and designs to make the baskets more appealing to buyers. Like textiles and sandpaintings, baskets have evolved from crafts made for tribal use to art objects intended for collectors.

The coiled Hopi circular tray (also called a plaque) and baskets shown are undated by unidentified weavers but in all likelihood were created by females weaving specifically for the market in the second half of the twentieth century. The bright colors, strongly delineated designs and tight coiling show a high degree of skill. The designs include a stepped motif symbolizing rainclouds and a recurring human-like figure that can be identified as a katsina (also called kachina), representing the spirit world. In Hopi cosmology, the katsinam are the spirits or personifications of natural phenomena, personages, qualities or concepts. They are found in different forms, including in dances, in three-dimensional carvings and ceramic figures, and in two-dimensional depictions in paintings and baskets. Central to Hopi ceremonialism, the popular katsina dolls made for collectors carry no spiritual power.

WE

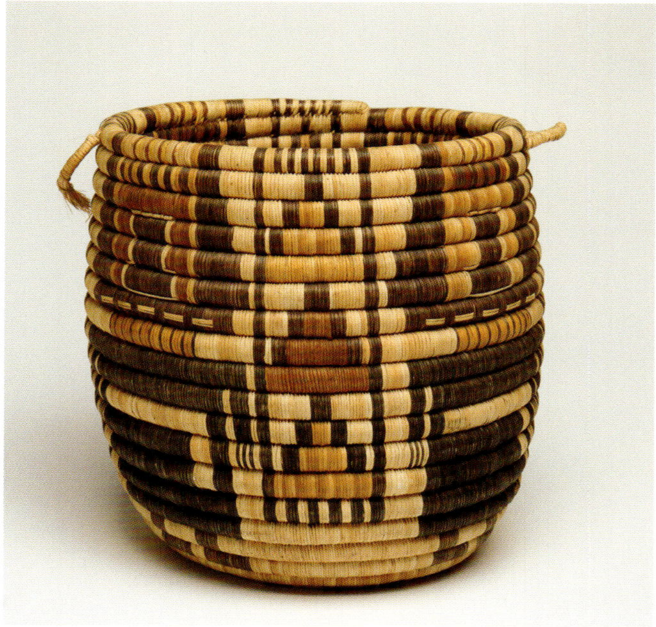

Unknown Hopi basketmaker. *Hopi Coiled Basket*, twentieth century. Woven yucca, 11 x 13 in. diam. 1982.013.001a. Museum Acquisition Fund.

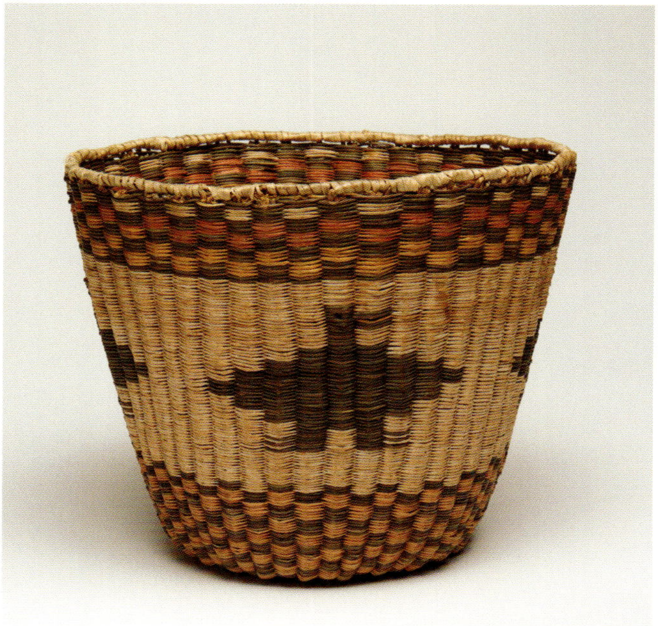

Unknown Hopi basketmaker. *Hopi Wickerwork Basket*, twentieth century. Woven yucca, 10½ x 13¾ in. diam. 1982.013.001c. Museum Acquisition Fund.

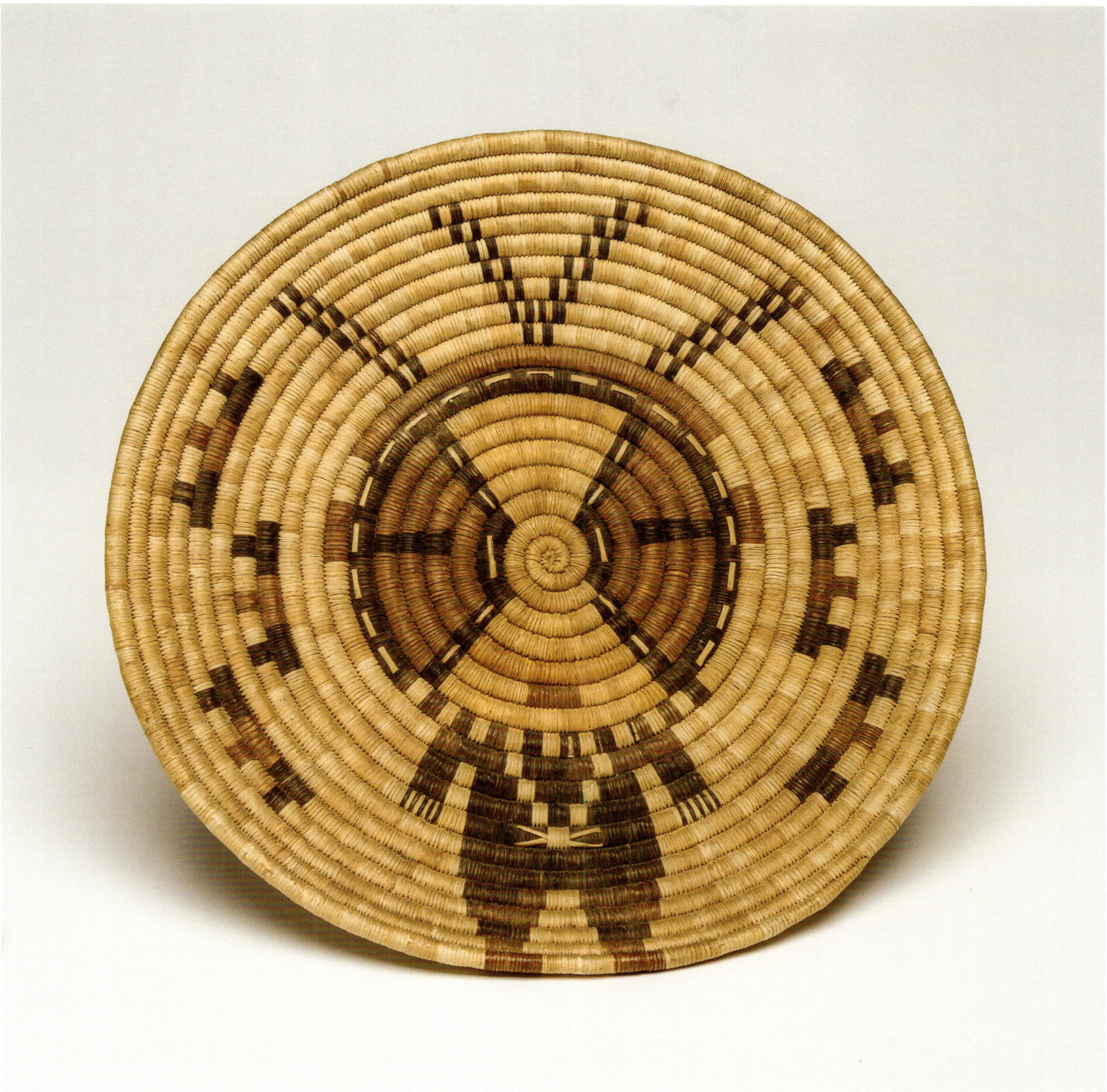

Joseph Imhof

(1871–1955)

Untitled (Study for Untitled Lithograph), Early twentieth century

Pencil on tissue, 15½ x 11½ in.

2004.004.013

Gift of Bill and Mary Cheek

Preparatory drawings and studies are a vital component of the art historical record and the effort to study an artist, but they are not often exhibited or viewed by the general public. The twenty-nine preparatory drawings created by Joseph Imhof in the collection of the Museum of the Southwest offer enticing portraits of the Pueblo Indians that captivated Imhof for most of his life.

Imhof has a fascinating biography, born to a family of German immigrants in Brooklyn and studying art while traveling the world. At the age of seventeen he started working as an artist for Currier & Ives, Lithographers, later opened a bookstore and then sold it to fund a trip to Europe to study painting. He started sketching and painting American Indians while watching Buffalo Bill Cody's Wild West show in Belgium. Imhof and his wife traveled to New Mexico often, and in 1929 they bought a house and studio in Taos. They were able to finance their move to Taos with funds from a printing process the artist had invented in 1921 that used invisible color. Imhof lived and worked in Taos until his death in 1955.

Throughout his lengthy career as an artist, Imhof used his drawings, paintings and lithographs to document the daily lives, rituals and ceremonies of the many different Pueblo people who lived around him. Imhof had a guest room for his Indian subjects, believing that he had to know the men and women before he could paint them. His drawings show individuals with highly defined features and piercing eyes, conveying a sense of personality and specificity. He almost always conveyed exact anatomical proportions and worked with gridlike compositions, seen in the background of the study for an untitled lithograph. This drawing has the words "Nofi-to/Red Hills/Tewa," likely the sitter's identification. Whether in drawings, lithographs or paintings, Imhof's portraits always capture the essence of the subject and the attention of the viewer.

WE

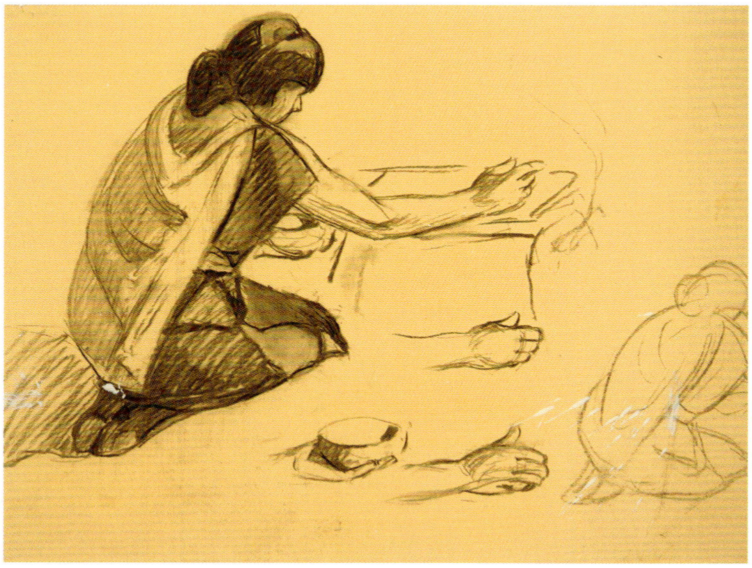

Untitled (Indian bust), early twentieth century. Charcoal on paper, 19½ x 14 in. 2004.004.025. Gift of Bill and Mary Cheek.

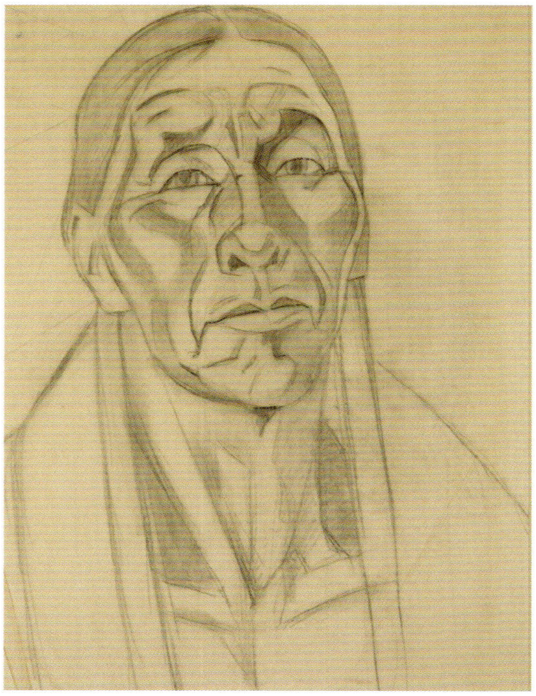

Study for *Making Wafer Bread*, from Corn series, early twentieth century. Charcoal on paper, 17½ x 23½ in. 2004.004.017. Gift of Bill and Mary Cheek.

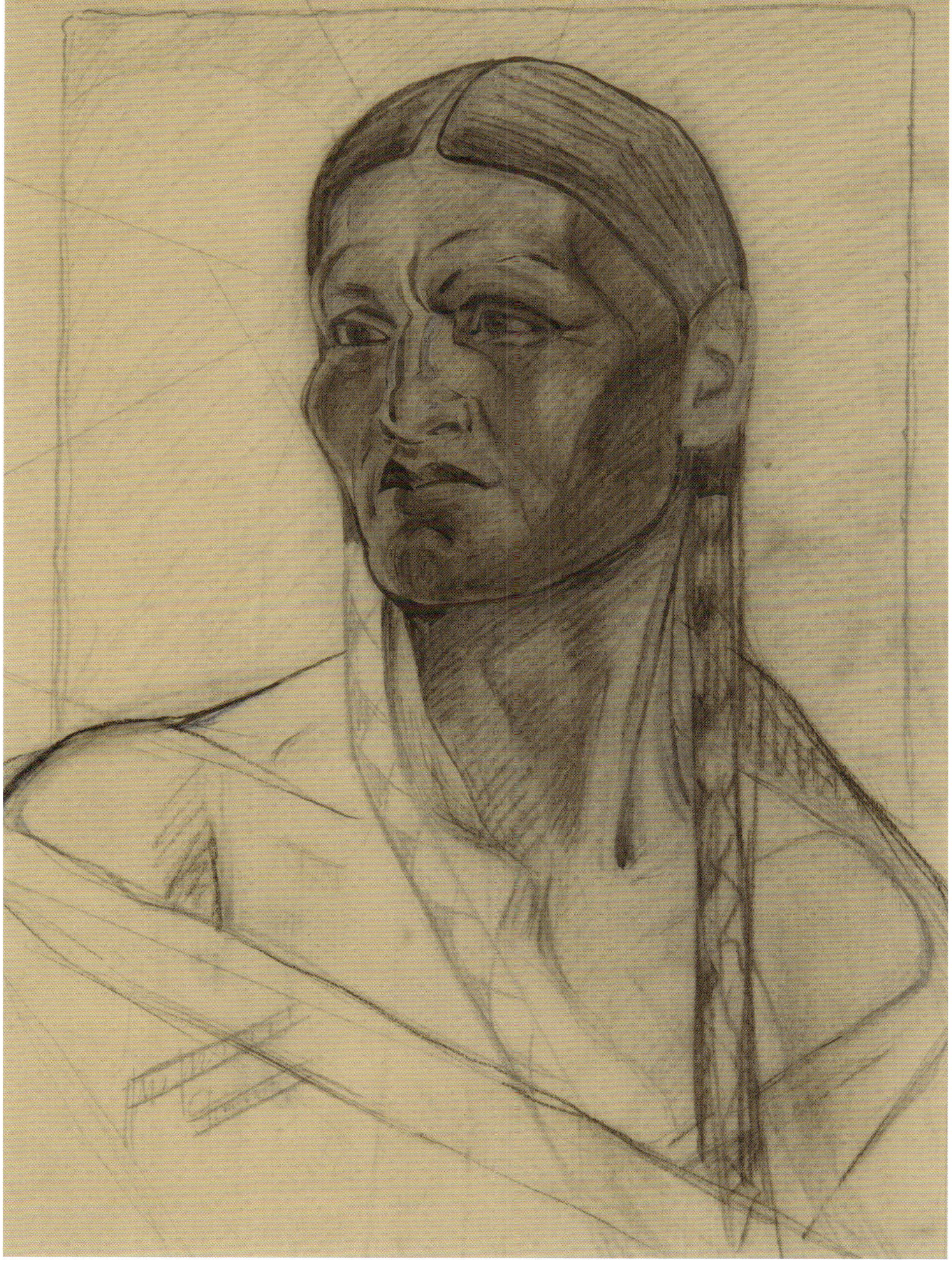

Glenna Goodacre

(b. 1939)

Crossing the Prairie, 2001

Bronze, 69 x 36 x 30 in.

2006.008.001

Gift of Lulene and Arthur Oldham

THE FACES AND FIGURES OF GLENNA GOODACRE'S SUBJECTS are skillfully represented with care and attention to detail that allow viewers to personally connect with the works. Goodacre began her career as a two-dimensional artist in Lubbock, Texas. Her fascination with people and faces stemmed from her early drawings and paintings and continued to be her focus when her emphasis shifted to sculpture. Goodacre has created over 500 works with people as her subject matter, ranging from the Sacagawea dollar to the Vietnam Women's Memorial in Washington, DC, to the Irish Memorial in Philadelphia, represented in maquette in the Museum of the Southwest collection.

Goodacre's representational sculptures are real-life depictions of moments frozen in time. *Crossing the Prairie* is a bronze sculpture of a woman carrying a small child during the westward expansion of America. Goodacre has crafted the woman in this sculpture to have a look of determination and strength, a representation that permits many different interpretations of who the woman is and what her purpose may be. Like many of her other sculptures of women and children, Goodacre has treated her subject with a dignity and sensitivity that engages her audience and connects with a variety of events and emotions within the human experience.

Crossing the Prairie stands out among the collection of Goodacre's work at the Museum of the Southwest as a contrast to her exuberant sculptures of children in *Carefree* and *Facts of Life*. The collection gives a snapshot of the range and depth of Goodacre's work as a sculptor of people and life experiences.

MR

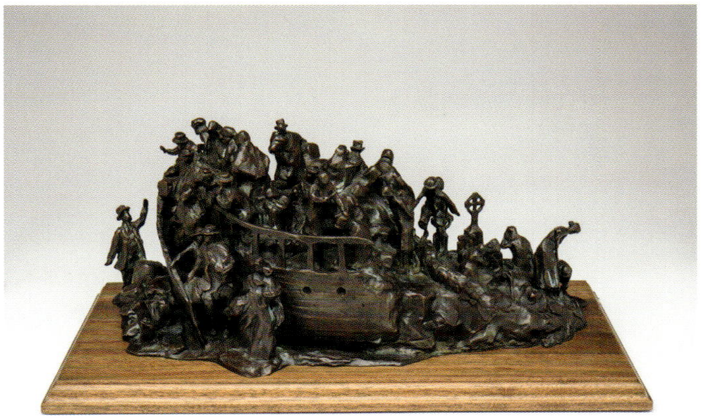

Irish Memorial Maquette, 1998. Bronze, 20½ x 8¾ 10½ in. 2006.010.001. Museum Acquisition Fund.

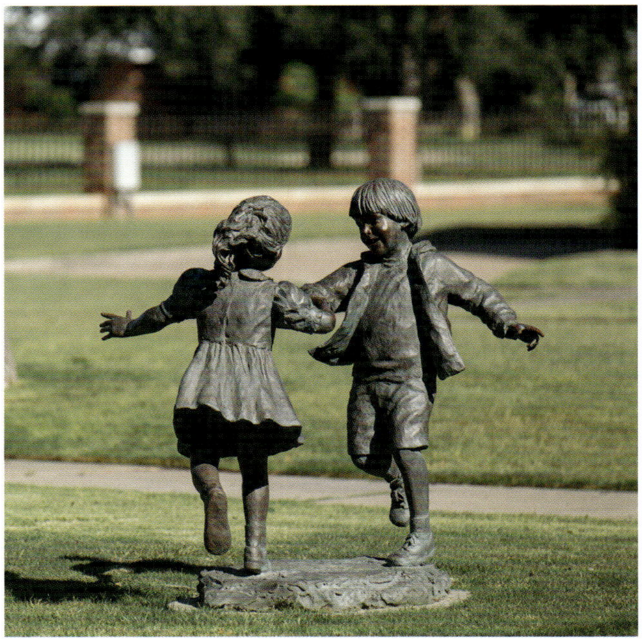

Carefree, 1994. Bronze, 53 x 48 x 43 in. 2001.003.001. Gift of Lulene and Arthur Oldham.

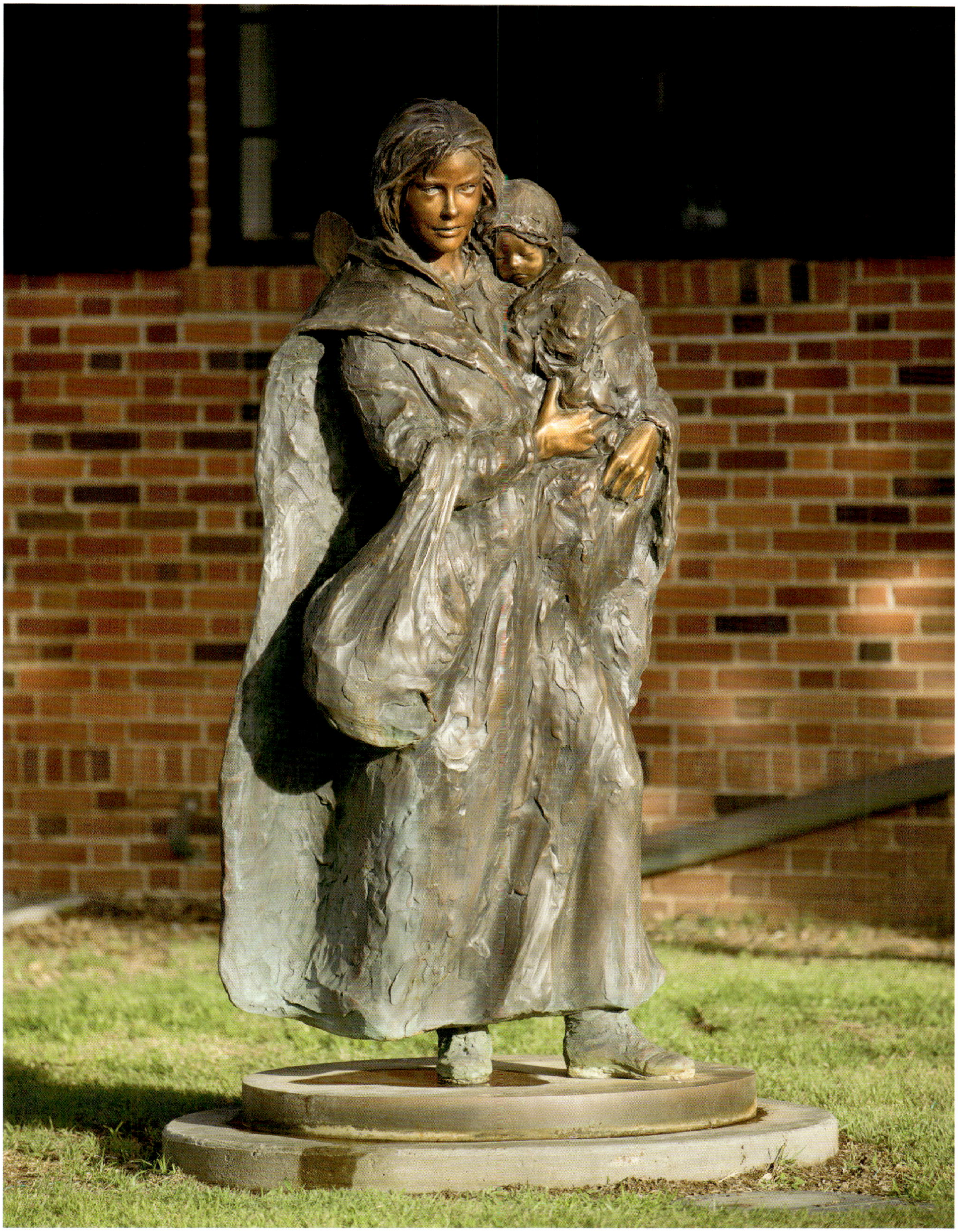

Veryl Goodnight

(b. 1947)

Back from the Brink, 2001

Bronze, 77 x 58 x 56 in.

2007.002.001

Gift of Arthur Oldham in memory of his wife, Lulene Oldham

THE GOODNIGHT FAMILY ENJOYS A LONG AND DISTINCTIVE HISTORY in the American Southwest. Colonel Charles Goodnight and his wife, Mary Ann, settled in the Texas Panhandle in 1888 where he established the Goodnight Ranch and built a new home in the fledgling town of Goodnight that bears the family name. The family home is listed on the National Register of Historic Places and is open to the public as the Charles Goodnight Historical Center.

The large bronze work, *Back from the Brink*, located on the front lawn of the Museum of the Southwest, was created in 2001 by Veryl Goodnight. A distant relative of Charles and Mary Ann, she was intent on commemorating the efforts of Mary Ann Goodnight who in the 1880s noticed the diminishing numbers of bison on the Texas plains. With her husband's assistance, Mary Ann Goodnight captured several calves and kept them protected, ensuring the longevity of the southern herd. This sculpture depicts Mary Ann bottle-feeding the baby bison that she and Charles rescued. The State of Texas owns the descendants of the rescued animals and cares for them at Caprock Canyon State Park in Quitaque. Had it not been for the care and concern of Mary Ann and Charles Goodnight in bringing the bison "back from the brink," the bison might have become extinct.

Goodnight does not limit her artistic production to sculpture; she has established both painting and sculpture studios on property she and her husband own in southwestern Colorado, where she grew up. The primary subject of her paintings is related to animal life and, as did Rosa Bonheur, Goodnight paints her subjects from life. She has said, "The primal partnership of animals, humans, and the land is at the core of my work."

MBW

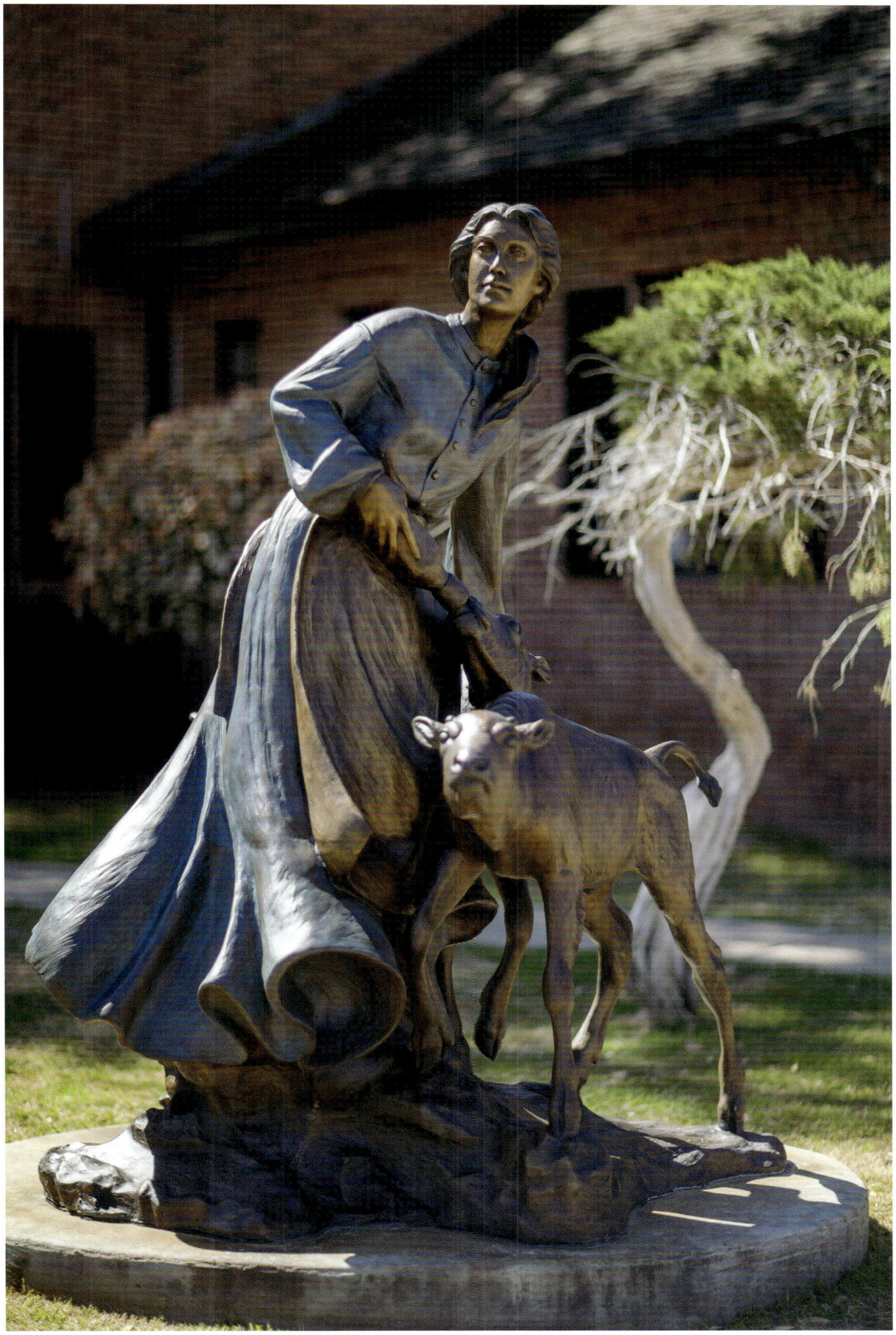

Lydia Quezada Celado de Talavera

(b. 1960)

Black-on-black Mata Ortiz Olla, 2007

Ceramic, 12½ x 8½ in. diam.

2007.003.001

Gift of Jerry Boyd

Mata Ortiz, Chihuahua, Mexico, is the town associated with the revival of the ancient pottery of the Casas Grandes culture. Lydia Quezada is today one of its chief proponents. Her brother Juan started the town's modern ceramic practice in the 1970s and remains well known for his work in the field. Many Mata Ortiz potters learned, in part, through examining pottery shards from the nearby ruins of Casas Grandes. While the black and red polychrome shards were the early inspiration for style and technique, the Quezada family and other artists in the community used them as a jumping-off point to create vibrant and modernist pottery in a variety of forms and designs. However the pieces are still hand-built without pottery wheels and hand-painted, using local sources for the paint and tools.

In addition to faithful reproductions of Casas Grandes ceramics, many painted pots incorporate Pueblo Indian designs found in the work of San Ildefonso Pueblo potter Maria Martinez, as well as those of the ancient Mimbres culture. Some artists are now creating pots with completely abstract geometric designs, some use rainbow hues, and there are many sculptural ceramics in the shape of reptiles, coyote and bison.

Black-on-Black Mata Ortiz Olla shows Quezada's striking balance of matte and shiny black surfaces, a firing technique she created and perfected. The complex patterns she creates use continuous lines, synthesizing abstract geometric patterns from different sources. The irregularly shaped rim draws the eye up further, giving the whole piece a swirling effect. Another ceramic by Alma Flores illustrates another popular style of red and black geometric pattern evoking the ancient shards but with a modern twist of repeating diamond patterns.

WE

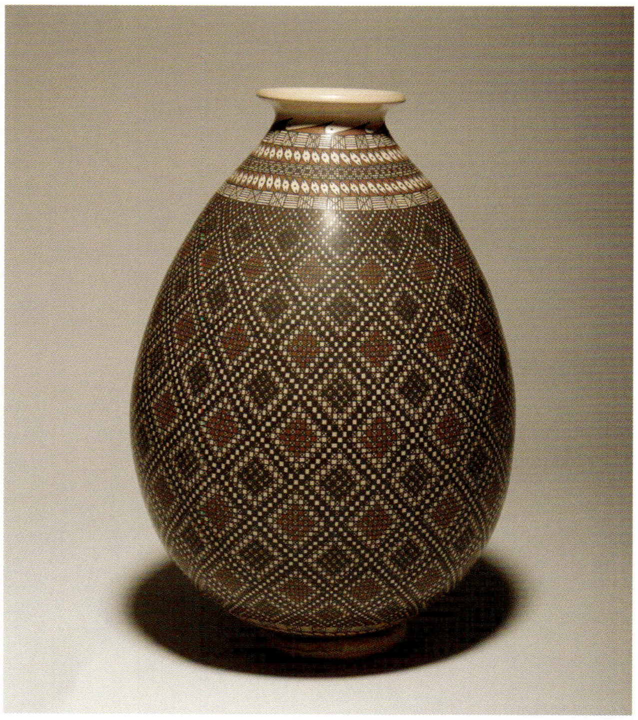

Alma Flores. *Polychrome Mata Ortiz Olla*, 2007. Ceramic, 14 x 9 ½ in. diam. 2007.003.002. Gift of Jerry Boyd.

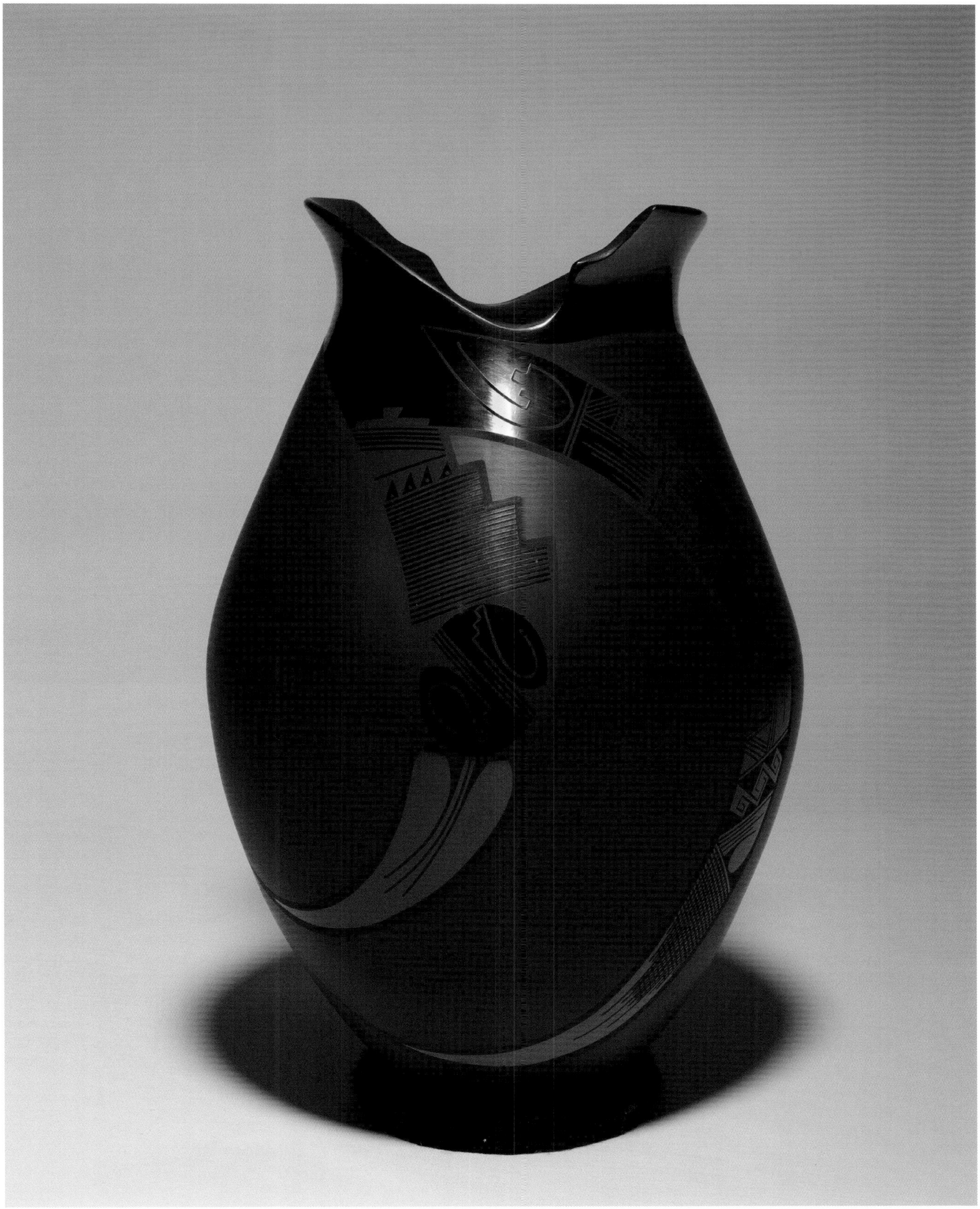

Jesus Moroles

(1950–2015)

ZigZag Diamondback Totems, 2007

118 x 6½ x 11 in. (left);
118 x 12½ x 10 in. (back, right)

2007.007.001, 2007.007.002

Gift of Mrs. Barbara B. Duke, Mr. and Mrs. Michael E. Klein, Mr. and Mrs. Jeff C. Shatto, Mr. Duke Edwards and Mr. and Mrs. Bradford Moody

Ritual, whether through the patterns carved into the stone or the creative process itself, is an important characteristic of Jesus Moroles' work. The artist did not start with drawings or plans for his sculptures. Instead, Moroles allowed the stone to guide his creations, leaving some portions raw and sculpting others. Combining the natural surfaces of the torn granite with the polished surfaces, the artist encourages his audience to view, touch and ponder the harmonious synchronicity of the two. He viewed his work as a commentary on how nature and humans interact.

ZigZag Diamondback Totems were designed as two separate sculptures but are placed together as a complementary pair on the Museum of the Southwest grounds. The physical presence of the totems and the combination of natural and carved surfaces suggest something akin to ancient structures, designed by man but worn down by nature and time. The vertical, zigzag movement of the totems, combined with alternating raised and carved textures of their surfaces, imparts a rhythm and the pulse of a dynamic conversation between the two pieces.

Art was a significant part of Moroles' life growing up in Dallas. He started selling his artwork as an elementary student and had his own silk-screening business in high school. He was later educated with a BFA at the University of North Texas. Moroles was an acclaimed sculptor and an active member of the Texas and Oklahoma art scene, serving as a mentor to young artists and as a board member for several cultural organizations.

MR

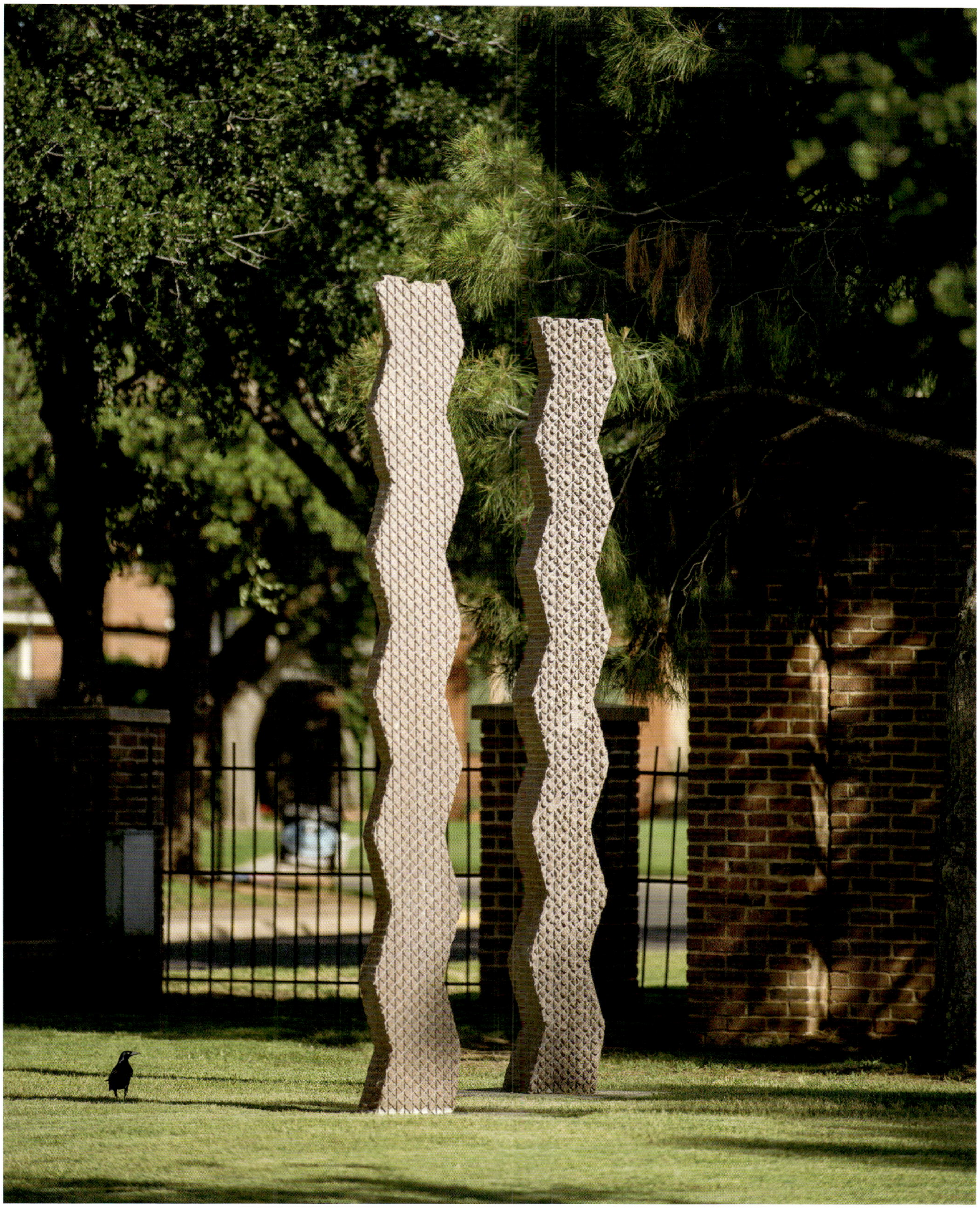

Burton Pritzker

(b. 1941)

Bushy Plane, 2009

Gelatin silver print, 18 x 12 in.

2010.001.001

Gift of the Artist

A student of architecture since the 1960s, Burton Pritzker is no stranger to the elements of art and design. An ongoing fascination with light is what ultimately moved Pritzker away from a career in architecture and into photography.

The Museum of the Southwest's collection of eighty-seven photographic prints make up the whole of Pritzker's Forgotten Planes series. Pritzker uses his camera as a tool to break down an object into its basic elements—shape, light, form and texture. The landscape that he creates in each photograph is given new life and renewed context. Changing the context of the object allows for a broader perspective; the object is no longer confined by any rules of perception and can therefore take on any life that the viewer chooses to give. Pritzker breathes new life into the forgotten, taking an object normally seen as insignificant and elevating its status. These photographs playfully contrast with the more traditional landscapes in the Museum of the Southwest's permanent collection.

In *Bushy Plane*, a horizon of shadows draws our attention to a foreground consumed with metal gears. Meaning and purpose are up to the viewer to decide, with only a glimpse of the object's former life in the lower left corner. In *Conflicting Theories*, a row of pipe is no longer a pile of scrap metal but a purposeful, repetitive arrangement. The titles of each image allude to a higher meaning, serving as a guide for the viewer navigating these new landscapes, but they are only suggestions. Pritzker's works are rich with possibility as he leaves their interpretation in the viewer's hands, his ultimate stance being that the viewer leaves comfortable space behind and enters a new reality.

KW

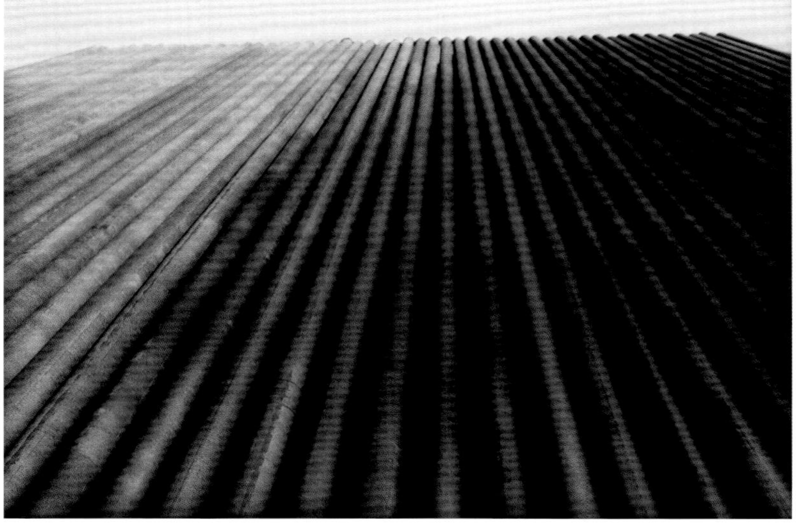

Conflicting Theories, 2006. Gelatin silver print, 12 x 18 in. 2010.001.022. Gift of the Artist.

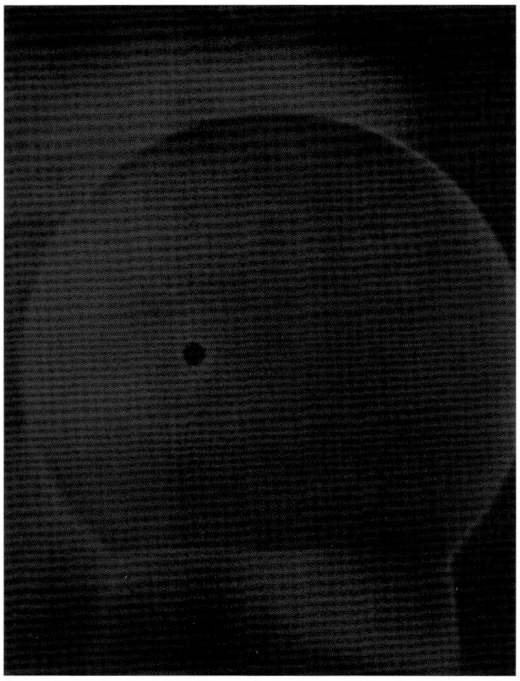

Looking to the Future, 2007. Gelatin silver print, 18 x 12 in. 2010.001.018. Gift of the Artist.

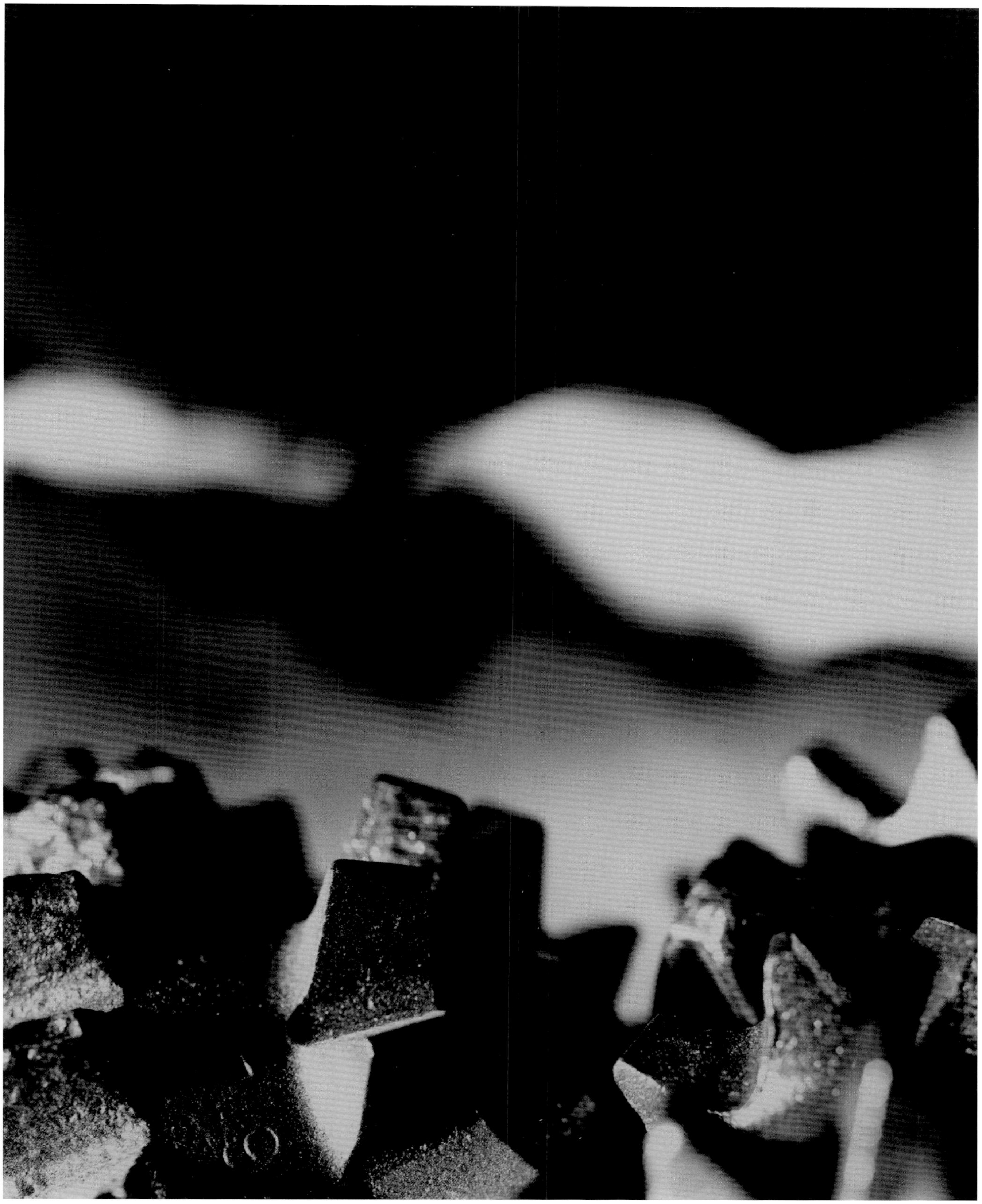

Danville Chadbourne

(b. 1949)

The Obscure History of Deception, 1994–2000

Mixed media, 28 x 28 in.

2013.005.003

Museum Acquisition Fund

San Antonio-based Danville Chadbourne's abstract sculptures are skillful assemblages of different materials that reflect the visual systems of cultures around the world. Born in Bryan, Texas, Chadbourne received a BFA from Sam Houston State University and an MFA from Texas Tech University. Chadbourne's sculptures can be found in galleries and museums across Texas. His extensive body of work and his artistic explorations in color, texture and form are represented in several sculptures owned by the Museum of the Southwest.

The abstractness of Chadbourne's art can be peeled away to reveal deeper art historical references and a striking and unique body of work. His color palettes are resolutely all over the map, with muted earth tones contrasting with bright and intentionally garish tones within the same work. This can be seen in *The Reinvention of Misrepresentation*, which also features a gridded structure open to numerous interpretations, with some viewers seeing a board game and others seeing some kind of map. He achieves different textures by incorporating found objects like the smooth river stone seen in *Sympathetic Beliefs—The Obvious Secret* or by creating a patina like that on *The Obscure History of Deception.* The surface treatment in this mixed-media wall-mounted sculpture gives the illusion that the object has recently been excavated from an archaeological site. The central form here is in the shape of a sacred bundle, an iconographic motif rich with symbolism found in almost all cultures from ancient Mesoamerica. This jade-green bundle, along with other evocations of Mesoamerican forms, such as quatrefoils, is a clear reference for those familiar with Pre-Columbian art. Viewers unfamiliar with this iconography, however, will have no trouble appreciating the bold aesthetic. The long and poetic titles of his works give viewers another type of abstraction, allowing for different kinds of interpretation.

WE

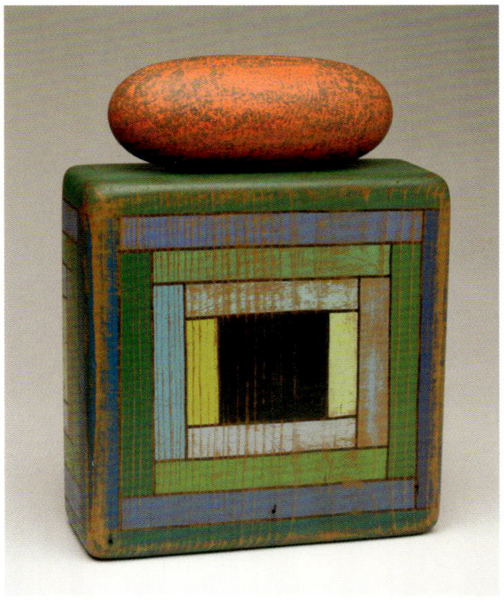

Sympathetic Beliefs—The Obvious Secret, 2002–2004. Mixed media, 15 x 11 x 4 in. 2013.005.001. Museum Acquisition Fund.

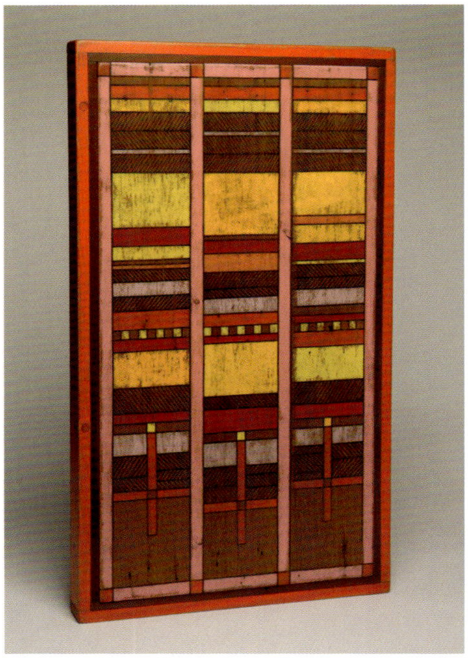

The Reinvention of Misrepresentation, 2008. Mixed media, 32 x 19 in. 2013.005.002. Museum Acquisition Fund.

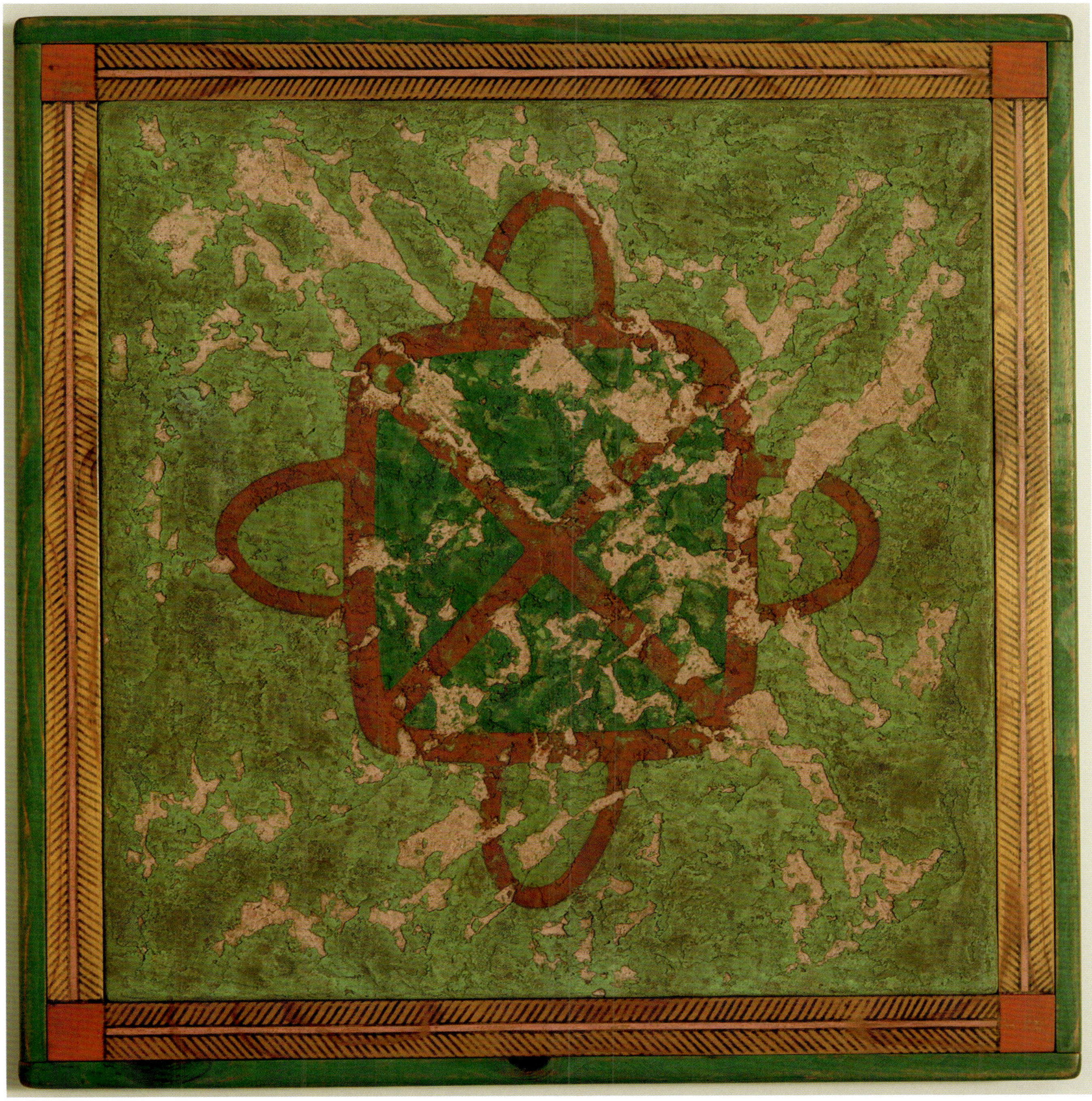

Tomy Lee Kentucky Derby Trophy

1959

Gold with jade base (shown with wooden presentation box), 20½ x 8 x 6½ in.

2015.001.052a–d

Gift of the Scharbauer Family

In 1956, after a successful career as a wildcatter, Fred Turner, Jr., and his wife, Juliette, decided to enter the field of thoroughbred horse racing. They purchased a horse from a breeder in England for $25,000, but Mr. Turner believed that this horse should have a companion for the travel back to the States. Tomy Lee was picked as the companion horse for $6,762. Tomy Lee soon began to outshine the primary horse and showed his worth by winning several races, culminating in the 1959 Kentucky Derby. Since 1875, Tomy Lee is only the second non-American-bred horse to win the Derby.

The tradition of the gold Derby trophy began in 1925 to celebrate the "golden anniversary" of the Kentucky Derby. Designed by George L. Graff, an industrial designer prominent for his Art Deco industrial light fixtures, the trophy features a jade base, solid 14-karat gold body and a horse and rider affixed on top of the lid. Each trophy also features horseshoe-shaped handles and an 18-karat horseshoe within which the inscription resides. Both trophies in the Museum's collection were supplied by Lemon & Son, a Louisville jeweler that crafted the Kentucky Derby trophies until 1999.

The only change to the original 1925 design is the 18-karat horseshoe. This element was flipped 180 degrees in 1999 for the 125th running of the Kentucky Derby to symbolize good luck. The trophy is entirely handcrafted, with only the horse and rider being cast by mold. To date, the Kentucky Derby trophy stands as the only solid-gold trophy awarded in the American sporting culture.

The "Run for the Roses" is considered the most exciting two minutes in sports. Every horse, jockey and owner is put to the test. Tomy Lee, along with jockey Bill Shoemaker, showed the racing community that dreams from West Texas can come true.

JO

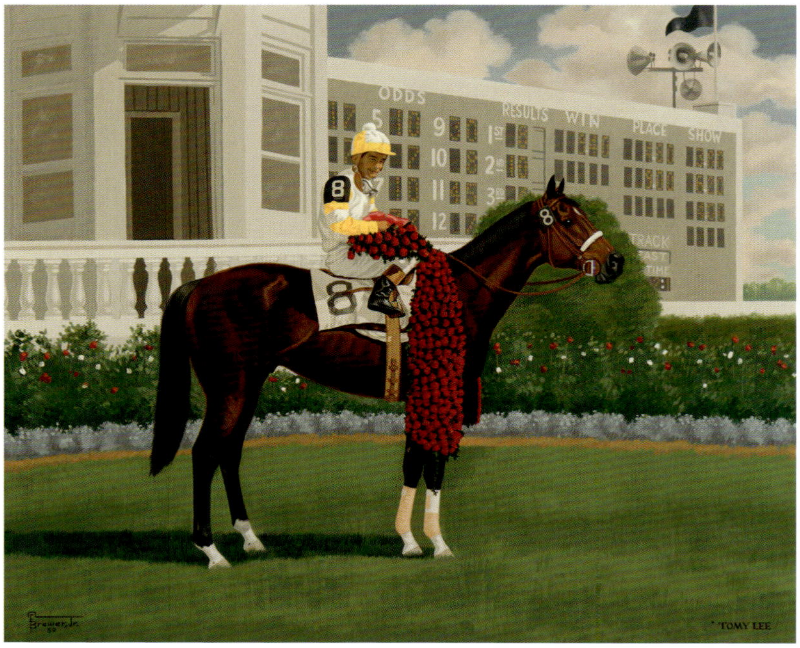

Allen F. Brewer, Jr. *Tomy Lee in Kentucky Derby Winner's Circle*, 1959. Oil on canvas, 33 x 39 in. 2015.001.136. Gift of the Scharbauer Family.

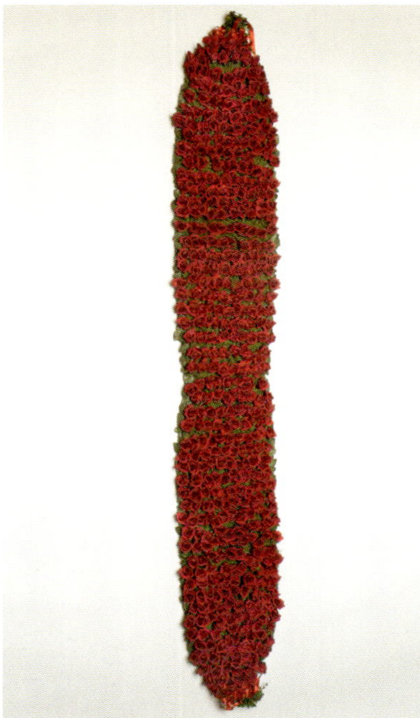

Alysheba Kentucky Derby Rose Blanket, 1987. Silk roses and fabric, 14 x 90 in. 2015.001.147. Gift of the Scharbauer Family.

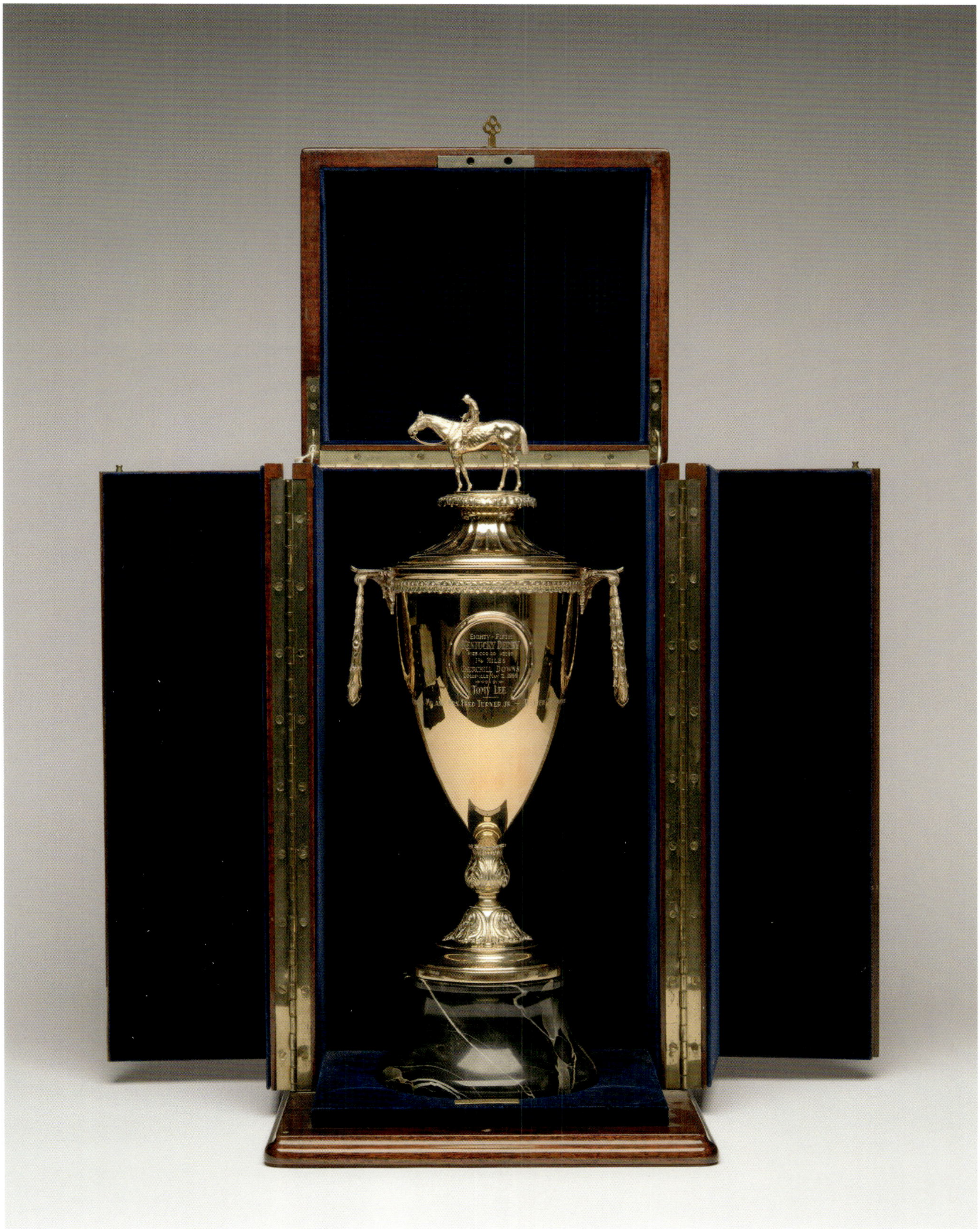
Eighty-Fifth
Churchill Downs
Tomy Lee

Alysheba Kentucky Derby Trophy

1987

Gold with jade base, (shown with wooden presentation box), 20½ x 8 x 6½ in.

2015.001.051a–d

Gift of the Scharbauer Family

In the early 1980s, Dorothy Scharbauer (née Turner) decided to reenter the thoroughbred racing world. She longed to recapture the glory and excitement of the sport and eventually hoped to reach another Kentucky Derby win, similar to that of her parents in 1959. The Scharbauer family had already participated in equestrian sports with her husband Clarence's preference for quarter-horse racing.

In 1985, Dorothy and her daughter, Pamela, bought Alysheba as a yearling and began the training process with up-and-coming trainer Jack Van Berg. Van Berg (who also grew up in an equestrian family) had an unknown connection to the Turner/Scharbauer family. Inspired by Tomy Lee's Kentucky Derby win in 1959, Van Berg named his fifth child Tommy after the winning horse.

Racing under Clarence Scharbauer's quarter-horse racing colors (the blue and white diamond), Alysheba quickly developed a reputation as the horse to beat. Throughout the racing season, a rivalry developed with other top horses such as Bet Twice and Ferdinand. Chris McCarron was selected as Alysheba's jockey by the family and Van Berg. His knowledge of Alysheba's movement allowed him to overcome a near fall during the Kentucky Derby race. "[Alysheba] did all the work," recalled the rider; "I've never ridden a horse that showed so much courage." McCarron narrowly edged out Bill Shoemaker (Tomy Lee's 1959 jockey) to capture the rose blanket.

Alysheba's spirit and determination during the Preakness and the Belmont Stakes captured the attention of the nation. While unsuccessful in winning the Triple Crown (losing at Belmont), Alysheba did earn the title of America's Horse after the 1988 Breeders' Cup Classic. During the 1988 presidential election (eventually won by another former Midland resident—George H. W. Bush) Alysheba received several ballot votes. At Alysheba's retirement a week after the Breeders' Cup Classic, signs were held up reading "Alysheba for President." Alysheba was retired as the richest thoroughbred to date.

JO

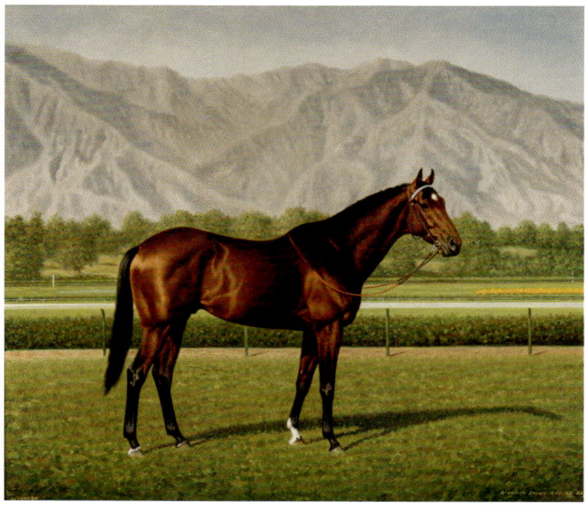

Richard Stone Reeves. *Alysheba*, 1988. Oil on canvas, 40 x 45 in. 2015.001.092. Gift of the Scharbauer Family.

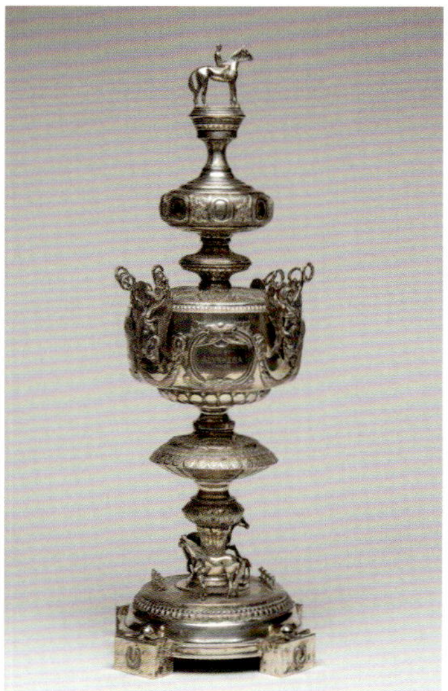

Alysheba Preakness Trophy, 1987. Sterling silver, 22 x 8 x 2½ in. 2015.001.048. Gift of the Scharbauer Family.

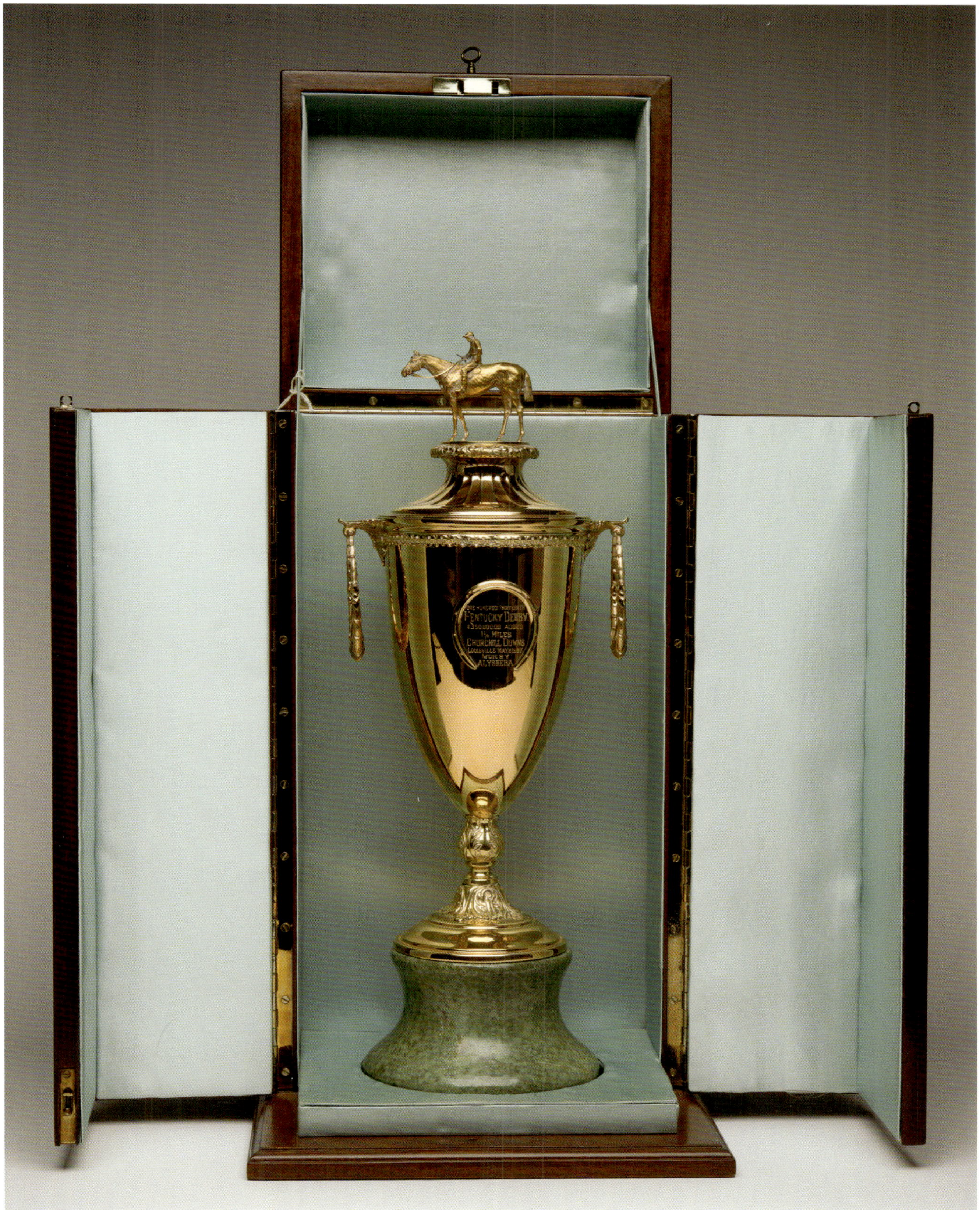
KENTUCKY DERBY
1¼ MILES
CHURCHILL DOWNS
WON BY
ALYSHEBA

Catharine Carter Critcher

(1868–1964)

Portrait of Frances Wyly Hall, c. 1920s

Oil on canvas, 19½ x 16½ in.

2015.002.001

Gift of Glenn and Louan Rogers

Not many young American women would have the courage to launch a school of art in a foreign country in the early twentieth century, but Catharine Critcher was the exception to many rules. She called the school the Cours Critcher and her goal in establishing it in Paris, in 1905, was to aid American students in gaining entry to art schools in what was then the world's art center. This was not a lucrative undertaking, so to supplement her income, Critcher served as a guide for American tourists during the summer break. In 1909, when the school closed, the artist-teacher returned home and began teaching at the Corcoran School of Art, where she remained until 1919, when she founded another school, the Critcher School of Painting and Applied Arts in Washington, DC. She stepped down as director in 1940 to devote her life to painting. Critcher spent many summers in Taos, where she was unanimously elected to the Taos Society of Artists as its only female member. Critcher noted that "Taos is unlike any place God ever made . . . There are models galore and no phones, the artists all live in these attractive funny little adobe houses away from the world, food, foes and friends."

This oil portrait is a recent acquisition of the Museum of the Southwest. The sitter, Frances Dawson Wyly Hall, has been described as having many of the same qualities as Critcher. She was an independent and determined woman who wrote and illustrated books related to the flora and fauna of Florida, including *Palms and Flowers of Florida, Shells of the Florida Coasts* and *Birds of Florida*.

MBW

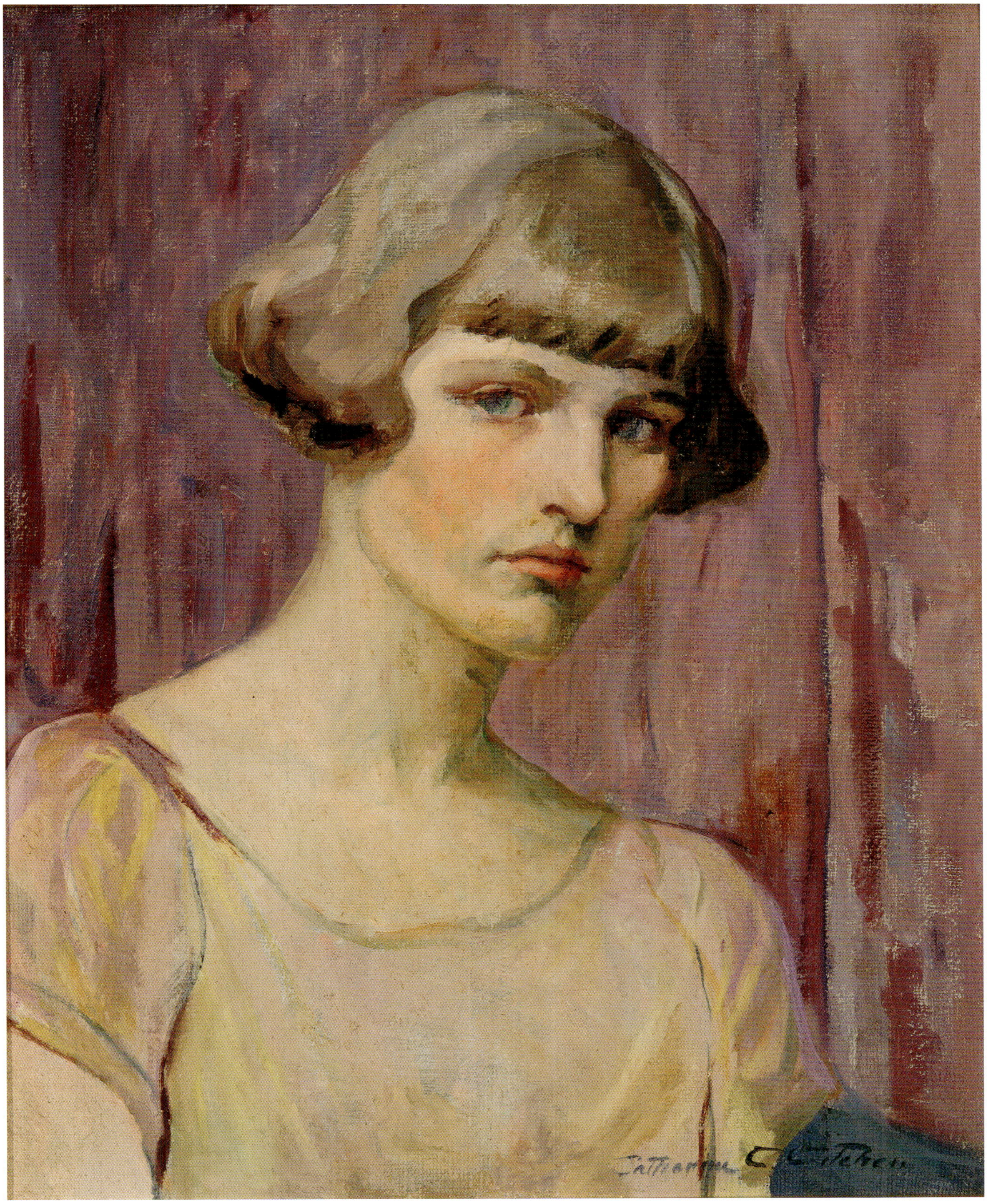

Catherine Lee

(b. 1950)

Shards, 1989/2004

Cast bronze with patination, glazed raku ceramic,
57 x 72 x 1½ in.
12 x 12 x 1½ in. (indiv.)

2015.003.001

Anonymous Gift in Honor of Dorothy Turner Scharbauer

Catherine Lee is interested in "absolute space." Lee's work consists of abstract forms using a variety of media from bronze to raku ceramic to graphite on paper. She refers to these disparate materials as being like speaking in different languages. Lee also identifies with the Minimalist style and considers herself a Post-Minimalist as well. Her work has been shown in many museums and galleries worldwide; currently the artist lives in New York City and the Texas Hill Country.

Lee's work, *Shards*, 1989/2004, is a series of twenty separate pieces created in cast bronze with patination, glazed raku ceramic and bolts. This particular work was selected for the Museum of the Southwest to complement Lee's *Harris (Hebrides II)*, a free-standing fabricated and patinated bronze sculpture. In seeing *Harris (Hebrides II)*, 2003, on the lawn of the Museum of the Southwest, the patina on this fabricated bronze work might remind viewers of the ancient nature of geological formations. *Harris (Hebrides II)* actually references the Isle of Harris, which is part of the Outer Hebrides off the western coast of Scotland. Both works, large and smaller (still a foot tall) share tonal gradations and similar forms. Although *Shards* does not indicate any specific place as does *Harris (Hebrides II)*, it might remind viewers of the landscape in Pampa, Texas, where Catherine Lee was born. The artist has said, "Where I grew up, the landscape was just nothing, it was flat, and there was nothing to stop the wind from blowing through an empty landscape. I'm working from that all the time, a really reduced perspective, a sense of vastness, of space."

MBW

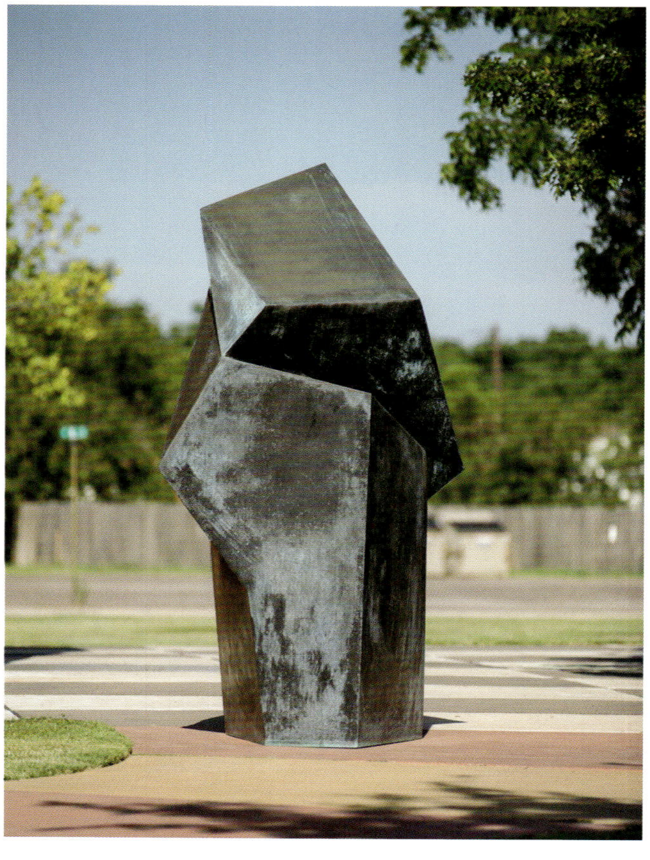

Harris (Hebrides II), 2003. Fabricated and patinated bronze, 102 x 48 x 39 in. 2015.003.002. Anonymous Gift in Honor of Dorothy Turner Scharbauer.

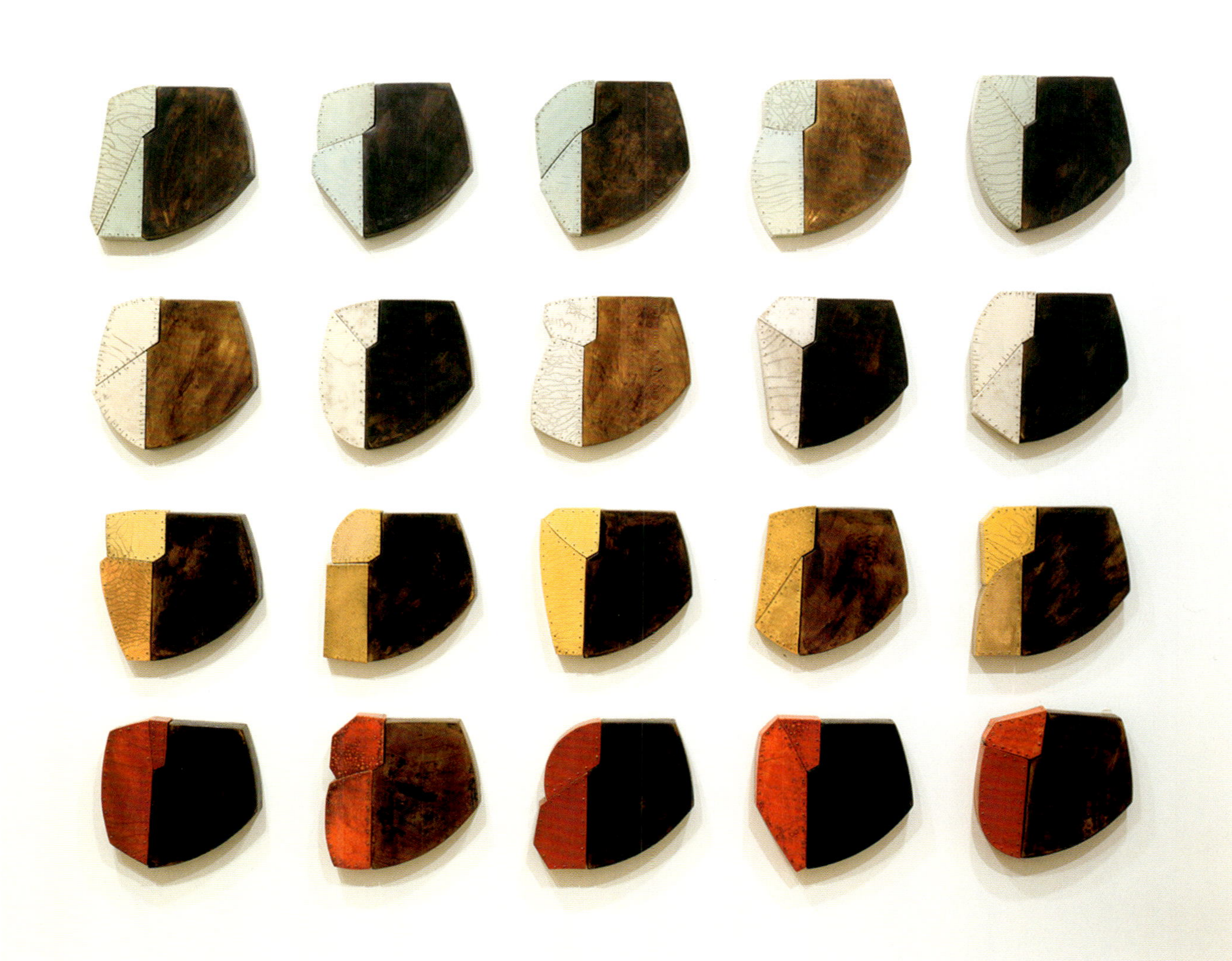

Katie Maratta

(b. 1952)

The Long Horizon (detail), 2012

Mixed media on archival fiber board, 1 in. x 70 ft.

2015.006.001

Museum Acquisition Fund

Using layers of ink and graphite, Austin-based artist Katie Maratta draws miniature landscapes dubbed "horizonscapes." Ranging in length from a few inches to seventy-five feet, Maratta's work is evocative of a long Texas road trip. Featuring wide open spaces, herds of cattle and endless telephone lines, the viewer travels the work as if riding in a car. In West Texas, road trips are common and they are long. Maratta seeks to remind viewers of the memories they hold of these long passes of time buckled into the backseat. "I believe," she has said, "that people in Texas are truly connected to their landscape." Her work allows time to stand still as she encourages the viewer to pause the drive and take in the scenery. Timeless snapshots mingle with modern-day elements: a Dairy Queen, wind turbines and pumpjacks.

Maratta refers to her work as having a beginning, a middle and an end; as being complete stories, journeys. More than mere drawings, Maratta's work becomes a performance piece. The viewer travels, experiences, stops, gazes, repeats. The act of viewing the work itself becomes artistic. A previous career as an illustrator led Maratta to be inspired by the small but spacious confines of the one-inch panels on which she creates her work. She is comfortable in black and white and shades of gray. In the galleries of the Museum of the Southwest, her artwork is often displayed with magnifying glasses for examining details. More than just a quirky novelty, these exhibition props serve to illuminate the contradiction in Maratta's work: she has found a way to cleverly fit the vastness of the Texas landscape inside a confined space.

KW

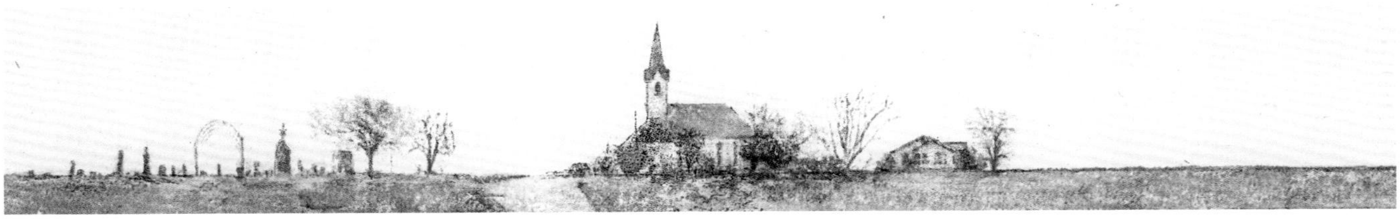

Contributors

WENDY EARLE is the Curator of Collections and Exhibitions at the Museum of the Southwest. She received her BA in History of Art from the University of Michigan and MA in Art History from the University of Texas at Austin.

JENNI OPALINSKI is the Collections and Exhibitions Manager at the Museum of the Southwest. She received her BA in History from Gonzaga University and MA in Museum Science from Texas Tech University.

AUDRIE PALMER was formerly the Development Director at the Museum of the Southwest. She received her BA in Journalism from the University of North Texas and a Master's in Public Administration from the University of Texas of the Permian Basin.

MELISSA ROWLAND is the Educational Outreach Manager at the Museum of the Southwest. She received her BA in Art and MA in Teaching from Austin College in Sherman, Texas, and obtained Principal Certification from Texas Woman's University.

KRISTEN WAGSTROM is the Curator of Education at the Museum of the Southwest. She received her BA and MA in Art History from the University of North Texas.

BRIAN LEE WHISENHUNT is the Executive Director of the Museum of the Southwest. He received his BFA and MA in Art History from the University of Oklahoma.

DR. MARIANNE BERGER WOODS is a professor of Art History at the University of Texas of the Permian Basin, focusing on the history of women artists and images of women in art. She received her PhD from the Union Institute and University, Cincinnati, Ohio.

Further Reading

Acton, David, Martin F. Krauss and Madeline Carol Yurtseven. 1993. *Gustave Baumann: Nearer to Art*. Santa Fe: Museum of New Mexico Press.

Breeskin, Adelyn Dohme. 1972. *Two American Painters: Fritz Scholder and T. C. Cannon*. Washington, DC: Smithsonian Institution Press.

Buechner, Thomas. 1983. *Norman Rockwell, Artist and Illustrator*. New York: Abradale Press.

Couse Leavitt, Virginia. 1991. *Eanger Irving Couse: Image Maker for America*. Albuquerque, NM: Albuquerque Museum.

Danzker, Jo-Anne Birnie, ed. 2013. *Nicolai Fechin*. Seattle, WA: Charles and Emma Frye Art Museum.

Eldredge, Charles, Julie Schimmel and William Truettner. 1986. *Art in New Mexico, 1900–1945: Paths to Taos and Santa Fe*. Washington, DC: Smithsonian Institution Press.

Ford, Alice. 1988. *John James Audubon: A Biography*. New York: Abbeville Press.

Grauer, Michael. 2012. *Texas Impressionism: Branding with Brushstroke and Color, 1885–1935*. Canyon, TX: Panhandle-Plains Historical Museum.

Hassrick, Peter, and Elizabeth Cunningham. 2008. *In Contemporary Rhythm: The Art of Ernest L. Blumenschein*. Norman: University of Oklahoma Press.

Hedlund, Ann. 2004. *Navajo Weaving in the Late Twentieth Century: Kin, Community, and Collectors*. Tucson: University of Arizona Press.

Heltunen, Vicki, and Rodger Rak. 1986. *Color, Pattern & Plane: E. Martin Hennings in Taos*. Orange, TX: Stark Museum of Art.

Hignett, Sean. 1984. *Brett: From Bloomsbury to New Mexico*. London: Hodder and Stoughton.

Hoppin, Martha. 2010. *The World of J. G. Brown*. Chesterfield, MA: Chameleon Books.

Kalil, Susie. 2011. *Alexandre Hogue: An American Visionary.* College Station: Texas A&M University Press.

Kissane, Sean. 2005. *Catherine Lee.* Dublin: Irish Museum of Modern Art.

Lowell, Susan, W. Ross Humphreys and Robin Stancliff. 1999. *The Many Faces of Mata Ortiz.* Tucson, AZ: Treasure Chest Books.

Neff, Emily Ballew. 2006. *The Modern West: American Landscapes, 1890–1950.* New Haven, CT: Yale University Press.

New-York Historical Society and Linda Ferber. 2009. *The Hudson River School: Nature and the American Vision.* New York: Skira Rizzoli.

Parezo, Nancy. 1983. *Navajo Sandpainting: From Religious Act to Commercial Art.* Tucson: University of Arizona Press.

Peterson, Susan. 1997. *Pottery by American Indian Women: The Legacy of Generations.* New York: Abbeville Press.

Porter, Dean, Teresa Hayes Ebie and Suzan Campbell. 1999. *Taos Artists and their Patrons, 1898–1950.* Notre Dame, IN: Snite Museum of Art.

Ratcliffe, Sam DeShong. 2007. *Jerry Bywaters, Interpreter of the Southwest.* College Station: Texas A&M University Press.

Reily, Nancy Hopkins, and Lucille Enix. 1998. *Joseph Imhof: Artist of the Pueblos; A Biography.* Santa Fe, NM: Sunstone Press.

Rushing, W. Jackson. 2004. *Allan Houser: An American Master (Chiricahua Apache, 1914–1994).* New York: H. N. Abrams.

Schiffer, Nancy. 1991. *Pictorial Weavings of the Navajo.* West Chester, PA: Schiffer.

Schimmel, Julie. 1984. *The Art and Life of W. Herbert Dunton, 1878–1936.* Austin: University of Texas Press.

Schimmel, Julie, and Robert White. 1994. *Bert Geer Phillips and the Taos Art Colony.* Albuquerque: University of New Mexico.

Sims, Lowery Stokes, Truman Lowe and Paul Chaat Smith. 2008. *Fritz Scholder: Indian/Not Indian.* Munich: Prestel.

Stewart, Rick. 1985. *Lone Star Regionalism: The Dallas Nine and Their Circle, 1928–1945.* Austin: Texas Monthly Press.

Townsend, Richard, Ken Kokrda and Barbara Moulard. 2005. *Casas Grandes and the Ceramic Art of the Ancient Southwest.* Chicago, IL: Art Institute of Chicago.

Traugott, Joseph. 2007. *Gustave Baumann's Southwest.* San Francisco, CA: Pomegranate.

Index of Artists

Credits

All objects were photographed by Daniel Barsotti, Santa Fe, NM, with the exception of Catherine Lee's *Shards*, photographed by the artist and *Back from the Brink*, photographed by Rafael Aguilera.

Every effort has been made to locate and contact the copyright holders of the objects illustrated in this book. If omissions are noted, please contact the Museum of the Southwest; corrections will be made in subsequent printings.

© Burton Pritzker
© Catherine Lee
© Danville Chadbourne
© Doug Hyde
© Glenna Goodacre
© Jesus Moroles
© Katie Maratta
© Lydia Quezada
© Veryl Goodnight
© Woody Gwyn
Allan Houser, Chiinde LLC
Doel Reed © 2015 Oklahoma State University Museum of Art
E. Martin Hennings, courtesy of Bridgman Images
Family of Jerry Bywaters
Norman Rockwell printed by permission of the Norman Rockwell Family Agency © 2016 the Norman Rockwell Family Entities
The Clark Hulings Trust
The Estate of Andrew Loomis
The Estate of Eric Sloane
The Estate of Everett Spruce
The Estate of Florence McClung
Fremont Ellis, The Estate of Frederick F. Ellis
The Estate of Fritz Scholder
The Estate of Gene Kloss
The Estate of Grant Wood/ Licensed by VAGA, New York, NY
The Estate of Oscar Berninghaus
The Estate of Peter Hurd
The Estate of Richard Stone Reeves
The Estate of T. C. Cannon
The Estate of William L. Lester
The Estate of Woody Crumbo
Thomas Hart Benton © T. H. Benton and R. P. Benton Testamentary Trusts/ UMB Bank Trustee/ Licensed by VAGA, New York, NY

This book is supported by a grant from The Henry Luce Foundation and other supporters.

Manufactured in Canada

Museum of the Southwest
1705 W. Missouri Avenue
Midland, TX 79701

The paper used in this publication meets the minimum requirements of the American National Standard for Information Sciences – Permanence of Paper for Printed Library Materials, ANSI Z39.48-1992.

Library of Congress Control Number: 2016950781

Distributed by University of Oklahoma Press

Photographer: Daniel Barsotti
Designer: David Skolkin
Copyeditor: Bonnie Lovell

Page 5: Detail of inlaid linoleum on Turner Mansion breakfast room floor.

Page 6: Detail of light fixture in Turner Mansion upstairs bedroom.

ISBN: 978-0-9978589-0-7 (hardback)

ISBN: 978-0-9978589-1-4 (paperback)